D0956338

Cleo

"A buoyant tale, heartfelt and open."
—*Booklist*

"Helen Brown's remarkable memoir took me on a journey that
threatened to break my heart, and right when I thought I
couldn't possibly bear to read another word, I realized that she
didn't break my heart at all—she opened it."
—**Beth Hoffman**, *New York Times* bestselling author
of *Saving CeeCee Honeycutt*

"Possibly the next *Marley & Me, Cleo,* by Helen Brown, is an
honest and unmawkish true story of ordinary people
rebuilding their lives after a tragedy, with the help of a kitten.
Even non-cat-lovers will be moved."
—*Good Housekeeping*

"Lively and admirably unsentimental . . . a salutary reminder
of the gratitude we humans owe to our companion animals."
—*Daily Mail*

"Heartwarming, fun, and romantic. *Marley & Me* fans
will love it."
—*Closer*

"This is an absolute must gift for yourself or
a cat-loving friend."
—*Cat World*

"Helen Brown's *Cleo* is not just a tender story about a cat and
a family facing the world again after a family bereavement. It's
also an epic, genuinely moving, funny, and ultimately,
uplifting. Don't be surprised to find yourself smiling through
tears after reading it."
—**Witi Ihimaera**, author of *The Whale Rider*

Cats &

Daughters

They Don't Always Come When Called

Helen Brown

CITADEL PRESS

CITADEL PRESS BOOKS are published by

Kensington Publishing Corp.
119 West 40th Street
New York, NY 10018

This is the American edition of the hardcover published in Great Britain by Two Roads, an imprint of Hodder & Stoughton.

All Kensington titles, imprints, and distributed lines are available at special quantity discounts for bulk purchases for sales promotions, premiums, fund-raising, educational, or institutional use. Special book excerpts or customized printings can also be created to fit specific needs. For details, write or phone the office of the Kensington special sales manager: Kensington Publishing Corp., 119 West 40th Street, New York, NY 10018, attn: Special Sales Department; phone 1-800-221-2647.

CITADEL PRESS and the Citadel logo are Reg. U.S. Pat. & TM Off.

First printing: April 2013

10   9   8   7   6   5   4   3

Printed in the United States of America

CIP data is available.

ISBN-13: 978-0-8065-3606-4
ISBN-10: 0-8065-3606-3

First electronic edition: April 2013

ISBN-13: 978-0-8065-3607-1
ISBN-10: 0-8065-3607-1

To cats and daughters,
who don't always come when called.

Contents

CATS & DAUGHTERS

Whisker's Tip

I never thought we'd end up with a cat crazy enough to want to go for walks. But felines change people. I should know that.

As evening shadows crawl across the kitchen, Jonah's footsteps drum down the hall. He appears in front of me, his red harness snared between his teeth.

"Not now," I say, peeling a carrot. "Dinner's only half an hour away."

His eyes widen to become a pair of lakes. He sits neatly in front of me, snakes his tail over his front feet, and examines my face. What do cats see when they look at people? They must be appalled by our lack of fur.

After a moment's reflection, Jonah, still carrying the harness, stands up and pads toward me. He balances on his back feet and stretches his impossibly long body against mine. Patting my abdomen with his front paw, he flattens his ears and puts his head to one side. Lowering himself to ground level again, he drops the harness at my feet and emits a baleful meow.

Irresistible.

Crouching, I clip the harness around his soft, athletic body. The cat arches his back in anticipation. His purrs reverberate off the cupboards.

"Cruel, too cruel!" I hear Mum's voice saying. *"Cats are wild animals. What are you doing to this poor creature?"*

It's strange how Mum stays inside my head, even years after she's gone. I wonder if it'll be the same for my daughters and they'll hear me wheedling and encouraging them when they're in rocking chairs.

In an ideal world, Jonah would be free to roam the neighborhood. But times have changed. We live in cities. Roads are plagued with cars.

A normal cat would hate going out in a harness. Three years with Jonah have taught me he's anything but ordinary. Apart from the fact he's learned to love his harness, his obsession with gloves, florist ribbon, and women's evening wear is beyond the realms of feline sanity.

He's complicated. While he can seem incredibly intelligent sometimes, he thinks cars are for hiding under. It's not that I want to keep him prisoner, but we live in perilous times. He needs to be safe.

Carrying him into the laundry room, I attach the harness to a leash, which is connected to an extension lead, allowing him as much freedom as possible. His purrs vibrate up my arms as I open the back door and place him on the grass.

Standing motionless for a moment, he lifts his nose to savor the warm evening breeze. Its perfume carries stories of mice and pigeons, fluffy white dogs, and cats—both friend and enemy. Tales my human senses are too primitive to detect.

Jonah charges ahead, straining at the lead, harness jingling, as we scamper down the side of the house. His youthful energy is exhausting. His confidence, terrifying. Not for the first time, he reminds me of our older daughter Lydia. In fact, sometimes I think this beautiful, headstrong creature is more like Lydia than like our previous cat, Cleo.

As Jonah pauses at the front gate to sniff the rosemary hedge, I can almost feel Cleo looking down from Cat Heaven and having a good chuckle. Half wild and streetwise, she thought harnesses were for show puppies.

Cats step into people's lives with a purpose. Many of these magical creatures are healers. When Cleo arrived nearly three decades ago, our family had been shattered to pieces by the death of our nine-year-old son Sam. His younger brother Rob had seen Sam run over and was traumatized. Yet I was so paralyzed with grief and anger toward the woman driver I was incapable of giving Rob the support he needed. Part of my anguish came from the thought of Sam dying alone on the roadside. As it turned out, I'd been misled. Years later, I received a letter from a wonderful man, Arthur Judson, who said he'd been on the roadside and stayed with Sam the whole time.

It took the arrival of a small black kitten called Cleo to make six-year-old Rob smile again. Cleo seemed to understand we were in crisis. Through cuddles, play, and constant companionship, she'd helped Rob embark on a new life without his older brother. For the first time I understood how profound the healing powers of animals can be.

Our lives changed after Sam's death and our hearts never healed completely. But through the years, Cleo stood guardian over us as we slowly pieced ourselves together. She'd curled around my expanding girth through a subsequent pregnancy, then kept me company during endless nights of feeding baby Lydia. A few years later she'd been my divorce buddy and, when I was ready, cast a feline eye over my pathetically few suitors to make sure I chose wisely. As it was, Philip—the first man Cleo approved of—turned out to be the right choice, even if he spends most of his life on a plane these days. Before our daughter Katharine was born, Cleo resumed her tummy-curling duties and was with me during the breastfeeding again.

Of all our children, Rob had forged the strongest bond with Cleo. She'd played kitten games with him throughout his boyhood and watched over him when he was struck by serious illness in his early twenties. That little black cat had seen us through grief, migration to Australia and, ultimately, a messy kind of contentment. Then, around the time Rob fell in love with the girl of his dreams, Chantelle, Cleo took a gracious step back and suddenly sprouted white whiskers. It was almost as if she felt her work was done with Rob grown up and happy, and our family on its feet, more or less. She was finally free to leave us and move on to Cat Heaven, if there's such a place.

I swore I'd never get another cat after Cleo. But when life

started getting complicated again, a so-called Siamese kitten exploded into our household.

This is the story of how one cat leads to another, and how rebellious felines and daughters have more in common than you might think. And how I learned compromise and medication can be okay.

Jonah's the cat I swore we'd never get. But as Mum always said, it never pays to swear.

Leaving

Your old cat chooses your next kitten.

"When are you getting another cat?" asked my neighbor Irene, leaning over the front fence.

What a tactless question, I thought. You don't go out shopping for another mum the moment her coffin has been lowered into the grave, do you?

I squinted up through sharp sunlight at Irene. She was wearing sunglasses and one of those silly hats from an outdoor shop. Laughing in an offhand way, I asked what she meant.

"You're always out there in the mornings talking to that shrub you buried Cleo under. It's not healthy."

Healthy? What would she know? I thought, staring into my coffee mug. Talking to a deceased cat after breakfast was harmless, and not half as batty as some of the other stuff I'd started doing, like wearing my clothes inside out and buying birthday cards six months in advance. Not to mention my increasing obsession with crosswords and television game shows. Besides, it was my choice if I wanted to converse with a dead cat.

"A friend of mine has just had three kittens," she continued. "Well, ha ha, I don't mean she *personally* gave birth to them . . ."

There's no end to the craftiness of people trying to offload kittens. "Just come for a look," they'll croon, confident the moment you've set eyes on some three-legged, half-bald creature with no tail your heart will liquefy. The trick is to get in quickly, right at the start. It only takes two little words. "No" and "thanks."

The thing is, there wasn't an animal in the biosphere that had a chance of replacing Cleo. It was a year since Philip had shoveled spades full of earth, damp and heavy, over her tiny body. I'd walked away to weep bitterly, Mum's voice scolding inside my head: "Don't be silly! It was only a cat, not a *person.*"

In many ways, Cleo had been more than a person. People come and go in any household, but felines are a constant presence. Over nearly twenty-four years, Cleo had been part of everything that'd happened to us.

But then cats and people never abandon you completely. I was still finding unmistakable black bristles in the depths of laundry cupboards.

"Why don't you come along with me and take a look at the kittens?" Irene persisted. "Fluffy and stripy. Gorgeous little faces."

"I'm not interested in getting another cat," I replied, the words coming out more vehemently than intended.

"Not ever?" she asked, adjusting her sunglasses on her nose.

As a hibiscus flower sailed from the tree above my head and landed with a plop beside my foot, I was surprised to feel a tiny bit tempted by Irene's proposition. Most people have hibiscus bushes but ours had sprouted into a twenty-foot tree laden with hundreds, possibly thousands, of pink flowers. It was so spectacular in summer we'd had a semicircular seat built to fit around its trunk so I could sit under it swilling coffee, swatting mosquitoes and doing Scarlett O'Hara impersonations. In autumn it wasn't so picturesque. As the days grew colder, every one of those flowers swooned to the ground like a Southern belle and waited to be raked up. Only one person in our household specialized in raking. If I went on strike and refused to scrape the hibiscus flowers away, they exacted revenge by rotting into slime. The rest of the family managed to tiptoe over the killer goo without doing themselves bodily harm. I skidded and fell painfully on the paving stones.

The same thing would happen if we got a new cat. Like everyone else in our house and garden, it would develop a giant-sized personality and I'd end up doing all the work. Another cat was out of the question.

"Never."

"You will," the neighbor said, waving a finger mysteriously at me. "Haven't you heard the secret of how cats come into your life?"

I feigned interest.

"Your old cat chooses your next cat for you," she said.

"Really?"

"Yes, and once your new kitten has been found, it makes its way to you whatever happens," she replied. "And it'll be exactly the cat you need."

"There's no sign of any cats around here," I said, yawning in the sun. "We obviously don't need one."

The neighbor reached up and picked a hibiscus blossom from the tree.

"Your old cat hasn't got around to choosing one for you yet, that's all," she said, then tapped the side of her nose, stuck the flower in her hat, and went off on her morning walk.

Watching her disappear down the street, I drained my coffee mug. The idea of Cleo trotting about in some parallel feline universe sussing out a replacement for herself was intriguing. She'd need to find an intelligent half-breed with heaps of street wisdom and soul.

But anyway, a new cat was off the agenda. After more than three decades of motherhood, I needed a break from nurturing. The kids were nearly off our hands. Once Katharine was through her final exams, I was going to take a gap year, sampling the world's great art galleries and all the other stuff I'd missed out on as a teenage mum. Another dependent—four-legged or otherwise—was the last thing I needed. I beamed a silent message to Cleo, if she *were* in Cat Heaven, *"Please no!!"*

Hard as I tried to forget, Cleo was everywhere. Apart from her remains under the daphne bush and the black bristles in laundry cupboards, her favorite sunbathing spot under the clothesline was still marked by a circle of flattened grass. Inside the house, memories were embedded like claw marks in every surface. The living room door still bore scars from Cleo trying to break in while we were eating takeaway chicken. When a shadow moved across the kitchen I had to tell myself it wasn't her. For the first time in twenty-four years, I could leave a plate of salmon on the kitchen counter safe in the knowledge it wouldn't be pilfered. Out in the garden and under the house, mice could safely graze.

Maybe the neighbor was right and I was grieving for Cleo on some level. Come to think of it, bewildering "symptoms" had set in around the time she died. Without going into detail, recent months had brought new meaning to words like flooding, leaking, flushing, chilling, and sweating. I'd become a mini environmental disaster zone. But when I'd raised the subject with women friends a couple of times I'd regretted it almost immediately. Their suffering was infinitely greater. Some made it sound like they'd hurtled straight from adolescence to menopause, interrupted by a brief interval of blood-and-guts childbirth.

Still, I was going to have to stop talking to the daphne bush. Word would get out. It wouldn't be long before people crossed the road rather than run the risk of bumping into me. Not that it worried me. We'd always been the neighborhood oddballs. Now every second house was being pulled down and replaced by a concrete monstrosity I felt even less at home. When Irene had shown me plans of her McMansion-to-be I'd struggled to conceal my horror. Not only was it going to overlook our backyard, its columns and porticos echoed several ancient cultures all at once.

The aspirational tone of the neighborhood was wearing me down. I'd never be thin, young, or fashion conscious enough to belong.

Changes needed to be made. Dramatic ones.

Another hibiscus flower fell, this time right into my coffee mug. That was it! So obvious, it was a wonder I hadn't thought of it before.

I rescued the drowning hibiscus flower from the coffee, flung it into the shrubs, and reached for the cell phone in the pocket of my track pants.

I'd escape the horror of watching Irene's Grand Design loom over us and years of raking hibiscus flowers in one hit. Never again would I listen for Cleo's paws padding across the floorboards. Or stumble over her discarded beanbags under the house. As for the daphne bush, it could retire from cemetery plaque status and go back to being an ordinary shrub.

Philip's prerecorded voice said he was sorry he couldn't get to the phone right now, but if I'd like to leave a message after the tone . . .

"We're moving house," I said, then pressed the off button with a satisfying click.

Arrival

A home is a second skin. A new one takes time to grow.

"Who'd live in a house called *Shirley*?" asked Philip, peering at the brass plate beside the front door.

Honestly, he could be so annoying sometimes. Our old house had sold faster than expected. We had to move out in four weeks. And here he was quibbling over a name plaque.

"Lots of houses had names in the old days," I said. "If you're going to call a house anything it might as well be Shirley."

It was clear he was unimpressed. Deep down, I knew he wanted to move into something white and modern, like a refrigerator. Instead, Shirley reared up over us in a children's-home-meets-Colditz style. Built early in the twentieth century, its red bricks and tiled roof whispered of an era when mothers packed their sons off to war, and sex before marriage was unthinkable. Any glamour Shirley might've possessed had long since evaporated behind cracked bricks and unadorned windows.

The brickwork ran in wavy lines and the gray stuff holding it together didn't seem entirely committed to the job. The orange roof tiles looked like rows of broken cookies, some of which appeared to be sliding earthwards. There was no reason to point any of that out to Philip. If we didn't find a house we wanted to buy soon we'd have to rent, causing more uncertainty and disruption.

I'd thought finding a new place to live would be simple, yet we'd spent weeks looking at town houses and inner-city apartments, demolition jobs and building sites. They were either too cramped, stupidly expensive, or spread over so many levels that rappelling gear should've been included in the price. We didn't want to downsize, but a Brady Bunch house in the 'burbs wasn't right, either.

I'd always liked the raffish inner-city suburb of Prahran (an Aboriginal name pronounced "Pran" by locals) so I'd been excited when I'd first spotted Shirley near the corner of an unpretentious cul-de-sac just off High Street. All the houses in Shirley's street had been built between the wars, giving the neighborhood a pleasing unity that is rare for Melbourne. Most were single-story, semi-detached affairs. I liked their white picket fences and quirky gardens. There was something *Alice in Wonderland*–ish about them. Thanks to a preservation order, apartment blocks and modern buildings were banned.

Unlike our current neighborhood, nobody living on Shirley's street appeared to be afflicted with a lawn-mowing fetish. In fact, there seemed to be an ongoing competition to see who could let the grass outside their house grow the longest.

Shirley's front garden, a rectangle of sandy soil alongside the double car pad, was technically a desert. Concrete paving stones masqueraded as a path to the front door. The only hint that Shirley might've once been a setting for family life was an ancient apple tree with a twisted trunk leaning against the veranda.

"C'mon," I said to Philip, "let's go inside."

But my husband refused to budge. He was still glaring at Shirley's brass rectangle nameplate, freshly polished for the open home inspection.

"We could get rid of that," I said, grabbing his arm.

"I don't see how. It's set in concrete."

I dragged him over the wooden threshold, uneven from decades of foot traffic, into the hallway. High ceilings. Drafty. A shaft of dusty sunlight settled on a pyramid of cardboard boxes. But something about it felt like home.

"Not exactly well presented," he observed.

"Can't blame the tenants," I replied. "They're being kicked out."

"Who sleeps in here?" he asked, inspecting a darkened room crammed with gym equipment and suitcases. "The Marquis de Sade?"

A real estate agent appeared like a specter in the doorway.

"This is the master bedroom, sir," the agent glowered, handing Philip a brochure and spinning on his heel.

"Ah yes, the one with the torture rack and excellent view of the neighbor's brick wall," Philip muttered.

Floorboards shrieked as we followed an aroma of mothballs across the hall to a smaller room with a boarded-up fireplace. Circular stains on the ceiling hinted at roof leaks.

"Looks like a baby's room," he said examining peeling teddy bear wallpaper.

"Or a study," I added, gazing out through a cracked pink and green stained-glass window to the apple tree.

We squeaked down the hall to the kitchen/family room, our voices echoing in the empty space. Philip pointed out the countertop, yellow marble speckled with brown blotches. Unusual, admittedly. A phone off the hook emitted a constant beep, like a heart monitor recording the decline of a patient.

Though Shirley was neglected inside and out, she was speaking to me. Tired, big boned, and possibly structurally unsound, we had a lot in common. It was like meeting a woman with sad, soft eyes—someone destined to be a friend for life.

"If the walls were a warmer color and we put up a few prints . . . and look!" I said, pointing out a whole wall of French doors. Unfortunately, they opened on to a patch of clay dominated by a single tree. I had to concede the back garden was even bleaker than the front. Roll-out instant lawn had worn through to dust. Melbourne had been in the grip of a drought, the Big Dry, for years. I'd read newspaper reports of small children who were so unfamiliar with rain they screamed on the rare occasions it hammered on their roofs. Water restrictions were so harsh, Melbourne households were back to 1950s consumption levels. Toothbrushing was a guilty necessity. We had a timer in the shower. Some people showered with a bucket, collecting gray water to fling over their gardens afterward. Buckets full of water and human skin cells are heavier than they look. Friends had sprained their backs hurling them about.

I missed the smell of rain, its softness and life-giving coolness. My eyeballs itched in the moistureless air.

Continuing on through the house, for every feature I found in Shirley's favor Philip found two against.

"This family area's a good size. The oak table could go here," I said, realizing almost immediately that I'd made a mistake venturing into oak-table territory. A relic from my first marriage, the oak table still had grooves on the edges where Sam and Rob had attacked it with a handsaw when they were preschoolers. Though Philip hadn't said anything, I was pretty sure he didn't share my affection for the thing.

"What if we get another cat?" he said. "There are heaps of main roads around here . . ."

"Come off it!" I snapped, wishing people would stop banging on at me about getting another cat.

How could I possibly open my heart to another feline only to have it torn apart again? If any new cat lived as long as Cleo had, I'd be seventy-eight by the time it died. Besides, Philip was right: Shirley's street looked like the Wild West, with every second lamppost featuring a REWARD poster with a photo of a lost cat.

He shrugged, went back down Shirley's hallway, and disappeared into another room. Sometimes I wished he was more malleable. Then again, if I'd wanted pliable I should have married a pot of Play-Doh.

I wandered back into the baby's room and looked through the apple tree's branches at the street. A man was strolling along the footpath on the other side of the road. I squinted to make sure my eyes were working. He was wearing a blue checked dressing gown—and it was two in the afternoon. This was definitely my kind of place.

"Look at *this*!" Philip called from across the hall. "The living room walls are *stucco*!"

My heart plummeted as I followed his voice. With lumpy white concrete walls rising from fraying green carpet the room had the ambience of a polar bear enclosure. Approximately half the size of a basketball court, it was empty and freezing. Running a hand over the glacial concrete, I wondered what it would take to hang a few paintings in there—mining equipment?

"Just look at those built-in mirrors over the fireplace and that carving above the windows," I said, quietly wondering how the living room could be made liveable. "You don't get that sort of attention to detail these days."

A stair rail of yellow wooden spindles led us up to a vast space opening on to two bedrooms and a bathroom. Some time in her recent history, Shirley had endured low-grade plastic surgery. A "teenagers' retreat" had been implanted in her roof on the cheap. It was an ideal set-up for two young women on the brink of independence, so Kath and Lydia would probably love it. We'd finally have room for sleepovers, and a few wedding guests for Rob and Chantelle's Big Day in six months' time. And who knows? Maybe even a grandchild or two.

Gazing out over the city through an upstairs window, I felt Shirley settling around me like an old friend. It reminded me of the old house I'd been raised in—a home full of laughter and secrets, with space for people to grow up in. It was the sort of house I'd always dreamed of buying. To top it off, my favorite café, Spoonful, was just across the road on High Street. It would be the equivalent of a cocaine addict living next door to his dealer.

I turned to Philip, who was absentmindedly kicking a lump in the carpet. He looked exasperated. I hated it when we had battles of will like this. He'd go silent and stick his jaw out while I'd get argumentative and repetitive. I had no energy for a fight.

"Don't you love it?" I asked. "It's got all the rooms we need, we'll give it character, and you'll get to work much quicker and . . ."

"But the *name* . . ." he said through gritted teeth.

"There are some great Shirleys . . ." I said. "Shirley Bassey, Shirley Valentine, Shirley Temple. And you've always been in love with Shirley MacLaine."

Silence.

"We don't have to call the house anything if it bothers you."

"That plaque's immovable."

"Nothing a pneumatic drill wouldn't fix."

"You love it that much?" he asked, defeated.

Love was hardly the word for it. As auction day drew closer, I became obsessed. Shirley was my soul home. Every day I invented excuses to drive past her. One evening I saw neighborhood kids playing cricket on the street. The scene was straight out of my childhood. In my dreams at night I roamed through Shirley's rooms, transforming them into *House & Garden* centerfolds. To my shame, I attended every open home inspection. The gleam in the agent's eye shone brighter each time I stumbled over the doorstep.

We ordered a building inspector's report, which concluded that Shirley had a few issues but was basically sound. On the understanding it might be possible to paint over the name plaque, Philip and I agreed on a price that would be our absolute limit for the auction in a few weeks' time.

I stay away from auctions due to twitchy arm syndrome. Whenever people start bidding, my hand leaps uncontrollably into the air. So on the day of Shirley's auction I hid around the corner clutching a takeaway coffee while Philip joined the throng of buyers and nosy neighbors gathering on the street outside Shirley.

After fifteen minutes or so, I assumed it would all be over and that it was safe to show up. But the crowd was still there, clustered in a knot. The atmosphere was grim, the way it must be toward the end of a bullfight. Philip was sitting on his hands on a concrete wall across the road from Shirley. To my disappointment, he was in observer mode.

"What's going on?" I asked.

"It's . . . it's . . ."

He was too engrossed in the drama to reply.

"Did you put in a bid?"

"Right at the beginning, but these two guys have gone way above our limit," he said, nodding in the direction of two men locked in a gladiatorial bidding war. The sum had reached a ridiculous price, but the auctioneer kept goading them up and up. Onlookers were mesmerized by the brutal spectacle.

Finally one of the men pulled a face, swatted an imaginary fly, and walked away. Electricity crackled across the crowd. Flushed with triumph, his opponent straightened, readying himself to declare victory. I secretly said good-bye to Shirley and steeled myself for a winter of renting.

Next to me, Philip shifted his weight, almost imperceptibly at first, then I watched open-mouthed as he slid his right hand out from under his thigh and slowly lifted it. Rising to his feet, he shouted a bid that was simultaneously terrifying and thrilling.

An outrageous amount. Where on earth would we find the money?

We both knew this could be our only offer, and one we couldn't afford in the first place. Insanity. But it was also one of the reasons I'd fallen in love with this man God knows how many years ago. On several occasions during our marriage when I'd gone beyond despair and given up on a dream, he'd done something breathtaking that had changed our lives. But never anything as wonderful and potentially disastrous as paying too much money for a house he didn't really like simply because he understood how much I wanted it.

Silence fell as the crowd—a many-headed monster—turned as one and focused its attention on Philip. Anyone who didn't know him would think he was standing there in a state of perfect calm. He hadn't changed color. His breathing was regular. He wasn't trembling or twitching.

I was the only one who knew what signs to look for. There they were—blue flames in his eyes. The auctioneer tried to prod the red-faced man into upping his bid by $500. Another 50 cents and we'd be in the gutter.

"Once . . ." bellowed the auctioneer and we waited for the enemy to swoop. "Twice . . ." Time stretched like a rubber band as we watched the hammer sail in slow motion through the air and . . .

The house was sold.

Unbelievably, to us.

Mystery

A cat never leaves you completely.

As the auction crowd dispersed, the agent invited us up the path into Shirley's family room, where the phone still bleated like a lost lamb.

All teeth and aftershave, the agent wrapped his hand around mine and congratulated us. He said the vendors would be pleased at getting such a good price for a house that was basically tainted.

Tainted? Like a Victorian maiden? The agent confessed that several months earlier Shirley had been "passed in" at auction— no one had offered the minimum bid. It'd lingered on the market ever since. I waited for Philip to shoot me a withering look, but he pretended to be engrossed in the agent's documents.

"You are a wonderful man," I sighed as we drove away, my hands still trembling from signing papers with so many zeros on them. "Are you sure we can afford it?"

"We'll work something out," he replied in the reassuring tone he'd used with customers when he'd been working at the bank. "We have some savings and I should get a pay raise at the end of the year with any luck. And who knows? Maybe you'll write a bestseller."

I squirmed in the passenger seat. His faith in my writing ability verged on pitiful. Supermodels would be size 18 before I produced anything like a bestseller.

After weeks of packing and planning, moving day finally arrived. I walked out the door of the mercifully never-named house we'd spent the last six years living in and said good-bye to Cleo and the daphne bush, promising I'd drive past every now and then to pay my respects. Movers heaved the semicircular seat into their truck and rattled off down the road. Melbourne's trees were dressed in autumn reds and golds as we drove to our new home, where the apple tree spread its branches in woody welcome.

Shirley's insides were cold and echoey. The oak table was dwarfed in its new family room, where the phone still bleated even with the receiver down. Some of our furniture fitted in better than others. The green couches looked good at the other end of the family room and the stone Buddha statue that'd sat on a window ledge in our old house settled comfortably in the alcove beside the couches. As I dusted it off, I remembered the day I'd bought it in a garden center—not for religious reasons but because I was struck by the tranquility of the statue's expression and hoped some of it might rub off on me.

As it turned out, I needed all the serenity I could get. Every house has a secret or two. Shirley had been hiding the fact she was a maternity ward for moths. Clouds of them flew out of every room, patting our faces with their soft brown wings. Alfred Hitchcock had missed a horror movie opportunity.

Watching the movers plonk the semicircular seat in plumes of dust under the tree in the back desert, I hoped we hadn't made a mistake.

Philip and I wondered aloud if we shouldn't have claimed the upstairs "apartment" for ourselves. The two bedrooms in it (one of which would've made a very nice study) were surprisingly spacious, each with a charming outlook over treetops and gardens, and the living area had views toward the city's skyscrapers, often outlined in tangerine sunsets. Instead, we moved our king-size bed and snore-proof pillows into a room across the hall from the Marquis de Sade. With a disused fireplace, plain white walls and no closets, our new bedroom was stark but sunny. I placed our wedding photo on the mantelpiece and hoped we'd get around to giving the room a personality boost. We decided to use the closets in the Marquis' gloomy chamber, which would also accommodate our chests of drawers, my Stair Stepper, and Philip's bike machine.

I cleaned out what had been the baby's room, painted the walls red, and claimed it as a writing space. My first "study" had been the oak table in the kitchen. I'd then graduated to a desk in the corner of a bedroom. This was by far the best work environment I'd had in thirty years of writing. It lured me away from *The Weakest Link* and helped me keep up with deadlines for the magazine and newspaper columns I'd been churning out for decades. I'd also recently embarked on a book about Cleo.

One of the reasons I didn't feel we needed a new cat was that as I wrote about her, Cleo seemed more alive than ever. Nestled in front of the computer in my new study, I could almost feel her coiling around my ankles. Nevertheless, my professional confidence as a writer was at an all-time low. Though I'd sent drafts of the Cleo manuscript to various agents and publishers, none had shown interest in the book. I decided I'd sign up for a weekend writers' workshop, hoping that might help.

During that weekend I was so impressed by the talent of the other students, all of them amateur, I was reduced to silence most of the time. At the end of the program we were invited to read our book ideas aloud. I scribbled a few paragraphs about Cleo and gave the last presentation. The room fell silent when I'd finished. Then people started asking questions. They wanted to know what had happened to the cat, and to our family. Several said they'd buy it if it was a book. That was when I began to realize Cleo and Sam's story had legs.

The course coordinator told me about Friday Pitch, run by Sydney publishers Allen & Unwin. Writers could e-mail their book proposals in on any Friday with the promise of a response the following week. It was for fiction writers but I thought I could be cheeky and send them a memoir.

Nestled in my new room I knocked the manuscript into shape while the girls settled in upstairs. Now I felt more confident our story might interest others, I fell into a routine. Armed with takeaway coffee from Spoonful, I'd write most mornings until my brain felt tired. Piecing our lives together in readable form helped me come to terms with some of the more painful experiences. If I wrote honestly enough, perhaps there'd be some healing in it.

Katharine and Lydia adored Shirley and loved their new living arrangements. Both easygoing girls, they'd always gotten along well, despite the seven-year age difference. Now that Katharine was a teenager they'd grown even closer, swapping clothes and makeup. Currently in the throes of a charity shop obsession, they delighted in bringing home stinky old clothes glorified with the name "retro." There was no tension over who'd have which bedroom. They quickly agreed Katharine would have the blue room on the left while Lydia took the one with apricot-colored walls on the right.

Moving into Shirley made me regret that we hadn't been able to afford a house of its size a few years earlier when Rob was still at home. With such a spread of age groups in the family, it was good to have more space.

If nothing else, having representatives from five different decades kept our regular family Sunday lunches lively. At a recent lunch, for example, Philip (b. 1962) had been wearing a T-shirt I'd talked him into buying because it had "Free Leonard Bernstein" emblazoned on the front. To Philip, Leonard Bernstein was some old musician he didn't listen to, like Leonard Cohen. He probably only wore the T-shirt because the design was retro-ish and therefore acceptable to his daughters. I (b. 1954), on the other hand, loved the T-shirt because I remembered seeing black-and-white reruns of the free concerts Bernstein gave to young people in New York. Katharine (b. 1992) knew who Leonard Bernstein was because she loved *West Side Story*. The first time Lydia (b. 1985) saw the T-shirt she studied it respectfully and asked in an Amnesty International voice, "Who's Leonard Bernstein and why is he in jail?"

Rob (Generation X) took a grumpy old man's perspective of Lydia's Generation Y. He thought she and her ilk had no idea what tough times were like and they expected everything laid on a plate, from jobs to technology. Lydia gave the impression she regarded

Generation X as a pompous lot. And as token baby boomers, Philip and I were easy targets for *all* the offspring. Not only had we stuffed up the world environmentally and politically, housing had been affordable for us, education free, and employers had practically begged us to work for them. Borderline Generation Z, Katharine was the only one safe in these discussions because nobody had profiled Generation Z fully yet. Chantelle (b. 1979) tended to listen in silence at family lunches, no doubt wondering what sort of family she was letting herself in for.

Each of our daughters was beautiful and precious in her own right. Katharine at fifteen was a tall pale blonde blessed with her father Philip's blue eyes and cursed with her mother's large feet. A born extrovert, she laughed easily and was never short of friends. Books, her violin, and musicals were among her many enthusiasms. She'd been thrilled to star in school musicals a couple of times, though always in male roles due to her height and alto voice: Wild Bill Hickok in *Calamity Jane*, Bert Healey in *Annie*. Short sopranos always scored the glamour parts. Katharine eventually agreed with my conclusion that most female roles were shallow compared to those written for men. Sunny yet sensitive, she was a conscientious scholar. In fact, I sometimes wondered if she took schoolwork *too* seriously. Katharine was desperate for a kitten. If we got one, she promised she'd clean its litter tray every day. Just as likely, the Dalai Lama was about to convert to Catholicism.

Lydia was a little shorter than Katharine with a pretty rounded face framed by straight gold hair. Her olive green eyes flashed with intensity. She'd inherited full lips and English skin from my first husband, Steve. Born just two years after her older brother's death, she was almost a female version of Sam, apart from the fact that she was left-handed. But from the start she made it clear she was in nobody's shadow.

Lydia never called me Mum. I don't know why. She'd just come into the world assuming we were equals. I wasn't entirely happy about being called Helen by my toddler daughter, specially when strangers dipped their heads curiously and asked where the poppet's mother was.

She'd seemed unruffled when Steve and I separated soon after her first birthday. Later on, she'd learned to love Philip as a father.

Nevertheless, the impact on a child born into a grieving household is incalculable. From an early age Lydia appeared burdened with a need to heal the world. While her friends hummed tunes from *Sesame Street*, she sang "Stand by Me." At the age of five she declared herself vegetarian, forcing me to lie about the content of the sausages on her plate. She even refused to eat chocolates molded into animal shapes.

I'd hoped Anglican girls' school might provide the consistency she didn't get being ferried between two households every other week. The school chapel was one of the few places where her loyalties weren't frayed. The Virgin Mother could be relied on to keep her mouth shut, and God wasn't about to argue over custody. She fell in love with the vicar and asked to be baptized.

We'd had our ups and downs, especially when Philip was transferred across the Tasman Sea to Melbourne, Australia. Thirteen-year-old Lydia railed against changing schools and countries. Once she'd made the adjustment, though, she became a high-achieving all-rounder.

Her final exams resulted in a scholarship to Melbourne University at the age of seventeen and a bewildering array of degree options. She chose economics and political science.

While her marks continued to be stellar through her undergraduate degree, the only work that put light in her eyes was with disabled people part-time.

She went apartment-hunting, then took a year off trailing through the Third World. With a lifetime's experience stored in photographic files on her phone, it was time for her to settle down. All she had to do was babysit her old teddies in her fabulous new bedroom and resume her studies.

I was too infatuated with the new house to notice that our older daughter had something else in mind—a project that was about to challenge me emotionally, mentally, spiritually, and in several other ways beyond my imagination.

Inspiration

Teachers appear in many forms.

Lydia and Katharine wasted no time injecting personality into their bedrooms. We heard thumps in the ceiling as beds were shifted, pictures hung. Junk shop expeditions were made. Katharine brought home 1950s movie posters and a floral bedspread. She lined her walls with books and draped party lights around her window.

Lydia didn't want me to see hers until it was finished. I already had a vague idea what was in there—not much apart from a chest of drawers and our old queen-sized bed. The fact she was sleeping in a bed of marital dimensions would have driven Mum to distraction. *("What's a twenty-three-year-old girl doing with a bed like that? Fancy encouraging her to have loose morals under your own roof!")*

While Lydia was busy decorating, she invited her boyfriend over for an exclusive preview. Tall and good-looking with dark hair bunched in a ponytail, Ned was a part-time jazz pianist. He had "one or two issues," which Lydia assured us were managed with medication.

Beaming, Ned nodded politely at me before bounding upstairs. I didn't mind Ned. At Rob's engagement party we'd danced together to "I've Got You Under My Skin"—a song that always reminded me of Mum peeling the eczema off her hands.

The eczema would've burrowed into Mum's bones if she'd been around to see Ned lumbering downstairs the next morning. His fisherman's jumper was fraying at the cuffs. I couldn't tell if the shadow on his chin was designer stubble, or just plain neglect. Everything about him screamed "work in progress."

Ned hummed nonchalantly as he poured himself a coffee. We'd never had a hummer in the house before. Lydia had spent the night at his place a few times, so I didn't mind him staying over. In fact, I was more comfortable knowing she was tucked up in her own bed, with or without a boyfriend.

Philip wasn't so happy. Striding into the kitchen in his work suit, he greeted Ned briskly and sat across the table from him. The temperature dropped several degress as the two males eyed each other over the cockerel on the cornflakes box. I got the impression there was one rooster too many in the room.

After Ned had gone, I asked Lydia if I could see her revamped bedroom. She shook her head. There were a couple of finishing touches she wanted to make. She'd show me later on, she said, after work.

"Who have you got today?" I asked.

"Teenage boys," she replied. "We're taking them to the aquarium."

"So you've got someone to help?"

"Yeah, they're pretty immobilized."

Waving good-bye from the veranda, I watched her stride down the path to the gray bus parked outside. How she managed to transport her clients around in it was beyond me.

Whenever she drove my car, she could barely execute a parallel park without scraping somebody's paintwork. In charge of the bus, she became a different person—capable, coordinated.

"Have you got a license to drive that thing?" I called, only half joking.

She shrugged, climbed into the driver's seat, and gunned the motor.

The occasions I'd seen her load clients—some with feeding tubes and oxygen tanks—on board, I'd felt humbled. No way would I have been that selfless at her age. Lydia and her friends walked their high-minded talk.

Some people criticize Generation Y as selfish, living off their parents and being perpetual students/layabouts with an impossibly high sense of entitlement. Some even blame the L'Oréal advertisement "Because You're Worth It." Personally, I've never known a more idealistic lot.

Lydia's involvement with disabled people began when she was sixteen and her class was encouraged to do voluntary work for a term. Her friends went for easy stuff like charity shop shifts. Our daughter had to go for something more demanding, which was how Alice, five years older than Lydia, burst in on our lives. While Alice's mental disability was mild, her personality was storm force.

The first time she came to our place, Alice's megaphone voice made Katharine dissolve into tears. Our visitor took a particular shine to Rob. While I was cooking dinner, Alice demanded to take a bath. I asked Lydia what we were supposed to do, but she hadn't been given guidelines.

I ignored Alice's unconventional request until her shouting became unbearable, upon which I filled the tub and handed her a towel. Hovering anxiously outside the bathroom door I asked if she was all right. "Fine," she yelled, and could I send Rob in now?

We ended up seeing Alice every week for about five years, gradually learning to respond to her demands as firmly as she made them. No, she couldn't have three pizzas or a sleepover in Rob's room.

After working with Alice, Lydia went on to care for many others whose needs were more complex. She learned how to transfer clients out of wheelchairs, feed them through tubes in their stomachs, give medication, and change adult nappies. She worked in a psychiatric hospital for a while, and as a respite carer.

People with disabilities had been important to her for almost a third of her life. She loved the work, and it had a social side.

She and Ned had met as fellow volunteers at a summer camp for young people.

I couldn't help smiling as the bus roared down the street. Our huge-hearted daughter claimed she wanted to make a difference in people's lives. I was surprised she couldn't see she was doing that already.

Later that day, she escorted me upstairs and opened the door to her room. I drew a breath. The shabby collection of furniture had been transformed into a chic Asian temple. Tibetan prayer flags bedecked her windows. Red cushions glowed against the walls. A small Buddha sat cross-legged between a candle and a photo frame, on top of a brightly painted chest. The effect was vaguely altar-ish.

"Fantastic!" I said, admiring the Tibetan wall hanging a friend had given her. "It's so . . . peaceful."

The room was perfumed with unworldly calm, as if it could detach itself and float away from the rest of the house.

Lifting the photo frame, I'd expected to see a family snap from our last holiday. Instead, I was greeted by the smiling face of a Buddhist monk. Actually, *the* Buddhist monk. The one we'd met years earlier when he'd been passing through Melbourne. At the time, word had gone out to our yoga group that a Sri Lankan monk wanted somewhere to give a meditation class. All he needed was a room that could hold twenty people who'd bring their own cushions to sit on the floor. A small ask. I volunteered.

Irene's net curtains had seizures the day his car pulled up outside our place. It was as if Queen Elizabeth and Father Christmas had rolled into a single entity and bestowed us with his presence. With a swoop of maroon robes and a pair of shaven-headed nuns in his wake, the monk sailed through our front gate.

In his knitted cap, gold-rimmed spectacles, and flowing gown, he was reminiscent of Yoda from *Star Wars*, except his ears were smaller and his sentence construction better. Radiating charisma, he accepted clumsy bows from Western admirers, most of them wives and mothers who'd spent a large part of their lives caring for others. Some were seeking inner calm; others were looking for the nurture they'd given away as if it had cost them nothing. Or enrichment. The few men who showed up in beads and Indian tops were too self-absorbed to be approachable.

I'd smiled obsequiously and bowed along with the rest of them. I didn't know a thing about monks or Buddhism, but I wanted people to feel comfortable.

We pushed the sofas back while they arranged their cushions and blankets on the floor. It was a squeeze. Those who were able to sat cross-legged and started drifting into meditative states to show the rest of us they were way past spiritual kindergarten. A comfortable chair was placed at the front of the room, along with a small table and a glass of water. Plus a vase of lilies. The monk liked flowers.

Once everyone was settled, I found a space near the back of the room, a couple of cushions along from Lydia. I was surprised she was even interested. Being eighteen, she had plenty of excuses to shut herself away in her room. But she sat effortlessly cross-legged, her eyes round with curiosity.

Expectant silence hung over the room as the monk eased himself into the chair and flicked his robe into elegant folds. He sniffed loudly and cast a benevolent gaze over us. I couldn't help giggling inwardly. No Christian priest, politician, or doctor could hope for this level of reverence. His audience was enthralled, not necessarily because they understood what he had to offer, but because of his otherness. The world had made us hard-minded and cynical about most things, but we still craved mystery.

The monk's voice was high pitched and sweet, but there was toughness at its core. Honey pouring over stone. He turned out to be an excellent meditation teacher. For the next hour we observed our breath, tamed our monkey minds, counted backwards, and breathed through different nostrils while trying to pretend our legs weren't giving us hell. We ended the session wishing ourselves and all sentient beings health and happiness.

As people stood to bow and leave their donations, the monk announced that the nuns would be delighted to bless our house. Philip watched perplexed while the two tiny women chanted and sprinkled holy water in the corners of every room. He wasn't over the moon about them sprinkling holy water on the television, but I assured him it wasn't every day that people were offered a house blessing. I followed one of the nuns into our bedroom while she christened our bedcover. Her eyes were so deep they seemed to go beyond the back of her head. There was kindness in them, hardship, too.

Once nearly everyone had gone, we stood with a few hard-core fans on the footpath outside the house to bid the monk and his entourage farewell. As he was about to climb into the back-seat of the car, he flashed a movie-star smile at Lydia. "Come visit me in my monastery in Sri Lanka someday," he said before bestowing a royal wave upon us all.

I laughed the monk's invite off, but Philip was wary, noticing the way Lydia's face had lit up. Even though she acted grown up in many ways, she was still young and impressionable, he said. Gullible, even. He thought the monk arrogant and manipulative with his charm. I told him to stop being a fusty old dad before nudging him back inside.

After the monk disappeared down the street, I'd assumed he was out of our lives. A photo frame in Lydia's bedroom was the last place I'd expected him to show up. Maybe she'd put him there because his beaming face and maroon robes toned perfectly with the new decor—a monk-ish style statement.

"He's my Teacher," Lydia said, taking the photo from my hand and replacing it beside the candle.

"Your *Teacher*?" I echoed, unsure what the word meant in this context and trying to piece together how a half-forgotten Buddhist monk could suddenly reappear in our house as a "Teacher." He certainly wasn't teaching her the three R's. We'd already forked out a fortune in school fees for that. Guru? Mind controller?

"You stayed in touch all these years?" I asked, straightening the Tibetan wall hanging and trying to keep my tone neutral.

Lydia was reluctant to answer.

"I've organized a few meditation retreats for him when he's been back in Australia," she said casually, gazing enigmatically through her window out to the sky where a crow flapped against gray cloud.

Something jarred inside my chest. I thought I knew my daughter.

We'd had battles of will over the years, but they'd been over trivial stuff like hairstyles and piano lessons. I'd learned the hard way that confronting her was pointless. Far simpler to let her dye her hair purple and grow out of it. But this felt more serious.

Flipping through my mental filing cabinet, I recalled her mentioning organizing the occasional meditation retreat. I'd encouraged her, thinking meditation might give her skills to deal with exam studies and stress in general. It hadn't occurred to me that the monk had been involved. Maybe I hadn't taken enough notice or asked enough questions.

I've never been one of those women who want their daughters to be their best friends, sharing jeans and bedroom gossip. Lydia was raised to be independent and strong. On the other hand, I was taken aback she'd felt the need to hide how important the monk had become in her life.

If she thought I'd disapprove of her exploring a spiritual path, she didn't know me very well. I'd always encouraged the kids to be open-minded about that sort of thing.

Surely I wasn't intrusive, the way Mum had been with me when I was young? The Gestapo had nothing on Mum when it came to interrogation. She'd delved so inquisitively into my life, I'd been forced to twist the truth quite regularly. But Mum was easy to shock. She had a long list of things she disapproved of—sex, left-wing politicians, Catholics, vegetarians, people from almost every foreign country . . .

I didn't disapprove of meditation or Buddhism. In fact, of all religions, I regarded it as the least offensive. But I couldn't help wondering why Lydia had chosen to shut me out from an important part of her life. Was it rebellion?

As I straightened a prayer flag, my mind spun into worst-case-scenario mode. I'd heard so many stories about young people getting sucked into religion and exploited by charismatic leaders. It was dangerous territory.

"Your room looks lovely," I said, swallowing all the anxiety that wanted to spill out.

I hurried downstairs and closed our bedroom door. If Lydia was in thrall to a Buddhist monk, and had been for years, it was probably too late to do anything about it. I reached for the phone and put it down again. Philip was probably in another meeting.

If only Cleo was around, she'd know what to do. She'd jump up on the covers and nestle purring into my stomach until I got my head around this.

Without Cleo, I had to find another form of comfort. Ten deep yoga breaths . . .

If I challenged Lydia and accused her of deception, I knew what she'd say. She was twenty-three years old, officially an adult. She had a right to keep secrets, even from her mother.

Especially from her mother.

Forbidden

The dreams of cats and daughters are invariably secret.

One of the good things about raising three children is whenever one of them is worrying you sick, chances are at least one of the other two is causing you no strife at all. They may even be bringing you joy.

Soon after we moved into Shirley, Rob and Chantelle acquired a kitten—or should I say a baby with four legs and a tail? A silvery Burmese with golden eyes, Ferdie was a friendly ball of fur. His stocky frame needed filling, which was good because Ferdie loved food almost as much as he adored his doting mum and dad. When Rob held the tiny creature baby-style in his arms, I gulped back emotion. His face was soft and tender as he smiled down at the little creature. Time folded back on itself and I could almost see six-year-old Rob nursing Cleo the same way. Except now Rob was very much a man, well over six feet tall, and the kitten looked like a toy in his arms. Thinking back over how Cleo had helped Rob laugh and play games again after his brother Sam's death back in 1983, I was touched to see him open his heart to another kitten. Cleo had taught Rob to trust life again. Ferdie was providing him with a gentle introduction to fatherhood.

Whenever we visited Rob and Chantelle in their new townhouse across the bay in Newport, Ferdie was the focus of attention. No kitten could have been showered with more devotion. From cat food to flea treatments, Ferdie was given the best of everything.

Watching Rob and Chantelle follow Ferdie's every move as he bounced around their townhouse, I smiled with delight. They were incredibly patient as the kitten attacked their furniture and their hands with equal pleasure. Now Rob was thirty-two and Chantelle twenty-nine, they were at the ideal stage to make fantastic parents of a two-legged, fur-free individual someday, if the stars aligned.

Ferdie was so adorable, I was tempted to bundle him up and bring him home with us for a visit. Not that I dared say anything, since I'd let everyone know my tough line on cats these days. In the meantime, I was in for a delightful surprise with the Cleo manuscript I'd been laboring over. After I sent Allen & Unwin a few chapters, the response from Jude McGee was immediate. She loved it. Contracts were signed and a deadline for delivery of the complete manuscript was set for September. Life was getting more multilayered by the week. I needed to get a move on if there was any chance of finishing the book on time.

As I waded through the early chapters, I realized it was nearly twenty-five years since we'd lived with a young feline. Watching Ferdie bouncing off the furniture I realized I'd forgotten how full-on kittens could be.

But there was also a wedding to organize. Having worn Roman sandals to my first wedding and a half-price suit to my second, I had no idea what twenty-first-century nuptials involved. Everything goes in cycles. Our parents had white weddings, so my generation rebelled and had hippie ceremonies. Rob and Chantelle were part of the Generation X swing back to church bells and tulle.

I bought a wedding etiquette book, *The Modern Wedding*, and soon understood how World War II could've been avoided. If Hitler had been preoccupied with planning a Modern Wedding he'd never have got around to invading Poland.

According to *The Modern Wedding*, while the bride's parents had traditionally shouldered most responsibility for a wedding, the groom's were more involved these days. With Chantelle's parents out of town, we obviously needed to do more than show up on the big day and have a good time.

The list of Must Do's was daunting. I hadn't realized that popular venues were generally booked up a year in advance. "Our" wedding was only a few months away. We needed to find a venue as soon as possible. A guest list had to be drawn up, invitations designed and sent, replies recorded. Photographers and celebrants, flowers, and a wedding cake had to be found. Plus cars, gift registries, hair and makeup, musicians, seating plans, and table decorations. And thank-you cards and gifts for bridesmaids and groomsmen. Not to mention the bridal dress. Rob and Chantelle were so busy working full time they didn't seem to realize that if they wanted a traditional wedding they'd have to carve out their nights and weekends to accommodate a schedule and stick to it.

Philip was at a work dinner and I was engrossed in *The Modern Wedding* one evening when Lydia floated downstairs in a waft of incense. *Meditating at 9 p.m.?* I thought. She was taking it seriously. When I showed her *The Modern Wedding* she said she couldn't understand the fuss. She'd rather get married on a beach. Generation Y Lydia was showing signs of swinging back in the hippie direction. Hang on a minute! Was she even *thinking* about marriage? Maybe her relationship with Ned was more serious than she'd let on.

Interrupting my thoughts, Lydia said she had something important to tell me. I tightened my grip on *The Modern Wedding*. The kitchen clock pulsed a heartbeat through the room. Could we possibly be faced with simultaneously organizing nuptials on the beach?

"I'm going to Sri Lanka," she said.

Sri Lanka? The flower-power wedding evaporated.

"You mean you'll go once you've finished your studies?" I asked.

"No. Soon," she said, avoiding eye contact. "In a few weeks' time."

"But Sri Lanka's in the middle of a civil war!" I gasped, dropping *The Modern Wedding* on the countertop.

"I've met people who've just come back," she responded with the confidence only twenty-three-year-olds can muster. "They say it's perfectly safe where I'm going."

A lead weight sank through me, anchoring my feet to the floor. This couldn't be happening. Didn't Lydia take even a passing interest in current events? Sri Lanka had been in the throes of civil war for nearly twenty-five years.

"Exactly where are you going in Sri Lanka?" I asked, trying to keep emotion out of my voice.

"The monastery."

Of course! So this was what Lydia and her monk had been cooking up over the past four years. Why hadn't she told me? I felt deceived. Philip had been right all along. The monk *had* been exerting some kind of power over our impressionable daughter.

"There are plenty of Buddhist monasteries around Melbourne," I said. "Why do you have to go all the way to Sri Lanka?"

"To learn more about meditation."

"There's no shortage of meditation classes in this part of the world," I countered.

"I'm going to help in an orphanage as well," she added, as if it might soften my attitude.

Admittedly it did, though only a little. Close to 30,000 Sri Lankans had lost their lives in the tsunami of December 2004. Families had been decimated. With its history of war and natural disaster, Sri Lanka had to be one of the most grief-stricken places on the planet. However, I was in no mood to sacrifice our daughter to its misery.

"The monastery's really remote, in the mountains in the south," she said, opening the fridge and slipping an organic blueberry into her mouth. "The war's miles away up in the north."

There'd been a serious gap in our daughter's education. Surely she understood war was something people ran away *from*, not toward. She'd been sheltered all her life, coated in SPF-30 sunblock every summer, and given the best education we could afford. Unlike our generation, she'd never met uncles who'd been maimed at El Alamein. Sepia photos of young men slaughtered at Gallipoli meant even less. She'd grown up in a world where supermarkets were always brimming with food. Lydia had no idea what she'd been protected from.

"Have you seen a map of Sri Lanka?" I asked, barely able to conceal my alarm. "It's a dot in the ocean. The north and south are as close together as Melbourne and . . . Warrnambool."

Warrnambool is a coastal town about three and a half hours' drive away from Melbourne. We'd taken a French exchange student there to see some whales. It'd rained and our guest hadn't been impressed.

In the face of Lydia's silence I asked her exactly how long she intended to be away.

She was vague. Months, possibly. *Months?!*

"And what does Ned think about it?" I asked.

"He'll be fine without me," she said, studying a crack in the floorboards.

"What about your study course? And your scholarship?"

The second hand on the kitchen clock froze. A spider sidled across the ceiling.

"They can wait," she said quietly.

"*Wait?!*" my voice rose to a quavering crescendo. "You mean you're going to throw away your *scholarship*?!"

Her eyes were damp and swollen. I couldn't remember the last time I'd raised my voice at her—possibly never—but a few tears weren't going to make me back down.

"You don't understand . . ." she muttered.

Three little words every mother loves to hear.

"This is something I need to do."

When did young people start *needing* to do things? Most previous generations counted themselves lucky if they lived long enough to raise a family.

"Why put your life at risk?"

"Plenty of my friends are doing volunteer work overseas," she said with infuriating serenity, as if I was the one being difficult.

"But there's a *war* going on in Sri Lanka!" I snapped. "They have *bombs* going off and terrorist attacks. Foreigners are being targeted. Can't you wait till the fighting's over? Or at least go to a country where people aren't killing each other?"

She looked at me as if I was an inmate of a mental institution in need of medication.

"You can't go," I added. "I *forbid* it."

Forbid? The word resonated back through decades to a similar situation, except it had occurred in another kitchen with wallpaper featuring hundreds of wicker baskets, and miniature prints of Hogarth's London on either side of the fireplace. Mother and daughter were locked in battle, though back then I was playing the role of impossible youngster and Mum was doing the yelling. "You're not even eighteen. You're just a child!" I remembered the anger on her breath and how I'd thought that in her teeth-gnashing, eye-rolling anguish she looked like one of Picasso's women. Her rage worked like a pitchfork, jabbing me into a corner. "I *forbid* you to get married!"

Dad was noticeably absent while this was going on. He was probably at work, or playing chess with his friend across town. Men are masters at keeping a low profile on these occasions. Mum's forbidding had made me all the more determined. Still, I hadn't been heading off to a war zone.

"The tickets are booked and paid for," said Lydia coldly.

Booked and paid for? I'd said exactly the same to Mum all those years ago just before my eighteenth birthday. *My tickets to Britain are booked and paid for. I'm flying across the world to marry the man I love. Defy me at your peril, old woman.*

Lydia's eyes had darkened to hazel blended with olive green. Maybe it was a trick of the light. For the first time I noticed her eyes were exactly the same color as Mum's.

"I'm leaving in three weeks. Good night," she added before fleeing upstairs.

Alone in the kitchen in anesthetized silence, I swallowed an urge to rip plates out of the cupboard and smash them against the walls. Much as I wanted to chase Lydia upstairs, grab her by the shoulders, and shake sense into her, I held back.

Lydia was determined to have her way. She'd made up her so-called mind. I knew the pattern from conflicts we'd had in the past, even over little things like choosing clothes. If I gushed enthusiasm for the pretty floral skirt, she'd inevitably want the plain linen one. The more I spurred her on, the more deeply she'd dig in her hooves.

A friend had drawn up her horoscope soon after her birth. He'd laughed and said he'd never seen anything like it. Lydia was a Taurus born in the *year* of the Ox and in the *hour* of the Ox. A triple whammy of bullishness. He said we were destined to lock horns.

I hurried to the computer and looked up Travel Warnings. It was not reassuring bedtime reading: "You are advised to reconsider your need to travel to Sri Lanka at this time because of ongoing civil unrest, the volatile security situation, and the very high risk of terrorist attacks. Attacks could occur at any time, anywhere in Sri Lanka, including the south."

I printed it out twice and forwarded it to Lydia by e-mail in case she tossed the printed version in her bin.

Two hours later, Philip and I lay side by side staring at shadows on the bedroom ceiling.

"Where do you think she got the airfare from?" he asked.

"Her father, probably. Hang on. Remember that money we gave her for her twenty-first?"

"You mean the study trip to China that never eventuated."

"She's not going to Sri Lanka. I'm forbidding it."

"Impossible," said Philip, the frustrating voice of reason. "She's over eighteen."

"I'll hide her passport."

"That's not going to get us anywhere," he sighed.

"She'll get herself *killed*!" I said, tugging the sheet into my neck and turning over to face the wall. It was all very well for Philip, I fumed. He hadn't carried her in his womb for nine months and nursed her with milk from his own body. He wasn't even her biological father. That was an unworthy thought, however. Even though he was Lydia's stepfather, there'd never been any dividing lines in his affection. He was as devoted to her as he was to his biological daughter.

Still, I thought, anger rising again, why couldn't he put his foot down and stop her?

Silent accusations hung in the darkness.

I blamed myself. If Lydia's father and I hadn't split up, she wouldn't be so reckless and defiant. On the other hand, if we'd stayed together one of us would probably be dead by now and the other in prison.

I blamed Lydia. The cheek of it, sneaking off to buy airline tickets.

I blamed the monk. How dare he lure our daughter away to his war-torn island?

I blamed television travel shows that present the Third World like a theme park offering endorphin highs along with extreme sports, booze, and everything else Generation Ys crave.

But I said nothing. Neither did he.

Even though Philip remained silent, he probably had accusations of his own to make. After all, whose fault was it for introducing Lydia to the monk in the first place?

He started making the whooshing noises that meant he was falling asleep. I was furious he could drop off so peacefully.

Thoughts spiraled as I lay awake. I remembered vowing I'd never behave like Mum when she'd tried to stop me going to England. Yet here I was in a similar clash of wills with my own daughter: me, convinced she was about to ruin her life; Lydia determined to go ahead and do it anyway.

Then again I shouldn't have been surprised. Lydia sprang from a long line of headstrong women who'd found ways to upset their mothers. Before she'd married, Mum had been "engaged" to another man and there'd been a scandal. Her cousin Theodora went to Paris in the 1920s and returned to live in sin with a German at the beach. Great-aunt Myrtle had smoked a pipe and advised me to do anything for love. And *her* mother caused ructions marching down the street of her country town demanding votes for women.

On the rare occasions Lydia's friends had confided in me about struggles they were having with their mothers, I'd always said the older generation had to give way. The younger woman must be free to carve her future. It's nature. In a pack of animals, the older ones lose pace and are devoured by predators. For the species to survive, youth must triumph. Confronted with the real thing from the old animal's perspective, I hated it.

Mum taught me how to deal with a woman whose strength matches your own. Yelling doesn't work. To handle another powerful woman you sometimes have to avoid confrontation and be stealthy. Rather than share information, it's better to make your own mind up and go ahead and do what you want. That's what I did when I wanted to get married too young. And exactly what Lydia was doing now.

I reached for the earplugs in the bedside drawer and willed myself to sleep.

Visitation

Good comes from good.

What does a good man do when he's worried about his wife freaking out over her daughter going to Sri Lanka and being her son's self-appointed wedding planner? He takes her to a wellness retreat in New South Wales. Even though Philip would've much rather been in a tent fending off crocodiles, he agreed to succumb to several days of detoxified living with me.

The wellness retreat was everything I'd hoped for: a combination of luxury, nature, and nurture. Grimy after a day's travel, we climbed the steps to a marble foyer that gleamed wholesomeness. We'd made a pact not to talk about weddings, Sri Lanka, or in fact any of our children for the next few days. This was a perfect environment to forget all that.

New Age didgeridoo music mumbled over the speakers while fountains chattered over volcanic stones. Staff flashed smiles that implied we too would be young, tanned, slim, and beautiful if only we could be disciplined and sensible.

I sucked my stomach in and bared unwhitened teeth in a middle-aged, overweight, city-living way.

Those health freaks didn't fool me. I knew the self-loathing it took to look like that. The exhilaration of losing twenty pounds a while back had been obliterated by the defeat of stacking them back on again, plus a few extra pounds I didn't have when I *thought* I was fat.

Then there was the revelation that I didn't actually feel that much better when I was thin(ner). In fact the "thin" version felt worse because I lived with hunger clawing my stomach all the time, and in fear that I was going to get fat again. After years of neuroticism I'd finally understood those who loved me would continue to put up with me fat or thin, and those who didn't ignored me. As a middle-aged woman I was pretty much invisible anyway. To pass unnoticed through an image-obsessed society is surprisingly liberating.

Refugees from the land of meat-eating, coffee-drinking, and wine-swilling hedonism, Philip and I were made to promise we hadn't stowed any caffeine or alcoholic contraband in our bags. I immediately wished we had.

The wellness retreat was famed for its week-long boot camp involving dawn-to-dusk physical challenges interspersed with soul-searching workshops.

Personally, I couldn't think of anything worse than a twenty-year-old Bear Grylls clone shouting me through an obstacle course. I wouldn't have gone near the wellness center if it hadn't offered the alternative "individual" package, where you could take part in workshops if you felt like it, and spend the rest of the time being massaged and aromatherapied to a pulp.

Bands of pink and orange stretched across the sky as our suitcases kerplunked over the gravel path to our villa. Spacious and modern with views over a valley, it was perfect. Oh yes, and the toilet paper was folded into a point and the towels were extremely fluffy. Opening the doors on to our deck, we let the warm night breeze comb our hair.

A group of kangaroos preened themselves before hopping lazily out of sight. I'd learned to love the Australian landscape with its giant skies and ancient, crumpled hills. The red earth and silver trees that had once seemed ugly and foreign now possessed unique beauty for me. No longer threatened by the emptiness of this land, and its potentially deadly wildlife, I savored the scent of eucalyptus gum on hot dry air.

Is it all right to mention here that we kissed? Not in a creepy,

please-don't-go-there-old-people way, like when an old walrus
of a Hollywood star lunges at a cosmetically renovated diva and
makes the entire theater cringe over their popcorn.

This was simply the kiss of a man and woman who've known
each other for twenty years, during which time they've spent
most of their waking hours putting other people first. Who were
just grateful to spend time alone together and have a conversation without someone else listening in and offering an
uninformed opinion. It was bliss to lie in bed between Egyptian
cotton sheets and use two towels each after a shower—none of
which had to be put in the washing machine later. Not by me,
anyway.

This place would purify our bodies, soothe our souls. We'd
be soaked and stroked, massaged and mentored in methods of
healthy living. After five days here we'd return to everyday life
happier, more balanced human beings. Our worries would evap-
orate.

Wind whistled a lullaby down the valley on our first night as
we slid between 1,000-thread counts of indulgence and slept
like stones.

It's hard to write about what happened that night except to
say it's one of the strangest events of my life. I've never been
particularly psychic, and yet . . .

Before dawn I woke to the sound of wooden blinds slapping
against the window. The wind had worked itself up into a
tantrum, and the air was hot and restless. Rolling over to find a
more comfortable position, I became aware of a human figure
sitting in a chair across the room. It was—of all people—Mum.

My chest melted at the sight of her. Even though she'd died
several years earlier, she seemed very much alive, her eyes blazing with love as she looked at me. In front of her a black cat kept
galloping impatiently across the floor, moving too fast for me to
figure out if it was Cleo.

Aware that this encounter with Mum might be short, I seized
the chance to ask her some questions. The cat zigzagged across
the room, as if urging me to hurry up.

"Is there a God?" I asked, feeling sheepish for being so unoriginal.

"Yes," Mum replied matter-of-factly.

"Have you met him?"

"No," she answered, with a tinge of regret.

"I miss you so much!" I cried, overwhelmed by a sudden sense of loss.

Mum had never liked it when people felt sorry for themselves. I'd sobbed like this once when she was dying and she'd just turned her head on the pillow and stared out the window at her camellias.

She began shimmering around the edges, her body melting away in the chair.

"What should I know?" I cried, desperate that she was going to disappear.

"Good comes from good," she replied before smiling enigmatically and vanishing.

Last thing I saw was the cat's tail melting into the shadows.

Getting back to sleep was impossible. It seemed melodramatic to tell Philip the moment he woke up. I waited till we'd showered and were on our way to an organic vegetarian breakfast. Philip has a surprisingly open mind for someone who works in a concrete tower.

"Was it a dream?" he asked as we wandered past the tai chi meeting point.

It'd felt more real than a dream but that was all I could call it.

"What do you think it meant?" he asked.

"Maybe it's about the book," I said. "If I keep writing from my heart, I think Mum was saying it could do some good—not just for me, but for other people as well. There was something really urgent about it, too. Mum and Cleo were telling me to hurry up and finish it. They don't want me to waste time."

The prospect of running out of time hadn't occurred to me before. It was something I was about to confront.

Inner Terrorist

Mothers and daughters share jeans and genes.

Five days and nights without coffee was enough for me. A detox headache drilled through my forehead. The moment we arrived back at Shirley I scurried across the road to Spoonful. Slurping my first latte of the day, I was grateful to be toxic again.

Winter had crept in while we were at the wellness retreat. Trees had shaken off the last of their leaves and stood shivering in their underwear against the pale blue sky.

I'd booked in to have a routine biennial mammogram a few days after we got home, but with Lydia due to fly out to Sri Lanka the day after the appointment it had moved to the bottom of my priority list. I'd lifted the phone a couple of times to cancel. Now I was back working on the Cleo book, worrying myself to distraction over Lydia, and scouring the web for wedding venues, there was hardly time for hypochondriac checkups.

The young doctor who'd done a breast examination a couple of months earlier had confirmed everything was fine and when I asked for a referral to the breast clinic, she'd said I hardly needed to bother. I could just as easily sign up for the government-sponsored program. It would mean a longer wait but the service was free.

I was about to accept her suggestion, but something stopped me. Instinct, maybe. Or one of the mood swings women my age are famous for. The doctor wasn't my regular GP and too young to understand the torment of middle-aged hormones. Besides, if I didn't have the mammogram now, I'd end up having to do it later, which would be more of a pain. Still, when I'd insisted on the breast clinic the GP had scrawled a referral with the level of enthusiasm I reserve for vampire movies.

Unless you're wired for photographic recall it's almost impossible to remember what you were wearing on a certain day. Some days are so devastating, however, the brain stores away irrelevant details. I recall, for instance, exactly what I was wearing the afternoon Sam died—a khaki skirt and matching shirt with a red trim. Ugly, but it was the eighties.

I also remember what I wore to the breast clinic that day in July 2008. To be honest, clothes are a source of frustration. I try to make an effort with my wardrobe. Sometimes, if a shop assistant gives the illusion of being helpful and isn't a complete liar, I can be talked into buying a few bits and pieces. I might even wear them for a day or two.

But my wardrobe inevitably gets whittled down to one pair of pants and a couple of tops that look okay and don't pinch in too many crevices. As long as they match the footwear worn the last three years in a row this, regrettably, becomes my uniform.

The weather was so cold on the morning of my appointment I dragged out my ankle boots with the wedge heels. They were so old I couldn't remember if I'd bought them the first time they were fashionable, or during their retro rebirth. The new velvet black pants compensated for scuffs and stains on the boots. As for the green shirt with embroidered shoulders in homage to John Wayne, it was the only thing I could find that was half ironed.

Anyone who's had a mammogram, or in fact any examination involving women's bits, knows to wear a skirt or trousers and a top that can be easily removed. It gives you negotiating power to keep at least half your clothes on. The John Wayne outfit was ideal.

I tried on the red hat that makes me look exactly like my mother. From what I can remember my grandmother had one a similar shape, a female version of the homburg favored by

Winston Churchill and Colin Farrell. There aren't many hats that suit the facial features of the females in our family, with our prominent noses.

There's something comforting about the thought of hundreds of forebears wearing the same hat shape through the centuries. No doubt my daughters, after experimentation with berets and floppy brims, would eventually do the same. I no longer minded looking like a carbon copy of Mum. Did this mean I'd finally grown up? A gray day could've done with a splash of red. But a hat meant hat hair. I put it back on the wardrobe shelf.

After scanning the obligatory trashy magazines in the clinic waiting room, I was summoned by the radiographer. "Relax," she said as she lined me up for the mammogram. "Stand naturally. Not quite there. A little to the right. Put your shoulder down. Relax." (*Couldn't she stop saying that word?*) "Move forward. Drape your right arm over the top of the machine. Hold that handle. No. Move back. That's it. Relax," she said, flattening my right boob between the equivalent of two paving slabs and running a garbage truck over them. "Take a breath. Don't move. Now hold."

She repeated the ritual three times and bustled back five minutes later apologizing, saying the images were underexposed and we'd have to do them again. I was surprised she was so incompetent. Alternatively, she could've been *faking* incompetence to lull me into a false sense of security. Soon after, she shepherded me into the ultrasound room.

Unlike the radiographer, who hardly talked at all, the ultrasound woman had verbal diarrhea. She spread warm goo over my boobs and ran her scanner over them. Usually I like to ask questions to draw these scientific types out of themselves. But I couldn't wedge a word in. She talked about her children, her grandchildren, the drought, and where she lived and wasn't it wonderful these breast-scanning services were available these days?

"You deserve a treat when you get home," she babbled. "No, you deserve *four* treats."

I wondered what was wrong with her. She wiped the goo off my breasts with paper tissues, helped me into a terry-cloth robe, and sent me off to sit in a vestibule.

I'm not a fan of confined spaces. The vestibule area was deserted apart from another stack of magazines, these mainly of the home decor variety. Thumbing through them, with their white kitchens overlooking improbably blue seascapes, I gradually became aware that the other patients had all gone home.

I'd been shut away, abandoned. I hadn't felt like this since primary school when the teacher locked me in the chalk cupboard one playtime. I was always in trouble for talking. Unease closed in around me in the breast clinic vestibule. All I wanted was to get dressed and go home.

"Oh *there* you are!" said an Indian radiologist in a white coat. An earnest gleam in her eye, she escorted me through a door labeled Assessment Room to inspect images of my right breast. The white blobs, dozens of them swirling like stars through the Milky Way, were calcification, she explained. Possibly an indication of irregularities in the cells. Careful language.

A primitive being inside me withdrew to the window ledge and watched the scene warily.

The doctor made an appointment for me to see a surgeon and have a biopsy the following afternoon. She asked me to bring a support person.

Am I dying? I thought, suddenly numb to the core.

At the same time, I seemed to split into several people, each with their own perspective. The primitive creature shadowed me, stumbling into the elevator, crossing the road, and climbing into the car. She watched curiously while I examined the backs of my hands resting on the steering wheel. With their prominent blue veins inherited from Mum, they were unmistakably part of me. Life pulsed through them now, but maybe not for much longer.

My fingers trembled as I punched Philip's number into my phone. He slid out of a meeting to answer the call. His voice was light and tender. Of course he'd be my support person tomorrow.

I wanted him to sob and say he didn't want to lose me; that I wasn't allowed to die—something to make it real.

But I was trying to stay calm for his sake, and vice versa. He asked if I wanted him to come and get me. *Yes, yes! Take me away. Save me!* But a cool, logical voice said no thanks. My car would end up stranded in the city.

Only minutes had passed but I was already imagining how the family would cope if I moved on. It would be new territory for Philip. Apart from his grandparents, he hadn't lost anyone close before. I concentrated on being strong for him.

I knew that one person would understand. Rob and I had been through so much together. We'd grieved in different ways for Sam, and in some ways still were. We'd found distraction and delight together in Cleo, the black cat who'd remained a living connection with Sam for nearly a quarter of a century. Having suffered ulcerative colitis and having his colon surgically removed at the age of twenty-four, Rob knew exactly how it felt to be alone and frightened inside your own skin.

When he answered his phone and heard my news the emotional connection was immediate. His words were cautious, but I could tell he was living and breathing it with me.

"It's nowhere near as bad as what you went through," I said. For the first time since the ominous mention of irregular cells, I was back inside my body being honest. We both understood what the clinic was doing, drip-feeding information to prepare us for the worst when the test results came in tomorrow.

Clicking the phone off a while later, I felt surprisingly serene. Maybe some kind of chemical had kicked in, but talking to Rob had put things into perspective. Even if it was worst-case scenario and I was about to choose music for my funeral, it didn't seem too terrible in the scheme of things. Losing Sam had been far more harrowing. A life snuffed out before it's barely begun. That's tragedy.

I switched the car radio on. Liquid jazz folded into the four o'clock news. A train crash in northern Egypt had killed forty-two people; a chunk of ice seven miles square had broken off Canada. Nothing like listening to the news for reassurance things could be worse. That's not even thinking about the ones who don't warrant a story—children stricken with serious illness; people who live with bitterness or despair.

The last news item announced that the Sri Lankan military had captured a major town in the northern district of Mannar from the Tamil Tigers . . . Sri-bloody-Lanka.

If there was one platinum lining on this cloud, I thought, it was that Lydia would have to cancel her trip. No way could she trail across the world to sit on a mountaintop now. I thanked God/Buddha/Mother Earth for "irregular cells."

As the car followed the curve of the river under a steely sky, I considered other possible upsides. The clinic people hadn't found a lump, so it couldn't be too bad. On the other hand, they were taking a more than casual interest in our family history. My sister Mary had undergone a mastectomy a few years earlier, and two aunts had died of breast cancer.

Another good thing sprang to mind. If it *was* serious, I finally had an excuse to give up my twice-weekly personal training sessions.

The girls were in the kitchen when I clattered down the hall and dumped my bag on the table. My babies, my daughters, were practically adults. They deserved the truth.

"Looks like I might have some irregular cells," I said, bright and firm, like a schoolteacher announcing extra homework. The words bounced off the walls. Subtlety had never been a strong point of mine. "But it's all right."

What a lie. The girls' faces were oddly expressionless as they hugged me. Did they think I was faking it? Maybe I was, or it was a dream. The other me observed the scene from a spot above the fireplace.

The kitchen tap hissed as Lydia filled the kettle. She'd be ringing to cancel her flight soon. I sat on one of the green sofas while Katharine tumbled on the floor and leaned against my knees, facing away from me. I stroked her hair as she stared down at the book she was no longer reading. Perhaps she was weeping. Fifteen must be one of the worst ages for a girl to lose her mum.

I wondered if mothers and daughters rehearse for this moment on their first triumphant meeting on blood-spattered birthing tables. Every beginning has an end. It's fitting for the mother to go first.

Not just yet, though.

All three of us seemed equally incapable of comprehending the implications. I loved my daughters with every cell in my body. But if some of those cells were irregular, killer cells, I might have bestowed a terrible curse on them. My efforts to help them become strong women would mean nothing if I'd passed on terrorist genes.

"Are you okay?" Katharine asked, her tone breathless and childlike, reminding me of the time I'd fallen over skating, and she'd hauled me up off the ice. She'd only been seven or eight years old then. The pain in my tailbone had been agonizing but I'd assured her I was fine. Mummies were always fine.

"Of course," I replied, play-acting again.

"But there's a problem with your cells," said Lydia, dropping tea bags in the pot.

"Apparently," I replied in an absurdly upbeat voice. "That's why it took so long. They took heaps of images and this daft woman used baby talk."

I didn't feel bold enough to broach the subject of whether Lydia would stay home now. She'd understand the gravity of the situation and do the right thing. Or Philip would talk her into it.

Tea was okay, but not enough. Reaching into the back of the cupboard behind the electric frying pan, my fingers curled around the consoling shape of the cognac bottle. It'd helped when I'd been in an unworldly state of shock after Sam's death. After the initial sting in my throat, the liquor eased through me like an old friend.

Philip arrived home early from work. The girls chopped vegetables for a stir-fry. I told them about the four treats I was supposed to have and they laughed too loud.

So this is what it's like when you have irregular cells, I thought. *People laugh at your jokes.*

"They catch things so early these days everything's going to be fine," I said, scrubbing out the wok afterwards. Yet I was already taking a step back from the three of them. From my viewpoint above the fireplace, I envisaged father and daughters getting on without me. They were loving and good to each other. They'd stick together.

How could I possibly leave them?

Waking for the third time that night I counted my blessings—great husband, terrific kids, living in a city with exemplary health care.

Starting awake the fourth time, I saw the faces of women friends who'd died circling above me. Lydia's nanny, Anne Marie; a neighbor who'd had a young family; Mum's friend Vicky; Aunt Edna, and more . . . They'd all been felled by the disease that strikes one in eight women. The one that starts with abnormal breast cells.

Sometimes it seemed I knew more angels than living people.

My last thought before falling asleep was that Philip would be hopeless on his own. I'd have to hunt out a new wife for him.

Abandoned

Willful daughters were born to defy strong-minded mothers.

Next morning I waited for Lydia to announce she'd canceled her trip. After breakfast she sailed downstairs in a pale pink shawl and invited me out for coffee. She suggested Globe for a change, a café not far from our old house. I let her drive my car, partly because I couldn't trust my reactions under the circumstances.

Globe glistened with mirrors and polished wood. Staff had changed since we used to go there. Assuming she was going to tell me about her change of plans, I ordered two lattes (one soy) and prepared to act surprised.

The best thing you can talk about when one of you has a potentially life-threatening illness is something else. I asked Lydia how Ned was doing. Apart from chronic lateness and the occasional fanciful idea (taking part in medieval battles with rubber swords in city parks), he was keeping his symptoms under control, she said.

Lydia had always downplayed Ned's symptoms, but hearing voices inside his head sounded a bit serious. She'd been encouraging him to stop smoking, lose weight, and smarten up his wardrobe. He wasn't responding well. He still smoked and never wore the "new" clothes she found for him in charity shops. I asked what'd happened to the scarf I'd knitted him. She said there'd been no sign of it. I smiled. Man makeovers almost never work.

"Maybe he'll wear something decent to take me to the airport tonight," she said offhandedly.

The words were too shocking to absorb.

"You're still going?" I asked, suddenly chilled.

"I can't change my plans now," she said, stirring her soy latte.

I couldn't believe Philip hadn't spoken to her, insisted she stay home for a few weeks at least.

"But I might be seriously ill," I said, sounding weak and pathetic.

My daughter stared into her soy latte. If our situations were reversed . . . but she'd seen it countless times. There's nothing I wouldn't do for her.

Did she think I was indestructible?

"This trip is important to me," she said in her therapist voice. "I've been saving for it for ages. And . . ."

"And what?"

"It's hard to explain . . . but . . . I'm thinking of becoming a Buddhist nun."

"*A what?!*" Café patrons glanced up anxiously from their newspapers.

There had to be some kind of mistake. The poor child was confused. Youthful experimentation with spirituality was one thing. Turning her back on her education, her family, and future to become Buddha's bride was unthinkable.

I had no problems with Buddhist nuns in theory. If any of my friends announced their daughter was about to be ordained, I'd probably make admiring noises. As "quite a spiritual person," I'd always encouraged people to embrace the nonphysical. But I wasn't prepared for my daughter to take it so seriously. Did that make me a hypocrite?

I'd once seen a Western girl with a shaven head dressed in maroon robes striding down a street near the university. There was no way Lydia could roam around looking like that.

"It's that monk, isn't it?" I mumbled.

Lydia's face closed in. She stared back at me defiantly, her eyes brimming with tears.

"Do you think it'll be easy for me?" she said, standing up and preparing to flee. "Shutting myself away from everyone I love and kowtowing to nine-year-old monks just because they're boys?"

She came from a long line of feminists. It wasn't in our genes to prostrate ourselves in front of anyone.

Rebellion. That's what this was about. Willful young women defy their mothers in order to discover who they are. Not so long ago she'd been writing a sex column for a student magazine. I wasn't sure what was more shocking. My daughter the sex columnist or my daughter the Buddhist nun.

If she wanted to rebel, why couldn't she just get a tattoo?

"What about your scholarship?" I asked, trying to control the tempest whirling inside.

Lydia nudged her chair under the table and glanced sideways.

"Do you have any idea how many kids would give their eyeteeth for a scholarship like that?" I said, standing to match her height.

"It's not working for me," she murmured, hurrying toward the doors. "I've had enough of economics and poli sci."

I reminded her that convents had been dumping grounds for women for centuries. If a man wanted to get rid of his wife, or an unmarriageable daughter, he packed her off to a life of prayer and chastity. The number of convent ruins in Europe, and the size of them, is appalling proof of that. While I didn't know much about Asian nuns, I'd heard they had miserable lives, sweeping, cooking, and performing menial tasks for superior male monks.

"Where are you going?" I asked, following her.

"Home to pack," she said, flushed with emotion. "I'll walk. Thanks for the coffee," she added, before disappearing into a stream of shoppers.

I stood at the counter in disbelief. What century was she living in? Dropping a tip in the jar, I recalled how I'd dragged her as a little girl along to some of the antics my New Age friends had got up to in the nineties. Crystal healers and aura readers had seemed harmless at the time, but maybe they'd tipped her into some wacky spiritual zone.

While our daughter walked home to prepare for monastic life in a war zone, I drove into town to enter a different battlefield.

If you want a steady support person, Philip's your man. He sat beside me in the hospital waiting room later that afternoon, studying a yachting magazine while I worked through a book of crosswords. He appeared not to be emotionally burdened in any way. Maybe this forbearance came from his army training, or from his years at boarding school.

The waiting room had a loathsome smell of fear. A raucous machine spat coffee from a pipe. Undrinkable sludge. Whoever chose the floral arrangement had a sick sense of humor. They'd placed a vase of arum lilies—didn't they know lilies symbolized death?—in a prominent position beside the tropical fish tank.

I pointed out the driftwood sculpture to Philip. "Better left on the beach," he muttered. It was his way of saying he hated everything about the place, too. I loved him for that.

A cheerful woman called my name and Philip followed me into the surgeon's office. Lined with pale wood, it was a pleasant room with brochures about handling emotions and various other inconveniences. A regulation box of tissues sat on the desk. A nurse in the corner typed into her computer. I wondered if she was there to provide emotional backup for the patient—or a witness in case patients turned litigious.

"How did this happen?" the surgeon asked me in a tone that was alarmingly tender as we peered at images of the swirling planetary system inside my right breast. The nature of her question was unnerving. She sounded like a mother soothing a child who'd fallen off a tricycle. I'd eavesdropped on enough doctors to know they have a good idea what's wrong long before they tell you anything.

"What's your feeling?" I asked, deploying journalistic training (i.e., ask questions that don't have yes/no answers).

"Do you really want to know?" she asked—meaning, do you

really want to sell Bibles in Baghdad/put your head in a pot of boiling porridge?

No! Stop right there, thanks. I'll just hop outside and pretend it's yesterday when I was in here having a routine mammogram. But it was too late.

"I think it's malignant." Her sentence smashed across the room like a crate of empty bottles. There was silence while I examined the splinters.

"But I haven't got time to be sick," I told her. "I'm writing a book."

Surely she'd take my busyness with the book into account and tell my malignant cells to go on hold.

"What's the book about?" she asked politely.

"Healing," I replied. I didn't have the energy to go into detail. She smiled wryly. There was far too much knowledge in her eyes.

I glanced down at her hands. They were small, almost dainty, with efficient-looking fingers.

"Brave" and "positive" are words associated with people in this situation. I could summon up neither. Cancer patients, especially if they're film stars or rock singers, are often described as wanting to "fight this thing." There wasn't an ounce of aggression in me. I felt like a creature in a wildlife program caught between the jaws of a powerful predator, its teeth sinking into my neck. I simply wanted to implode quietly in the corner.

"The growth is large," she continued gently. "It's spread across the breast."

"Mastectomy?" I asked.

"Yes," she answered.

Hang on. Couldn't we strike a deal here? Couldn't she make do with a lumpectomy like the ones I'd read about in magazines?

She said a lumpectomy was impossible considering the size of the growth. Performing a lumpectomy would mean taking the whole breast anyway. I glanced across at the man I'd met twenty years earlier; the man who'd been mad enough to marry me. He silently examined his fingernails. I needed to know the dimensions of the catastrophe.

"And the other breast?"

"Possibly it will have to go, too. We won't be sure until the biopsy and MRI results are through."

"Do you think I'm going to . . . ?"

"You've had enough information to absorb for one day," she chirped. "Let's hope I'm wrong and the growth's harmless."

Her words disintegrated into gibberish. She wrote a prescription for sleeping pills. The days would be easier to get through, she said, if I'd had a decent night's sleep.

The clinic nurse handed me a psychologist's business card. A shrink? *Hell no*, I thought, but slipped the card in my handbag anyway. I was going to need all the help I could get.

In the biopsy room a man who could've been mistaken for a model train enthusiast attacked my breast with a miniature ditchdigger that had a staple gun attached. The local anesthetic had little effect. His gun discharged four painful shots before he was satisfied he had a sample of the offending tissue.

Outside the clinic, beside the car, I wept into Philip's neck. Trees in a nearby park waved their arms in sympathy. I'd encountered death before—my son, both parents, and various friends. But I wasn't ready to clasp its bony claw. Not just yet.

I wanted to be around for Rob's wedding in January. Katharine still needed a mother. And Philip would be hopeless without someone to trim his ear hair.

The concept of dying—of shaking free of my body—was okay, providing it was relatively painless. What I couldn't face was the prospect of leaving my husband and kids.

That evening, forks scraped through risotto while I recounted the day's events. The girls nodded solemnly, uncertain how to arrange their smooth young faces. I'd sometimes wondered what they'd look like once life had etched a few wrinkles in their features. Perhaps now I'd never find out.

After loading the dishwasher, Lydia went upstairs. Any

minute now she'd tell us she'd changed her mind about Sri Lanka. There'd be smiles, tears, and forgiveness.

An iron weight formed in my chest as I heard the thump of her suitcase on the stairs. She appeared clothed entirely in white, pure and unapproachable, the way monastery students are required to dress.

A knock on the front door revealed Ned, his eyes blazing. I couldn't tell if he was hurt, excited, or confused. All of it, possibly. Filling the doorway with his presence, he seemed taller and broader than usual, almost physically threatening, as if he was challenging us to try and thwart his role as abductor.

One after the other, we kissed Lydia good-bye. My lips had no feeling as they brushed her cheek. This wasn't happening. She wouldn't, *couldn't* abandon me . . .

A rush of brisk night air. The door clicked shut. She was gone.

Roaring with tears, I ran to the bedroom, slammed the door, and flung myself on the bed.

Lydia loved orphans. Her devotion to people in wheelchairs was beyond comprehension. She'd drop everything to attend a fund-raiser for refugees. Eggs from caged hens were repulsive to her. She loved the environment so much she preferred riding my old bike to driving and wanted me to start a compost heap. Possibly she loved Ned, the Buddha, and her monk as well. Lydia's heart was so huge the whole world basked in the shimmer of her loving compassion.

How come she found it so hard to be kind to me?

Rage

Life's too short to eat spotty bananas.

Once my chest stopped heaving, I turned the pillow over. It was wet. I had no energy to change the pillowcase.

Philip opened the door a crack. I told him to go away. There was nothing he could do. Besides, someone needed to be with Katharine.

I popped a sleeping pill out of its plastic bubble, swallowed it, and waited for the chemicals to kick in. The bedside light gleamed harshly on books I'd started reading in my pre-cancer life. The American War of Independence wasn't so riveting anymore. Our wedding photo beamed across the room. Philip had more hair then. I had less fat.

Next to the photo sat a small cat statue Philip had brought back from Egypt, and a miniature plate Mum had loved. On the plate was a painting of a wild beach in mauves and blues. The scene resembled New Zealand, but the plate was made in Denmark.

According to magazine editors bereft of ideas, a woman's personality is revealed by the contents of her handbag. They should try investigating the lower drawer of her bedside dresser.

My top drawer held the usual run of spare earplugs, crosswords, sore throat lozenges, pens, scraps of paper, a magnifying mirror to pluck rogue moustache hairs, a tube of hand cream I was never going to finish, lavender oil to sprinkle over our pillows.

The lower drawer was a pharaoh's tomb of priceless worldly goods. A plastic tiki pendant Sam bought for me at a fair months before he died; handmade Mother's Day cards covered in wobbly writing and glitter. Among them was a more adult card from a couple of years earlier. It had a picture of two flamingos, one large bending protectively over a smaller one: "Dear Helen, Happy Mother's Day. You raised me well. I love you. Love Lydia."

I'd hoovered up the "I love you" and stored it under my ribs.

Under the cards was an ancient tape recording of Mum singing for national radio in 1953. She'd chosen a maudlin song and the accompanist dragged along too slowly, but underneath the hisses and cracks of time her contralto voice was richer than burgundy.

I wished Mum was still here. She'd have sorted Lydia and told the surgeon she was imagining things. On the other hand, perhaps Mum had been watching over me all along, giving me a heads-up at the wellness retreat just before things turned to custard.

If good comes from good, maybe cancer really *is* the angry disease some say it is. Years of pent-up rage could wreak havoc on the immune system. I had plenty to be mad about.

Pouring everything out on paper might help. Reaching for the top drawer, I grabbed a pen and scribbled a list of people I had "issues" with: provincial editors who'd rejected my column; those who'd frozen me out of their lives, let me down, or decided to become Buddhist nuns. Plus a list of resentments, some admittedly petty.

I am sick of:
- Changing toilet rolls.
- Being the only one who does any cleaning around here.
- *And* being a one-woman laundromat.
- Always choosing the spotty banana, so the others can have perfect fruit.
- Letting them hog the most comfortable chair.

- People saying, "What's for dinner?"
- Then saying, "Spaghetti bolognaise *again*?"
- People checking best-before dates. Like I'm trying to poison them.
- When someone finally touches the vacuum cleaner having to praise them as if they've spun sink-hole hair into gold.
- People rolling their eyes when I ask for help with technology.
- Never-ending deadlines for columns, and now the book.
- Saying yes, I'd love to attend the tennis luncheon/Tupperware night when it's a lie. I don't even play tennis.
- The garden. It's the only thing I don't look after, so it's the Gobi desert.
- Spending too many hours waiting for Philip to get home at night and then snarling when he does because dinner's burnt.
- Trying and failing to be a good corporate wife.
- Forgetting what fun was.
- Feeling tired. For weeks and years, infinitely worn out.

I belonged to the generation of females who aimed to Have it All. Instead of learning from Mum's mistakes, I'd tried to squeeze more in and made things worse. No wonder almost every middle-aged woman I knew pleaded exhaustion.

Not only had I shouldered the domestic roles Mum railed against, I'd striven for a "successful career." During the solo mother years, I'd been too tired after a day at the newspaper to give the kids the attention they deserved. Parenthood and work were frantically woven together in a safety net that was continually collapsing under me.

My efforts to be a good corporate wife for Philip were laughable. At one memorable function, imagining I was entertaining a lawyer from Sydney with my wit, I was startled when he glared and said, "I haven't been lectured at like this since I was at university." Then there was the Qantas Business Class debacle. Accompanying Philip on one of his trips, I followed him on a leg-stretching stroll through Economy. At the stop of the stairs on the way back to our seats I was apprehended by a hostess who snapped, "You do realize this *is* the Business Class section, madam?"

And now to top it off, my daughter was dumping me for a Buddhist monk.

Still, it's impossible to believe that cancer is really caused by repressing anger. I'd known plenty of angry people who died of heart attacks, and easygoing types without a shred of rage in them who'd succumbed to the disease.

Not that I'd gone out of my way to get the lousy thing. At fifty-four I didn't smoke or take HRT. I seldom drank more than a couple of glasses of wine (red for antioxidant qualities). Yoga and Pete the trainer were a regular part of my life and I was no stranger to organic produce.

But I had no control over genetics. Or the lingering impact of Sam's death, divorce, remarriage, and shifting countries. The menopausal hormone tornado wouldn't have helped, either.

Environment, too. I remembered the evenings our parents took us to play on Paritutu Beach in New Plymouth back in the 1960s. Nobody had known back then that a nearby factory was pumping out Agent Orange for the war in Vietnam.

At least, they weren't supposed to. A bright orange stream gushed from the cliffs into the sea, creating the perfect lure for kids raised on *The Wizard of Oz*. Our city wasn't emerald. It was orange! I remember the alarm in Dad's voice when he called us back. Too late. Mary and I had already run barefoot through the magic river. He told us to wash our feet in the sea.

Then there was the night we were sitting at the dining room table when someone noticed red clouds outside the window. We hurried outside to take a look. The entire sky glowed redder than a sunset. Awe-inspiring and freakish. Dad said it was because of the atomic testing going on in the Pacific. He thought maybe we should shelter inside.

For all the theories, there was only one I could rely on: getting cancer is bad luck. With breast cancer the plague of the female species it wasn't a case of "Why me?" but "Why *not* me?"

If it was too late and I was dying—well, everyone has to die of something.

I reached for a fresh sheet of paper.

Things I want to see/do before I die:
- Revisit Paris and the Loire Valley. See Monet's garden at Giverny and the palace at Versailles.
- A Northern European cruise. Yes, we *are* that old!
- San Francisco, and the North American fall.
- Visit Chicago for the art galleries and New York for Broadway and more galleries.
- Las Vegas. Why not? I'd always wanted to see Western Civilization taken to its logical conclusion.

Clichés, admittedly. But things become clichés for good reason. On a third piece of paper I wrote

All I really want is:
(my pen hovered over the paper)
- A friend.

I had fabulous friends, but their lives were overflowing with family and work commitments. I didn't want to add to their worries. There were other friends, too. People I listened to with a view to helping them piece their lives together, not the other way round. I'd always shouldered the role of the strong Earth Mother for them. Perhaps I was afraid of my own vulnerability.

What I needed now was someone who understood suffering, but padded lightly over heartache. Who didn't continually twist the subject around to their own problems. Who'd be there for me night and day without it being a chore. A friend who knew when to wrap arms around me, and when to quietly leave the room. Someone who could make me laugh.

I smiled when I read my list of friend requirements. Understanding on that level was almost beyond human. It sounded more like a cat.

Climbing down on my knees, I felt under the bed for a silver cardboard box full of wedding paraphernalia. Sliding it out from under the mattress base, I removed the lid and turned it upside down. Photos of glamorous brides and opulent venues fluttered to the floor. My pages of complaints and dreams fitted neatly inside in the silver box. I closed the lid.

Philip's anxious face appeared around the bedroom door. Darling man. He placed a glass of water on the bedside table and helped me into bed.

"Where do you think she'll be now?" I asked.

"Lydia?" he said, pulling the sheet up to my chin and kissing me gently. "Up in the air still."

I imagined her picking through her vegetarian dinner on a plastic tray while her plane inched across the Indian Ocean.

And dropped gratefully into a hole of unconsciousness.

Amazons

A circle of women—many who have just one breast.

I woke in better spirits. Morning light filtered through the blind. Philip lay beside me. We rose early and headed across the road for coffee and still-warm bread.

Whatever today's outcome, things would be fine. I knew that from a program I'd seen about Stephen Hawking's view of the universe. The fact we're all made from stars was profoundly comforting. Our bodies are literally composed from the stuff of heavenly explosions. We never die. We revert to stardust. Dust to dust.

I hoped I could be as brave as Mum had been. When she was diagnosed with terminal bowel cancer, she'd treated it lightly. "I'm floating out to my island," she said with a dreamy smile. "It's so beautiful over there. I can almost see it now. I'm going to Bali Ha'i." What was it with women in our family and islands?

I wondered how much of it had been an act for our benefit. Probably more than we realized. As the cancer distended her abdomen and turned her skin the color of candle wax, Mum spent her days comforting visitors and phone callers who couldn't disguise their grief.

When she wasn't in pain, she was a beacon of happiness, claiming these were some of the best days of her life. Alone in her room with me one afternoon, she raised a bony finger and said, "Learn from this. Watch me."

The local vicar visited her town house to find out if she had any sins to offload. I ushered him into her bedroom and closed the door. Mum wasn't an official churchgoer, but she'd sung in the choir. Singing was her form of worship, she'd always said. The vicar emerged a few minutes later looking flustered. He said he'd never met someone with such a spiritual approach to dying. Checkmate. Part actress, part guru, Mum bedazzled us all.

I'd perched on her bed and taken notes while she choreographed her funeral. She didn't want things starting on a downer, so chose "Morning Has Broken" for the opening number. After that she wanted her friends from choir to line up in front of the altar and sing "Make Me a Channel of Your Peace," which had become one of her favorite songs. The words attributed to St. Francis of Assisi were a neat summation of mother love—"Grant that I may never seek so much to be consoled as to console, to be understood as to understand, to be loved as to love with all my soul."

"I'm so excited," she said about the funeral. "How many people do you think will show up?"

"Oh, I don't know," I said, trying to think of a huge number. "A hundred and fifty?"

"Is that *all*?" Mum looked devastated.

"Well, no. Probably double that."

Settling into her pillows, whose whiteness matched her chiseled face, Mum looked satisfied.

"When they're carrying my coffin out, someone will have to sing 'Bali Ha'i,'" she instructed.

Mum had been famous in town for her role as Bloody Mary in the 1963 Operatic Society production of *South Pacific*. I asked if she knew of a local whose voice was good enough to match hers. Her response was firm. A decent international recording would be required. Sarah Vaughan, perhaps.

"It'll be a great do," she sighed. "I wish I could be there. Though I suppose I will be in some way."

I doubted I could ever be that strong for my children. Compared to her, I was a coward, an amateur.

Even though we'd had our conflicts, largely about sex and

marriage, Mum and I had been close. When we fought it was only with mirrors. I still sometimes dialed her phone number just to feel a connection with her.

A journalist herself, Mum had pointed me at a typewriter from an early age. I'd rebeled, of course, and ended up exactly where she'd wanted me. When we knew she was dying I'd experienced a guilty surge of freedom. At last I'd be free to smash the mold she'd squeezed me into. But it was too late. She'd carved me in her own image.

When Philip and I met at the clinic that afternoon the surgeon had good and bad news. It was cancer. The growth was unusually large at nearly seven centimeters across. The cells, however, appeared to be noninvasive. They wouldn't know for certain until after the surgery but once my right breast was lopped off, and assuming the left one was clear (pending MRI results), I had every chance of a normal life span.

Normal. Life span. Hallelujah! I could have kissed her, but the desk was wedged safely between us. Surgeons aren't touchy-feely types, which is strange considering how deeply they delve into people's flesh during working hours. Walking through the city after the appointment, I savored wintry sun on my face. Naked branches stretched across baby-blue sky. A seagull on top of a statue rearranged his feathers and glared down on the crowds huddled in their coats against the cold.

I meandered through a sea of impassive faces engrossed in iPods and cell phones. The world had gone Asperger's. Bent over little boxes, white wires dangling from their ears, people were compulsively attached to realities that didn't exist. Connected to the abstract but disconnected from their living, breathing lives, they were half robots. I wished they'd stop for a second to absorb the beauty around them, the ephemeral nature of being human. Our visit here is so short.

In the waiting room of the MRI place next morning, a questionnaire asked if I was claustrophobic. "Somewhat" I scribbled between yes and no. Apparently some patients need general anesthetic before they'll consent to being slid inside the giant vagina that is an MRI machine. Birth in reverse.

The medicos were back to calling me "dear." A radiographer stabbed my arm, dear, where dye was going to be pumped through during the procedure. I wanted a sign stuck on my forehead for the benefit of every nurse, doctor, scanner operator, bloodsucker, and pusher of probes and trolleys: Dear dears. Please don't call me "dear."

A nurse warned me it would be noisy in the MRI machine and gave me headphones with the choice of jazz or classical. Usually I'd go for classical, but tastes of medical people are unpredictable—see the arum lilies. Wagnerian opera or "The Funeral March" could have a devastating effect. Jazz felt safer.

Two nurses packed me on a trolley like meat on a tray, buzzer in hand in case I freaked out in there. Lying on my front, a boob protruding through each of two holes, I glided into the machine's womb with "The Girl from Ipanema" tootling in my ears. "Tall and tanned, and young and lovely . . ."

I'd always hated that song, even more so now that I was feeling almost the exact opposite of an elongated Brazilian beauty—short and white, old and ugly. Thank God it was soon drowned out by head-smashingly loud buzzing.

"Are you all right, Mrs. Brown?" a male voice asked through the headphones.

I was reassured by the youthful tentativeness in his voice, the sunshine in his Australian accent. And the fact he didn't call me dear. "Yes," I shouted, though shouting probably wasn't necessary.

The buzzing was replaced by rhythmic ringing. It was like being lodged inside a giant bell. I thought of Lydia in Sri Lanka and imagined myself meditating alongside her to the strikes of a monastery bell. Together in a mysterious land, and at peace. Except the bell could've done with silencers.

I drifted to another time, a day at the beach after sixth-form exams, skipping school with Jan. Glittering black sand, a mandarin sun hovering over the horizon. Poised between childhood and maturity, it was a perfect moment—my first adult experience of bliss.

"You did well," said the red-headed young man who belonged to the MRI machine voice.

"How could I not?"

"Some people move."

To my relief the MRI gave the left breast the all clear.

Later that day I called my sister Mary in New Zealand. Her voice was calm and gentle over the phone. Having had a mastectomy eight years earlier, she understood what it was like.

"You won't be as lonely as you think," she said. "There'll be a circle of women. It happened for me and it'll happen for you, too. So many women have been through this thing, they know how to help. They'll draw close and give you more strength and support than you can imagine."

I hadn't heard that tone in Mary's voice since we were kids and she was the older sister, the Protector. Any distances adult life had forced between us evaporated. She'd lost her left breast. I was about to shed my right. Between the two of us we'd have a perfect pair.

It was as if we were back sharing the bedroom with daffodil wallpaper again. In the mornings I'd gaze across at her dark curls wrestling on her pillowcase and feel such crystalline devotion. We did everything together—playing dolls and listening to radio serials late at night until my eyelids drooped.

Then one day it ended. Mary acquired a new blue transistor radio and started listening to *Top of the Pops*. She bought a bikini and told Mum she wanted a room of her own. Mum explained to me that Mary, being five years older, was growing up and her interests were changing. Unable to understand why Mary wouldn't want to play dolls and listen to *Life with Dexter* with me forever, I was exiled into a smaller bedroom with tree wallpaper next door to the toilet.

Mary offered to come and stay for a while after I came out of the hospital. I accepted with gratitude.

Under the shower that evening, I examined the right breast that would soon disappear, hurled into one of those hospital furnaces and sent up into the sky to become part of a cloud, maybe. The thought was unexpectedly reassuring. I liked the idea of my body tissue drifting above the city on its way to joining the solar system.

Pert and springy no more, the breast had exhausted itself feeding four babies. And okay, possibly playing a minor role in attracting a mate or two. I ran my fingers across the nipple under which the enemy lurked. Apart from being bruised from the biopsy, it still felt the same. No lump. If anything, the malignant region felt slightly indented.

Losing a breast couldn't be *that* bad, I thought. When I was a girl, Mum had told me how Amazon warrior women hacked (and sometimes burnt) their right breasts off so they could shoot arrows more efficiently. Good old Mum. She always enjoyed imparting information about the peculiarities of human behavior. Under her tutelage I absorbed Enid Blyton along with images of African slaves packed like cheese crackers into slave ships.

Perched on Mum's knee, I'd imagined Amazons pounding through the jungle, their single breasts flapping, before hurling themselves off rope swings and landing with a splash in the Amazon River. Finding out the Amazons weren't in fact from the Amazon jungle but from somewhere around Turkey was one of the mild disappointments of adulthood. Anyway, if Amazons hacked their boobs off without modern anesthetics, I couldn't have much to worry about.

The front doorbell jangled. I hesitated to respond. Probably it was Katharine late home and feeling too lazy, as usual, to dig her key out from the bottom of her bag. I plunged into my dressing gown and stomped down the hall, my lecture ready to roll. Things were going to have to change around here. People were going to have to be more independent . . .

"This is the last time . . ." I said, swinging the door open.

A tall male figure hovered in the evening shadows. It was

Ned, hands in pockets, looking more disheveled and wild-eyed than usual.

"Sorry, I thought you were Katharine," I said, suddenly feeling uncomfortable in the dressing gown, though he didn't seem to notice.

"Have you heard from Lydia?" he asked, distracted.

"No," I replied, still resentful he'd kidnapped her and taken her to the airport. "She probably arrived at the monastery a few hours ago, I suppose. Have you?"

"No," he said, examining his boots.

Clearly I wasn't the only one hurt by her departure. Tying the dressing gown firmly around my waist, I invited him inside and filled the kettle. We, the mutually rejected, could at least share a hot drink. I opened the fridge. He staggered and grasped the kitchen counter.

"Are you okay?"

"Not too good," he said. "I've stopped taking my medication."

My grip tightened around the milk container. Lydia had always been vague about Ned's condition. She disapproved of people being labeled. It was manageable providing he kept up with his pills. Otherwise, he lost touch with reality and heard voices again.

My only experience with people like him had been in a newsroom years earlier, interviewing a distraught mother whose son, after flushing his pills down the toilet, had jumped into the lion's pit at the zoo.

A journalist's training is handy in some ways, but it does make you catastrophize. The headline "Cancer Victim Stabbed to Death by Daughter's Lover" sprang to mind as I backed instinctively against the knife block on the kitchen counter. Dealing with Lydia's spaced-out—or, worse still, *not* spaced-out and potentially voice-hearing—boyfriend was the last thing I wanted just now.

I needn't have worried. A dejected Ned hunched over his coffee mug at the table and, sounding for all the world like a pair of jilted wives, we shared stories of our disappointment in

Lydia's heartlessness in not having contacted either of us. Poor Lydia; for all we knew she hadn't even got off the plane or made it to a place with cell phone reception.

Apparently satisfied by the coffee, our conversation, and the promise that whoever heard from her first would contact the other, Ned stumbled into the night. Rivals had become allies, temporarily at least.

That evening, every time the phone rang I leaped at it. There were calls from Rob and Mary, but nothing from Lydia.

In the days that followed, being a patient became a full-time job. In between going to various test appointments we had to make momentous decisions.

During this time, my surgeon announced she was going on holiday and I'd either have to wait a month for her return to have the operation (giving the cancer cells five more weeks to use my body as an amusement park) or she could refer me to another surgeon. I chose the referral, though this meant adjusting to the more flamboyant style of her colleague.

The option of reconstructive surgery was another considera-tion. Even though the eight-year age gap between Philip and me felt less important these days, Philip was still a "younger man." I wanted to reduce the shock of massive physical change—for both of us, frankly.

A silicone implant was the simplest choice. Alternatively, I could choose a more complicated process involving harvesting the roll of fat that sat companionably on my lap to make a new bosom. Flab into fab! I loved the sound of that.

A reconstructive surgeon showed us photos. She was proud of her work, which to the untrained eye resembled carnage from World War I. She could make nipples out of anything . . . toes, ears. She knew how to slice muscles off a back and bunch them up for a boob, except she preferred doing implant surgery.

I wanted to find a surgeon who preferred transforming stom-ach rolls into boobs. Across town we found our man. Greg had been to lots of international conferences and he specialized in flab to fab. His photos weren't quite as brutal as the previous surgeon's display—though maybe he was just a better photographer.

I was becoming an expert observer of surgeons' hands. Greg's were confidence-enhancing with their short fingers and freckles on the backs. A compact man, he was boyish and, for a surgeon, outgoing. With his pale complexion and reddish hair, he could've been a Highland piper in a previous life. I liked and trusted him almost immediately.

Mastectomy plus reconstruction—I was told—would involve three surgeons and several assistants, six to eight hours under the knife, and a recovery period of three months (assuming the patient was a twenty-year-old Olympian with an incredibly high pain threshold, I thought later). Greg would leave a scar the shape of a smile stretching across my abdomen from one hip to the other, cut conveniently low so I could still wear a bikini. As if.

At the same time he planned to simultaneously perform a reduction on the left breast so the new pair would match. Scarring around the breasts would be artfully concealed.

My optimism wavered. What Greg was proposing wasn't a renovation so much as a full body refit. Putting myself through all that would be the equivalent of simultaneously bungee jumping, climbing Everest, and playing in the World Cup Rugby final.

"We live in a breast-obsessed society," said Greg.

Rubbish, I thought. Driving home, I stopped at some traffic lights and saw a sculpture I'd never noticed before. It was constructed entirely of concrete breasts.

A DVD about breast reconstruction lay on the kitchen table. I wasn't keen to examine its contents. Apparently the reconstructive surgery would take longer to recover from than the mastectomy itself. Still, even though I'm no Pamela Anderson I didn't fancy running around like an Amazon for the rest of my days.

Watching the DVD with Philip, I emitted involuntary yelps.

How could those women talk so brightly about the massive scarring on their bodies?

Maybe I'd give reconstruction the swerve. But then I remembered a friend describing how shattered she'd felt waking up after her mastectomy to see a vast empty space where her breast had been. Reconstruction might be a physical hurdle, but it could spare some psychological trauma.

Getting three surgeons to show up in the same operating room at the same time was like arranging for Lady Gaga, Angelina Jolie, and Queen Elizabeth II to attend the same charity event. The medics shuffled their diaries around and found a date to suit them all in three weeks' time. It felt like forever.

Preparation

It's what's inside that counts.

Two nights after Ned's visit, the phone rang close to midnight. Answering it, I was relieved to hear Lydia's voice, though it was a bad line that made her sound as if she was in a submarine.

She apologized for the lack of contact, explaining that it was the rainy season and the phone line to the monastery had been down. The impersonal cheer I heard in her voice left me cold.

Like a wounded lover, I held back on information and waited for her to ask. Yes, I was fine, but not really. There were long silences. I told her about Ned's visit. Oh yes, she said offhandedly. She'd e-mail him sometime.

A parrot squawked in the background. The monastery really was in some kind of jungle. With little enthusiasm I asked what she'd been up to.

Meditating, she said, then went on to tell me that the monk and nuns had conducted a ceremony for me in a cave. There'd been chanting. Special, she said.

It sounded like a touching scene, intriguing even, but anger quickly flared. "So they know I'm sick?" I asked. "Don't they think you should be here right now with your family?"

Silence again. "I don't know what they think," she replied.

Though I wanted to understand, to be reasonable, I still felt too raw. "I'm sick and you're not here," I said quietly. Silence.

If only she could say it once. The word I longed to hear—Mum.

"You don't love me!" I wailed, sounding wretched and deranged.

The Sri Lankan parrot screeched. I couldn't gauge her response. Was she impatient, resentful . . . or weeping?

"I do. I really do," she said after interminable silence. The line crackled and went dead.

The phone rang often during the three weeks leading up to surgery. My sister Mary and Ginny in New Zealand. Julie my yoga teacher and numerous others phoned. Lydia's calls were less frequent. Either the lines were down or she was too busy attending ceremonies.

I tried to concentrate on upbeat diversions, like helping Rob and Chantelle prepare for their wedding. The big day was just five months away.

They'd chosen a wonderful venue: an old convent in the country town of Daylesford, an hour and a half's drive from Melbourne. The tiny chapel oozed a blend of romance and spirituality. A few steps away from the chapel, the reception area opened on to balconies with views of silver-green hills nudging a vast sky. Eucalyptus on the breeze added a touch of air freshener.

They'd also booked a photographer and band, and a celebrant had been found, though she kept forgetting their names. However, organizing these things turned out to be just the first tier of sorting out the Modern Wedding.

I'd had no idea there was such a thing as wedding cake *emporiums* until I found myself wandering through a grotto of gateaux with Rob and Chantelle. For those who considered gilded flowers too restrained, there were cakes smothered in ostrich feathers and sequins. Rob announced it wasn't how a cake looked but how it tasted that mattered. The shop assistant asked if he'd like a tasting and presented him with a plate of what looked like plastic cubes.

"This isn't cake!" he muttered, munching one thoughtfully. "It's not even made with real eggs. Let's get out of here."

I was impressed by Chantelle's pragmatic approach to

weddings. Instead of ordering a multi-thousand-dollar gown
from a boutique, she'd found a designer who worked from
home. She'd then treated her mother and me to glimpses of
tasteful fabric samples in subtle pink. Crystals and pearls were
on the agenda. She had an aversion to veils. With her dark hair,
peachy complexion, and vivid blue eyes, she was going to look
stunning.

Like every straight man alive, Rob was proving himself a
shopping bore. In every wedding-related shop we'd dragged
him into he acted as if we were holding him hostage. But I
enjoyed the outings. Every mother wants her son to have a
beautiful wedding, and nobody deserved one more than Rob.

In between times, I was preparing for the surgery physically
and emotionally. Finding 100 percent cotton nighties that
didn't resemble something a granny might expire in proved
impossible. I ended up buying three in shades of blue, inappro-
priately frilly, and a pair of navy slippers decorated with
dachshunds. The shop assistant asked if I was going away somewhere. Yes, the hospital, I replied, getting evil pleasure out of
watching her smile fade.

Appointments were made to see Jodie the hairdresser, the
psychologist (why not?), and David, a friend blessed with
exceptional flair in furnishings. Our bedroom was too stark to
feel sick in. The bedside tables bore circular scars from thousands of morning cups of tea. If I was going to be incarcerated
there for weeks, it might as well be jollied up.

Not that David was feeling particularly happy, his partner
having traded him in for a younger model and run off to Perth.

"I want to end it all!" he moaned as he flicked through his
curtain samples. "I'm going to jump off Westgate Bridge. But
only if there's media to cover it."

Fortunately, a shattered heart had no effect on David's
taste—which was impeccable as ever. He found two bedside
tables, one tall and pale, the other compact and deliberately
distressed by some Asian workhouse slave, no doubt.

Beautifully mismatched, the tables made a perfect pair—like

all the best relationships. With new lamps and semitranslucent curtains (off-white, fine Italian lawn) I kidded myself the bedroom was going to be stylish and new-smelling enough to make me look forward to the months ahead.

When David mentioned there was enough curtain fabric left over for the Marquis de Sade room, I said *why not?* Maybe off-white curtains that only three people on earth would realize were breathtakingly expensive would reduce the gloom factor. I decided to have the stairs recarpeted while we were at it. Pale, elegant carpet to match the pale, elegant life I had yet to begin.

I've no idea what men do when they're preparing to go into the hospital. A woman—well this one, anyway—clears out her kitchen cupboards. Into the bin went sachets of satay sauce circa 2001, plastic barbecue knives (who bought *them?*), muesli bars nobody liked. Maybe seagulls at the local landfill would appreciate them. Surgical mishaps aside, I'd be coming home to pristine cupboards, more or less.

In the back of the fridge I checked out some stewed apples destined to fester. I examined them closely and reckoned they had only a day to go, even by my standards. I spooned the apples into tiny bowls, tossed in some dried fruit, and sprinkled them with crumble topping. Delicious, they said that night, scraping the bowls so clean they hardly needed to go in the dishwasher. The fools.

A brochure encouraged me to spend the days leading up to surgery constructively, filling the freezer so the family would survive while I was in hospital and I wouldn't have to start slaving the minute I returned (when my arms would be too weak to lift pots and plates).

No wonder women get cancer in their breasts, the great symbols of nurture. Heading home from the supermarket with three months' worth of washing powder and toilet paper, my style behind the wheel was less aggressive than usual. Life, for all its imperfections, felt so very finite and precious. Immersed in thought, I missed a turn and found myself meandering through an unfamiliar neighborhood.

Managing the reactions of others was sometimes harder than dealing with my own. The word "cancer" had such an extraordinary effect I wondered if a name change couldn't be considered. "Tulip" perhaps (somebody kindly left a bunch on the doorstep). "I have Tulip and you needn't worry." Because some friends reacted as though I'd told them they were dying. Once the news settled in, they arranged their faces in a slightly different expression that implied that they thought I was dying.

"Is there anything I can do?" has to be the most commonly heard question by anyone diagnosed with serious illness. It's a safe ask, as the patient can be relied on not to say, "Well, yes, actually the upstairs loo is blocked and a wild animal's scrabbling in our attic. Bring poison and a plunger."

No, the air fills with a balloon of silence. The sufferer says, "Not just now thanks; you're so kind. I'll let you know." Irritated by the weakness of that response, I invented a new one: "Pray for me." I didn't say it solely to make people feel awkward, as it sometimes clearly did. I was hardly in the gold medal department for praying myself, but I was open to the idea that prayers of the practiced and sincere can pack a punch.

"My life's a mess, too," said an acquaintance, who by all accounts lived like a princess. "Our basement flooded and we're having a hell of a time with the insurance company."

"You've just reminded me," said another. "I'm way overdue for a mammogram."

Others were more upbeat, even though life wasn't treating them kindly. Jodie the hairdresser had a tattoo for every failed love affair. There wasn't much blank space left on her body. She planted a kiss on my cheek and wished me luck. She said, like me, her aunt had also had a vasectomy.

"You *not* sick!" shouted Sophie the wonderful cleaner who did her best to tidy our house up every two weeks. "My uncle is very important doctor in China for woman's breast. He say stop drinking coffee. Drink more tea. And *don't think you are sick*! When you think sick you get sick. After you get out of hospital I find you good Chinese doctor. Help you get strong. He will make your face red again."

The house was much tidier and smelled faintly of lemons after she left. I felt momentarily cheerful.

I decided not to respond to earnest messages asking after my health on the answering machine. There was an edge of relief in some of the voices. They didn't want to go through the awkward business of talking to me. They felt safer leaving a recorded message . . . and so did I, just listening.

A few well-wishers deposited alternative therapy books on the doorstep. Having watched a dear friend die of breast cancer having refused all conventional treatment and dosing herself on mistletoe injections, I wasn't tempted—or not just yet anyway. First I'd take whatever modern medicine had to offer. I did, however, start going to the old Chinese woman who did acupuncture around the corner.

My plot to escape the gym failed. Peter, my trainer, pointed out that I'd need strong arm and abdominal muscles to speed recovery. As an act of kindness, he started giving me lighter weights. He offered to visit the house twice weekly when I felt strong enough after hospital. I said I'd think about it.

Sleep and more sleep. I couldn't get enough. Shock, maybe. Katharine nestled beside me in bed some afternoons and read *Kidnapped* aloud. Once she'd wrapped her tongue around the wild old-fashioned language, *Kidnapped* was riveting. No wonder Samoans called Robert Louis Stevenson "*Tusi tala*"— the storyteller. He put Hollywood action writers to shame. It was a relief slipping away to a world of adventure and danger of a different kind.

"All we need now is a cat," said Katharine one day, pausing between chapters.

I smiled back at her. Katharine sometimes has the ability to read my mind. A kitten curled up on the blanket would have completed the picture, all right. An affectionate fur ball would calm my fears and be my constant companion through whatever lay ahead. A friend beside me even when the house was empty.

But the timing was all wrong for a new cat. I had enough on my plate.

The shrink had a tea bag string draped over a mug half filled with muddy fluid. It reminded her to drink, she explained. Otherwise she got migraines.

No wonder, I thought, *listening to people moaning all day.*

I was willing to keep an open mind about seeing a psychologist providing she didn't use the word "journey." Everything's a journey these days, from climbing Everest in a wheelchair to having your underarms waxed. "Journey" reduces everything to the tidy dimensions of a television script. If I'd wanted to be on a breast cancer journey, I'd have bought a ticket.

The shrink was mercifully down-to-earth and practical. She asked me to make a list of household tasks and stick it on the fridge for Philip and Katharine to work through. She suggested I write a list of friends who could be relied on to bring a meal to the house once a week while I was recovering. I couldn't face the thought of troubling the busy, stressed-out people I was fond of. The last thing they needed was to be making soups and casseroles for me. Was I too proud, or simply a failure at friendship?

She offered tools to help me step back from negative emotions. For instance, instead of saying "I hate 'The Girl from Ipanema,'" I was supposed to say, "I'm having a thought that I hate 'The Girl from Ipanema.'" The idea was to encourage me to take a step back, instead of just reacting all the time, and accepting emotional reactions as reality. Likewise, instead of feeling angry at Lydia for taking off to Sri Lanka, I was to think, "I'm having angry thoughts about Lydia . . . etc." Though I wasn't confident shoving a few extra words in was going to make much of a difference, there was no harm giving it a go. The technique was possibly a Westernized version of the Buddhist concept of detachment. According to Buddhist teaching, most human suffering springs from attachment. There's some truth in that, but it's the power of attachment that makes mother love so fierce. Without attachment, the human race would never survive.

The shrink also taught me a powerful new phrase: "My health comes first."

My initial response was cautious. Favored by hypochondriacs and neurotics since time immemorial, "My health comes first" gives you a license to be annoying: "Yes I'd love to adopt your guinea pigs, but my health comes first."

Nevertheless, the psychologist's phrase did provide an excuse for something I felt like doing anyway—letting go of stuff that was too hard, or not relevant any more.

I'd been writing weekly columns for newspapers and magazines for thirty years. That was long enough.

Being a weekly columnist is perpetual high-wire walking. Dreading going stale or losing my touch, I'd always suffered performance anxiety. If anything it'd grown worse with each year. I couldn't recall the last time I'd slept soundly through a Sunday night knowing there was a Monday-morning column to write. It was time to let go.

I contacted all the editors who ran my syndicated column and said I was taking a break. What I really meant was retiring, though that word had the air of a tomb about it. I was touched by the warmth of the editors' responses, along with countless e-mails from readers. The only commitment I decided to keep up was a monthly piece for *Next* magazine, who'd asked me to write a breast cancer diary.

Louise and Jude at Allen & Unwin, who were waiting on my half-finished *Cleo* manuscript, were more than understanding. Jude had been through a bout with breast cancer herself just a year earlier. She canceled the September deadline for the book, and said I could restart whenever I felt ready. In truth, I wasn't sure I'd ever return to working on it.

The day before I went into the hospital, I revisited Susan, the Chinese acupuncturist. The purpose of her needles (in the calves, forehead, scalp, and ears) was to promote calmness and stimulate the immune system. Behind a depressing array of faded cartons of herbs and the occasional dead fly in the window, her rooms always appeared empty.

Looks were deceiving, though. Susan had a steady flow of clients stretched out on rows of beds behind floral shower curtains. There was no point trying to hide our problems. We heard them all through the curtains. An old woman was seeking help for her arthritis. A younger man had done something to his back, though it was getting better. I had no idea what they made of my cancer.

"Close eyes and listen to music," said Susan, smiling gently before disappearing behind the curtain. I waited for sounds of ancient China but was disappointed to hear the sort of New Age Muzak favored by the average spa. In the background I heard a microwave ping and wondered if Susan was mixing some exotic herbs. But the sound of cutlery scraping against a bowl confirmed she was having lunch.

Susan and I developed a sort of relationship. She was pleased when I said her needles had a calming effect (though after phone calls from Sri Lanka I usually had to revert to Western-style sleeping pills). Susan said I must go to China and write about it because it's a very beautiful country. China vs. mastectomy. Tough choice.

Strolling back up Shirley's dusty steps the day before my surgery, I made up a mantra: Today I have cancer. Tomorrow, with any luck, I will not.

Philip, Katharine, and I went out for dinner at a café up the road that night. We had champagne, too, of course. We laughed when the waiter spilled an explosion of chocolate sauce over our table-cloth. Life seemed gloriously simple and worth celebrating.

A familiar tune started oozing through the loudspeakers— "Past the Point of No Return" from *Phantom of the Opera*. I'd never liked that song. Now it was reminding me there was no going back. The operating room was booked, the surgeons getting an early night (I hoped) for a big day tomorrow. Nil by mouth after midnight. In a few hours' time I'd be handing my body over to strangers. I wasn't brave, just seasoned enough to accept there were no choices.

Back home, I laid out clothes for the next day—the black trousers, green shirt, and ankle boots with the scuffed heels. No hat. Same as I'd worn to the clinic that first time. The three blue nighties and a toilet bag were packed, though I'd probably forgotten something.

I glanced at the bedroom clock perched on the smart new bedside table. Five to midnight. Probably mid afternoon in Sri Lanka. I swallowed a sleeping pill. Breathe. Relax (I hated the word relax, I thought. No, I was having a *thought* about hating the word relax!).

Drifting off, I imagined a giant hot air balloon. Into it I loaded the wedding, the columns, the book writing, my fears about tomorrow, Sri Lanka . . . and watched them float away into the crisp night sky.

As I dropped into a deep hole of sleep, I imagined my hands curved around the warm softness of Cleo.

Reunion

Daughters, like cats, are only ever on loan.

"You're going to forget most of this," said my old friend Greg, his face a halo of light, in the operating room. It's easy to develop strange attachments to people when your survival depends on them.

Next time I saw Greg, he was wearing a red shower cap and seemed extremely perky. I assumed I was having an inappropriate dream about him. Would my hormones never leave me in peace?

"It went well," said Greg. "We're confident the cancer's been removed."

Oh. So it wasn't an erotic fantasy. A stab of pain from an unlikely place, on my left side just under the ribs. Plastic snake. A drainage tube, a voice explained. Soon after, I was being wheeled down a gray corridor, mesmerized by the thousands of little holes in the ceiling. Do hospital architects have any idea how much time patients spend studying ceilings? An oxygen mask sucked like a starfish at my face.

"Your husband's waiting for you," said a nurse.

Sounded romantic, I thought. What could be sexier than six drains, a drip, and catheter with matching oxygen mask? Oh, and legs encased in loud, hissing plastic tubes—something to do with reducing the risk of clotting. I was trussed up like Tutankhamun.

It was good to see the darling man, though he looked tired

and worried. The only thing worse than being in a mess is upsetting people you love. I sent him home to sleep as soon as was politely possible.

Back to nothingness.

Drifting in and out of consciousness, I became aware of a new sound over the hissing support hose. A female voice rolling over unfamiliar phrases. The words were musical and soothing. And loving, like a lullaby. Except none of the words were recognizable. A painkiller high. Obviously.

I opened my eyes to focus on a point near the window where Philip had been. A willowy profile and a head, pretty and feminine, was outlined in the shadows. *Lydia?!* The hospital drugs were playing tricks. I dropped reluctantly into a pool of semi-consciousness again.

Fighting through the haze of narcotics some time later, I looked over to where I'd seen the hallucination of Lydia. To my amazement, the figure was still there sitting ramrod straight in the chair beside the window, her eyes half closed. The words tumbled off her lips and wrapped around me. Chanting.

Lydia slowly became aware of me looking at her. She paused and smiled at me. Radiant light filled the room. Leaning forward, she placed three cool fingers on my forehead. And disappeared. Hospital drugs are so trippy.

Next thing Greg was standing over me comparing breast reconstruction to gardening. In the way a newly transplanted seedling requires water, he said, a new boob needs blood. The next twenty-four hours were going to be crucial. If my irrigation system did its job properly my transplanted tummy fat would "take" and assimilate into its role as my new right breast.

"And if it doesn't work?" I asked in a weak, breathy voice.

"Then we'll all have a good cry, wheel you back to surgery, and weed it out."

That took my mind off cancer cells.

A nauseatingly vivid print bore down from the opposite wall. Abstract; a coastal scene. A man's face was hidden between the beach and the cliff. If I could've climbed out of bed I'd have hurled it out the window. Except the windows didn't open.

A nurse, May from Malaysia, introduced herself and exchanged the oxygen mask for little tubes, one for each nostril—like the ones Tom Hanks had when he was dying of AIDS in the movie *Philadelphia*. They were surprisingly comfortable and less claustrophobic than the mask.

"Isn't it great your daughter's here?" said May, scribbling notes on a chart.

"Lydia?" I whispered in the pathetic little voice that didn't belong to me.

"Is that her name? She certainly amused us with that chanting. I'm broad-minded, though. Healing takes all shapes and forms. I thought it sounded lovely."

"She's here?"

"Yes, she said she's just flown in from Sri Lanka to see you. She brought you these," May said, pointing at three candles in the shape of lotus flowers on the window ledge.

It hadn't been a dream after all. Lydia had left a month ago with no mention of returning. She must have flown home to be with me. My eldest daughter cared. Overriding my pain-racked body and fuzzy brain, a new sensation coursed through me. Joy. Pure joy.

Lydia was actually here, living and breathing in this hospital. Three candles sat on the window ledge to prove it.

"Wait till you get home before you light them. We can't have naked flames in here. Oh and she also brought this . . ." May added, holding up an old lemonade bottle half filled with amber liquid.

"Holy water," she said with an amused twinkle. "I'd recommend boiling it before putting it anywhere near your lips."

"Where—?" I croaked.

"I sent her downstairs for a coffee," said May. "She looked tired. She'll be back soon."

Lydia's silhouette appeared in the doorway. A white shawl

was draped around her shoulders. With her long sleeves and high-buttoned neck, she looked almost Victorian.

This was a very different young woman from Lydia the sex columnist, or the stroppy little girl who'd once confessed to mooning cars from a motorway footbridge. She'd been under the influence of an Unsuitable Friend at the time, but had admitted that shocking innocent motorists wasn't devoid of thrills.

It was hard to imagine the saintly being at my bedside was related to the vibrant, opinionated little girl who loved climbing door frames and diving fearlessly off cliffs into Lake Taupo.

I scanned her face for familiar landmarks—the chicken pox scar above her right eyebrow, the memory of a dimple in her chin. I was saddened to notice her eye sockets were hollow, the lids almost hooded, reminiscent of Gandhi after one of his hunger strikes. Yet as she moved toward me she was obviously still the same young woman I loved so much. I'd never seen such tenderness in her eyes.

"You're too thin," I wheedled. It was exactly the sort of thing Mum would have said.

Lydia blinked, possibly to repress annoyance.

"I love you," she said gently.

"Love you, too," I responded, feeling wretched for having started on the wrong footing. I should've been first to say "I love you." Or at least, "Thank you."

"Are you thirsty?" she asked. I nodded. She passed me a paper cup from the bedside table and prodded a straw into my mouth. Slurping tepid water, I felt weak and helpless. Holding the cup steady, Lydia was the powerful one now, the nurturer.

As I sank back into the pillow, there were a hundred questions I wanted to ask. What had made her change her mind about staying in Sri Lanka? When had she made the booking to come home and who'd paid for it? How come she'd lost so much weight? Had she been sick, or had she deliberately starved herself?

More important, how much further did she have to go to prove she was a separate entity who in no way "belonged" to me? I was willing to keep my end of the bargain and let her sail into adulthood on her terms. When would she realize she no longer had to rail against me so stubbornly?

The only sentence I had energy to piece together though was: "When did you get here?" A stupid question, but thoughts kept slipping through my head like jelly.

"A few hours ago. I came straight from the airport."

The tubes around my legs hissed. My brain was enveloped in cloud again.

"Can I chant some more?" she asked quietly.

I wasn't that keen. Not if it was making the nurses laugh. I needed them on our side rather than making jokes about us being a family of fruitcakes.

Mum and Dad had raised us Church of England, but I'd ticked "No Religion" on the hospital form. When a pastoral caregiver had stuck her head around the door asking if I'd like to pray with her before they wheeled me off to surgery, I'd waved her off. Her morbid expression implied she'd spent too many hours in front of the mirror practicing sympathetic looks.

Too weary to string words together, I nodded for Lydia to go ahead. May smiled and said she'd be back in a few minutes.

My daughter settled into the chair again, closed her eyes, and drew a breath. I felt uneasy verging on irritated at first. Her words were utterly foreign. They could've meant anything. Nevertheless, there was benevolence in them. And they undoubtedly meant something to her. She believed they had significance, even power. I let the chanting wash over me like waves on a windswept beach . . . and fell asleep.

I could've slept for hours, days even, if they'd have let me. But May stirred me every half hour to record vital signs and unravel my dressings to listen for a pulse inside the new boob. As night dragged on she said I had low blood pressure and a fever. It was of no interest to me. All I wanted was sleep. Turning toward the darkened window I saw Lydia's profile, straight-backed and motionless. There was no need to reassure or entertain her. She was meditating.

★ ★ ★

The night dragged on for weeks. I hungered for sleep. Toward dawn I hallucinated about being a prisoner of war. Soldiers jabbed me with spears every time I drifted off. Yet May was such a dedicated nurse she was more angel than prison guard. Every time I turned to the window Lydia was still there, silent and unmoving, asking for nothing. The constancy of her presence gave me strength. All the doubts I'd had about her caring melted in the dry hospital air.

There's no real time in hospital. The outside world peels away. Nursing shifts tick over. Rain scatters black diamonds across the window—not enough to put an end to the drought, though. Dark sky fades to gray.

The hospital shook itself awake. Brisk footsteps, clattering pans, and nurses' chatter brought the day alive. Trolleys bearing patients, food, and medical equipment rattled down the corridor outside my room.

A sullen girl from Eastern Europe plonked a breakfast tray in front of me. Cornflakes in a plastic bowl and a tea bag. The smallest task was barely possible now my arms and legs were out of action. Lydia raised the spoon to my lips, then held the cup while I slurped tea.

She looked weary. I urged her to go home and rest. She pressed her cheek against mine. Suddenly, I remembered the question I really wanted to ask. A simple one, but loaded.

"How long are you here for?"

The tubes on my legs hissed and sighed. If she was planning to leave the next day my heart would shatter.

"As long as you need me," she replied.

My head sank back in the pillow. That was all I'd wanted to hear.

In the days that followed, my room filled with flowers. I felt deeply grateful to family and friends who'd sent them. An outsized card signed by all the women in my yoga group featured, inexplicably, a Siamese kitten.

The circle of women my sister, Mary, had talked about was

already forming. They sent cards and e-mails, which Philip printed out and brought in. Some, he said, had left casseroles on the doorstep at home.

From the capsule of my hospital room, ambitions and deadlines flattened to nothing. A mastectomy is the ultimate reminder that the only thing that really matters is love and kindness.

Regrets? There weren't many, except I'd taken life too seriously on the assumption there'd be decades to spare for frivolity. I'd spent countless hours shut away from the world bent over keyboards producing probably millions of words. Instead of living life, I'd spent too much time writing about it.

Lydia, Mary, friends, the yoga group, and readers who'd e-mailed in—sometimes I could almost feel the circle of women around the bed. Their good wishes and prayers seemed to fill the room. Some of the nurses felt it, too.

"This room has a lovely feel. I could stay here all day," said Nurse May before adding that my hair was a mess.

As she fished through my toiletry bag, I realized, with a creeping sense of shame, that I'd forgotten to pack a comb. Nurse Mary offered to buy one for me from the hospital shop. Returning soon after with the new comb, she stroked it tenderly through my hair. Kindness personified. I was unable to sit up and barely able to move my arms; self-grooming was out of the question.

Visitors. An elating, daunting prospect. Even though Lydia spent hours at my side, I didn't count her as a visitor because she didn't demand conversation or any kind of performance from me. She was more a presence, a lucky charm, providing reassurance and serenity by simply being there. She didn't mind if I drifted to sleep. Knowing she was there made it easier to sleep.

I longed to see the family, but not if my hissing legs and bottles of blood draped around the bed like macabre Christmas decorations caused alarm. Two figures appeared at the door that evening. Rob and Chantelle. Armed with bottles of mineral water and fresh limes, Rob knew exactly what was needed. He arranged my bed at the most comfortable angle, made sure the nurse call button was within easy reach, ran a watchful eye over the level of fluid in the drip. My mouth was dry as kitty litter and the mineral water spiked with fresh lime was nectar.

Philip's anxious face appeared regularly. He stroked my forehead, admired the flowers, and asked if there was anything he could do. The best gift he brought was our Bose radio from home. Tuned quietly to a classical music station, it provided bedside companions in the forms of Bach, Beethoven, et al. Mozart and flowers. What more could a girl want?

Another indispensable comfort was, oddly enough, a lamb-skin recommended by a nurse friend who'd been through similar surgery. Cast on my back for days and nights I welcomed its softness, and the way it seemed to let air circu-late underneath me.

During a day shift, a young nurse accelerated my drip. Nine liters later my abdomen was bloated with enough fluid to resem-ble a seven-month pregnancy.

Looking down at my distended abdomen bursting out of its corset, it reminded me of how Mum looked in her final days with bowel cancer. I felt nauseated. A ring of concerned nurses appeared.

"What's your pain level on a scale of one to ten?" one of them asked.

My stomach was a sack of broken glass. I felt on the edge of passing out, but didn't want them thinking I was a whiner. To be conservative I said six.

The nurses looked at each other. One of them said "As much as that?"

I was in too much pain to reply.

"It's subjective," the senior looking nurse said to the others. "If she thinks it's as high as six that's what it is."

Nurses will sometimes talk as if you're not in the room, call-ing you "she," which gives you an opportunity to eavesdrop and find out how sick you really are.

They decided it was nothing to worry about and gave me an injection. Greg's corset was exchanged for a softer body stock-ing. A few hours later, May appeared and wiped me down like a distressed baby who'd fallen out of its pram. She smoothed the sheets and settled me for the night. The woman deserved a sainthood.

Greg, a regular visitor, appeared soon after and announced his gardening efforts had succeeded. The transplant was thriving. I thanked him. He said it was the first time he'd seen me without my hair all over the place. The flatterer.

Encouraged, I ticked boxes for tomorrow's menu. Mediterranean Pasta with Spinach and Parmesan followed by Crème Caramel for desert. It looked haute cuisine. Hospital food's the same everywhere, though. The main course turned out to be made of cardboard, the Crème Caramel unapproachable.

Next morning, some drainage tubes were removed and the catheter was tugged out with a sting. I'd rather hoped to hang on to it. A permanent catheter would simplify plane trips and visits to the theater no end. And now I had to hobble, bent double like a hag in an old fairy story, to the loo.

Not only that, it was now necessary to confront the lonely fear of "sitting out." Perching on a chair next to a bed sounds simple; hardly even an activity. Good for you, too, according to the nurses. It opens your lungs and gets your blood moving in directions it never goes when you're lying down. The sitting-out chair was hard. My tailbone hurt. I stared longingly at the bed, willing it to glide over and envelop me. Twenty minutes of sitting out was more than I could achieve. I pressed the buzzer after a few minutes and asked to be helped back to bed.

Then there were the arm exercises the hearty physio insisted I do ten times a day. Standing facing a wall and creeping my fingers up the wall was barely possible.

I hadn't cried yet. Was something wrong? Philip brought Katharine, looking pale and falsely jolly. She wanted to show me a video on her camera of her school music concert. I agreed just to humor her. But as young soloists launched into the opening bars of "Bridge Over Troubled Water," just missing the top notes, my chest contracted.

The song reminded me of the pain that has always accompanied the challenge of being human, and the saintly beings who give solace through music and their own translucent purity—or (in some cases) hospital-strength medicine. For the first time since the last phone call with Lydia, I wept uncontrollably. Not the desperate barking of the previous episode but with the steady flow of an underground river.

Hospital time was both urgent and meaningless. The difference between going home on Monday or Tuesday could mean tears or elation. The woman two doors down who'd had surgery the same day as me was going home a day earlier. She was officially "doing better" than me. I didn't envy her. The idea of going home and learning to look after myself, specially with two drainage bottles attached, had no allure.

On some of her visits, Lydia helped me hobble bent double in a tangle of tubes and drainage bottles along the corridor. If I was feeling adventurous we'd catch the elevator downstairs. I'd venture into the hospital courtyard and gulp gallons of fresh air. Tainted with cigarette smoke, it was raw and exhilarating.

Days became cycles of routine—the sulky Eastern European woman with her cornflakes, then pills, surgeons' visits, temperature- and blood-pressure taking. It's surprising how quickly the adjustment's made. Probably the same thing happens in prisons. Comfort sprang from unusual sources—the tea bag sheathed in its blue envelope; diced canned fruit I'd never eat at home.

It was almost impossible to sleep with the hissing tubes massaging my legs. There was no point counting the hours of restless wakefulness. Four a.m. was much the same as four p.m., except there were no visitors.

Of all the night noises keeping me awake, the one that was most irritating was the sound of snoring across the corridor. How dare anyone indulge in the luxury of uninterrupted sleep?

On the third night, I became engrossed in a program about English architecture on the tiny TV high on the wall in the right-hand corner of my room. Admiring the Royal Crescent of Bath, my thoughts drifted to something that's a milestone after any operation. The first bowel movement.

I summoned Nurse May, who helped me creep to the loo, hanging on to her elbow. Draped with drainage bottles and wheeling my drip, I made sedate progress to the bathroom like a 110-year-old woman. Clutching the stainless-steel rail, I lowered myself on to the seat. May slid the door discreetly shut and said to press the buzzer if there were any problems. I sat anxiously enthroned while the television presenter continued his erudite description of how the city of Bath became extremely fashionable in the 1700s and how the stone chiseled from nearby hills contributed to architectural masterpieces.

Unfortunately, the commentary wasn't accompanied by any architectural masterpieces of an intimate nature on my part. Where was May anyway? There were no rustles or throat-clearing sounds from the other side of the door. She must've hurried away on some nursey business. I was alone and suddenly frightened.

A wave of dizziness. The harshly lit bathroom, along with the television presenter's carefully enunciated praise for the archi-tecture of Bath, merged into a sickening blur. With a clatter of bottles and tubes, I spiraled off the seat toward the floor, just managing to press the emergency buzzer on my way down.

The door slid open. A forest of nurses, including May, appeared above me.

"Get the commode!" snapped an authoritative voice.

"She's anaemic," said another. "She's been pale ever since she came out of surgery."

"Sleep deprived, too," said a third.

The old "she" again. Thanks for letting me know, girls.

"Her oxygen levels are okay, though," said May.

I was wheeled back to the room to be lowered painfully into bed. Glumness hovered for a while. The bedside phone screeched. In no mood for the Herculean task of answering, I flipped the receiver off with my hand and lowered my head into position.

It was the breast cancer surgeon, loud and a little breathless. Results were just back from pathology. She was confident the cancer had been removed. The growth was even larger than they'd thought. Another six months and it would've been absolutely everywhere, she said.

Absolutely everywhere. Wasn't there a rock song with a name like that? Thank goodness I'd ignored the GP who'd suggested I take the slow track to breast screening.

Wonderful news. So good I made her repeat it three times. To celebrate I was allowed to summon bedpans for the rest of the night. Pure luxury.

Next morning when I was ushered into the bathroom, I produced a masterpiece worthy of the Royal Crescent of Bath. Pale green, it was the color of Play-Doh, and probably a result of the pre-surgery scan when they'd pumped me full of radioactive dye. Bending uncomfortably to flush it away, I issued a silent apology to the environmental engineers who ran the municipal sewage ponds. The last thing they wanted was radioactive poo.

After breakfast, Nurse May hauled me out of bed and helped me into the shower. She said she'd seen the fear in my eyes in the bathroom the previous night, but I'd turned a corner today. When May said she liked the perfume in my hand cream, I made a mental note to send her some when I got home.

How painful it must've been for wounded soldiers, young and frightened with holes shot through their bodies. Almost every one of them must've fallen for a nurse. I was half in love with them myself, the competent ones at least. Good nurses are angels, kind and strong. I loved their gentle strength when they lifted me in their arms to rearrange my pillows or help me stagger across the floor.

Soon, however, I was going to have to get by without them. Very soon.

Entrapment

Never swear you're not getting another cat.

Clutching Philip's arm and creeping down the hospital steps, I entered a world of eye-stinging color. Winter gray streets and footpaths pulsated with vibrancy. The red of an advertising sign glowed so aggressively I was forced to look away. Maybe being in the hospital had heightened my senses. Or I'd forgotten to notice how vivid everyday life is.

Lydia and Katharine trailed behind us like anxious bridesmaids carrying my bags and what was left of the flowers.

It felt too soon to be going home. My abdomen was still swollen and a drainage tube somewhere below my right rib cage remained attached to its Christmas bauble bottle. I'd rather have stayed tucked up in the hospital until they'd removed that thing. But the nurses had made it clear enough. If I'd insisted on roosting in their airless corridors I'd have been ignored, pretty much. There were new patients to tend to.

Six nights in the hospital is long enough anyway: the food, the noise, the awful artwork. Presumably the nearly seven centimeters of high-grade cancerous growth removed from my right breast was now floating around in the clouds over our heads, merging with other particles and about to be drizzled down on the city. Technically, I had a pert new breast made from tummy flab and a reduced and lifted left breast to match. Somewhere underneath the bandages and swelling was a new woman. In reality, I was a patchwork quilt and felt like a wreck.

Driving home, Philip abandoned his usual Roman-taxi-driver-on-steroids technique and nursed the car along as if a bomb was lodged under the hood. When he pulled into our driveway, I looked up at Shirley. It was good to see the old girl. In my previous life I'd barely noticed the slope up to the front door. Today it looked like the path to Everest Base Camp. As I hobbled up the paving stones, drain sloshing inside a discreet pink drawstring bag, my lungs sucked and puffed. I felt like a building due for demolition. One nudge in the basement and I'd crumple.

Being home was good but frightening. The table was set for lunch, except for one glaring omission. There were knives and plates—but no forks. The old me would've sprung into the kitchen and slid the forks out of the drawer before you could flick a dishcloth. Now I could only sit and wait for someone to notice and do something about it. They didn't.

"Forks," I wheedled in my post-operative voice.

There was a pause bred from years of me leaping around to fix things before they'd started going wrong. Mother's syndrome. When does it start? Must be in those moments after birth when a woman sees her baby for the first time and feels like a god. Giving birth is the ultimate act of creation. No wonder Mother Earth was the first deity. She brought things to life and helped them grow. We handed religion over to men just to keep them occupied. Our devotion to our creations, our kids, has no limits. I'd heard an eighty-year-old woman angst over her sixty-year-old son as if he was still in nappies.

It's a two-way disorder. Mum becomes a compulsive nurturer. Dad and kids play the role of domestic dimwits. Once it sank in that I could not, would not, jump up from my chair to collect the forks, Lydia hurried over to the kitchen to get them.

Motherhood has a habit of turning women into martyrs. I'd always believed I was too liberated for that to happen. Yet the decades had eroded me into someone just as subservient and resentful as my own mother. Jeez, I had three aprons hanging from a hook beside the fridge! I even wore the one emblazoned "Desperate Husband."

There are no medals for being dictator of the small island nation that is a household. Maybe breast cancer would bring the dawn of a freer, more democratic society to our place. Perhaps I'd learn to step back and take care of myself more. It might be good for all of us.

I couldn't sit at the table for long. A hot dagger was digging into my ribs. Bed and the forgiving softness of the sheepskin were welcome relief.

It soon became clear that the new regime was going to require patience. I couldn't bend over to pick a towel off the floor. Or stoop to collect crumbs, or petals from wilting floral arrangements, the way I always had. It was time to adopt selective blindness like everyone else, and not notice anything below waist level.

The only suggestion Greg had given to ease the abdominal swelling was gentle massage. Limited arm movement made it impossible to perform the task myself. Understandably, there weren't many volunteers. To my astonishment Lydia stepped forward and offered her services. Twice daily she instructed me to lie on the couch while she rubbed almond oil on my belly. Her willingness to overlook my gruesome wounds, her tender dedication, was overwhelming. I'd never have been so physically intimate with my own mother. Lydia cooked meals, brought cups of tea, and took over the running of the household.

Whenever I asked about her time in Sri Lanka, her gaze drifted sideways. Her descriptions were vague. She'd meditated a lot, often more than twelve hours a day. ("How do you sit still that long?" I asked. "Oh, sometimes I'd get up and do walking meditations," she replied.) There had been outings with the monk, blessing a few bits and pieces, and taking part in ceremonies.

I still couldn't get a feel for the place and why it held such magnetism for her. The more I probed, the less willing she was to talk. Nevertheless, I was so overjoyed to have her home I didn't want to do or say anything to make her uneasy.

When I asked what had happened to Ned, she looked away and said they'd broken up. Another No Go area.

Assuming her father Steve had paid for her return fare to

Melbourne—there was no other possible way she could have afforded the ticket home—I wrote him a fulsome card of thanks. For all the disagreements we'd had in the past it was heartening to know he understood the importance of family.

Soon after I posted the card, I dreamed Lydia's monk was sitting in a pool of light at the end of our bed and laughing good-naturedly. With his maroon robes folded neatly around him and his bald head gleaming, he looked so amiable my animosity toward him faded temporarily. I wanted to thank him for the cave ceremony, but by the time I'd woken up properly the monk had disappeared.

It was the second outlandish visitation I'd had in a couple of months. Maybe it was just a matter of time before I'd be wandering down streets muttering to myself. There had to be some explanation for the visitations. The first one with Mum in the wellness retreat was probably due to caffeine withdrawal. And the monk to a hangover from hospital drugs.

Steve didn't reply to the thank-you note, but our relationship had never been straightforward.

Forbidden to vacuum, lift anything weighing more than a couple of pounds, drive, or pick things up off the floor, I struggled to adapt.

"Don't bend over like that!" Lydia snapped as I stooped over to pick an envelope off the floor. Her tone was sharply maternal. The power dynamic had changed.

A patient is so called for good reason. In the early days after surgery, progress had been fast. In hospital I'd woken one morning suddenly able to creep to the loo. Once I was home, improvement slowed. Some days I even went backwards. A drive to Rob and Chantelle's for pizza one night was surprisingly harrowing. I'd forgotten to wear the surgeon's "corset" that held the ghoulish grin of stitches in my abdomen together. It was a lovely evening but I was wrecked the following day. Then there was the night I spent bonding with Katharine watching *Doctor Who* with a hot-water bottle on my stomach. I'd forgotten that a wide strip of flesh there had no feeling. In the morning it was bright red and accessorized with two large blisters.

Other times, I felt a lot better, like the day I asked Lydia to stop at the drugstore and buy leg waxing strips. As if I needed to volunteer for more pain.

The delight of my sister Mary's arrival was immeasurable. The dark brown curls of her girlhood were lighter these days, and tamed by regular visits to the hair salon. Having stayed in the town we grew up in, her outward style was conservative, but her perspective surprisingly broad. She'd raised three children with her husband Barry and continued to work as a substitute primary school teacher. Her pupils had grown up to be cops and car thieves, opera singers and opticians. There wasn't much she hadn't seen.

Some people deteriorate with each decade—and not just physically. Disappointment seeps into their bones and turns them bitter. Mary's one of those rare beings who grow more beautiful every year without even trying. The tenderness in her hazel eyes had intensified with time. Since her bout with breast cancer, she'd accepted that while life's not perfect, it's still pretty wonderful. I watched her savor a shaft of light on water, or the blue of a hydrangea flower. She'd learned how to live.

Unlike me and our brother Jim, Mary was always the Quiet One. You'd think a reserved person in a household of loud-mouths would lack power, but it turned out the opposite. Whenever Mary ventured a well-considered opinion in her calm, steady voice, we always listened. Still do.

When she wrapped her arms around me I was the little sister again, protected in her embrace. Nothing could hurt me now. She smelled of home.

Mary's easygoing presence in the house over the following days was medicine in itself. To the outside world we would've looked like two middle-aged matrons sifting through old photo albums together and drinking mugs of tea. Inside our heads we were the little girls we'd always been—Mary, wise and tactful; me, eager for her approval.

Every day I crept around the block, trying to walk a little

farther each time. Faced with steps to climb up or down I could almost hear my stitches screaming "Nooooooo!" Hobbling back from a 500-meter marathon, we bumped into Patricia from down the street. When we'd first moved into Shirley, Patricia had introduced herself and said she wasn't social and would prefer not being asked inside for cups of tea. Respecting her for that, I'd tried to stay out of her way. Fate had punished us both ever since, arranging for us to bump into each other constantly—at the supermarket; waiting for crossing lights to change. Trapped in another unplanned encounter, I asked how she was. Not too good, she said. She was having women's problems.

I hoped she wouldn't go on too long. My legs were getting wobbly. When she asked after my health, I hesitated. Telling her about the mastectomy could've been perceived as one-upmanship, so I said, "Good."

Patricia beamed at my sister and said, "She always looks well, doesn't she?" and trotted off down the street.

Sometimes Mary would say I was looking tired and excuse herself to catch a tram into town or go for walks. I sometimes worried she might need a higher standard of entertainment, but she assured me she was happy with her own company. On her last day with us she returned from an excursion with a twinkle in her eye.

"What is it?" I asked.

"I don't think I should say," she said smiling enigmatically at Lydia and me.

I recognized that expression from years back. The old "I know what you're getting for Christmas" smile.

"Come on! Tell us!"

Lydia stopped rattling the dishes in the sink and put her head to one side.

"Is it a secret?" Lydia asked.

"No," Mary replied. "Well yes, it should be. Oh, all right. The only reason I'm going to tell you is you've sworn you're never getting another cat."

"Of course I'm not getting another cat."

"Okay, then," Mary said, settling to her subject. "I've just seen the cutest Siamese kitten in a pet shop across town!"

My sister is in possession of what's commonly known as a long fuse. She doesn't get hugely annoyed or enthralled by anything much. When she does it's for good reason. Her eyes were positively blazing.

"What were you doing in a pet shop?"

"I was just walking past and I saw him. Well, I think it's a him. He's really special!"

Another thing about Mary is she has an eye for quality. Her taste is restrained, and exceptionally good. Any kitten she considered even half cute would be off the scale of adorability by anyone's standards.

Nevertheless, I was on safe ground. I had no intention of getting another cat. Not only that, I'd never been enamored of Siamese as a breed. While the ones I'd met were attractive to look at, they were far too full of themselves and yowly.

If I ever acquired another feline—which I wasn't going to—it would be a mixed-breed moggy like Cleo, preferably from an animal shelter. On top of that, in the unlikely-verging-on-impossible circumstance I'd *ever* consider another cat, it certainly wouldn't be one from a pet shop. Though I didn't know much about it, I'd heard rumors about kitten and puppy farmers who breed animals indiscriminately in their backyards with the sole purpose of selling them to pet shops on a no-questions-asked basis.

No "cute" Siamese kitten was going to wrap me around its little paw. Immunity was guaranteed. On the other hand, I'd just started feeling strong enough for a proper outing. A quick trip to a pet shop would be fun, and about all I could manage before crawling back into bed.

I climbed painfully into my clothes, packed the drainage bottle into my coat pocket, slapped a homemade beanie on my head, and creaked down the path. Lydia loaded me carefully into the front passenger's seat and drove the three of us across the river. A parking space was waiting right outside the pet shop. Hunched over my stitches, I hobbled through the doors with sister and daughter on either side.

If there's an opposite of a cancer ward, it must surely be a pet store. In this restless nursery of life the smell of damp newspaper and sawdust mingled with birdseed and something vaguely meaty. Budgies squawked, canaries whistled, puppies whined. Neon stripes of tropical fish flashed from inside their tanks.

A large cage about six feet high in the center of the shop soon drew us into its orbit. A handwritten notice on the cage door said "Burmese and Siamese Kittens. Please Do Not put Finger's through the Wire. It Spreads Disease."

I'm a fully paid-up apostrophe bore. So much so, Katharine reckoned I should have my own television show traveling the world striking out rogue apostrophes and restoring omitted ones on public signs. I was on the verge of protesting about the creative punctuation of "Finger's" before my attention was swiftly diverted.

About a dozen tiny kittens were curled up in bunches, some on the floor, others on a ledge halfway up the cage. They were all fast asleep—except for one. A pale kitten, considerably larger than the others, was scrambling up the inside of the cage wire with the aptitude of a world-class mountaineer. One paw after another he scaled the wall, trusting his entire body weight to the strength of the claws on his front feet. Higher and higher he climbed, until he was almost at the summit. Deeply engrossed in his challenge, every muscle in his body was focused on conquering the cage—and gravity.

Even from several feet away I could see he was beautiful—sleek and long limbed. Milk white, his faced was tinged with shadowy brown with matching ears, tail, and feet. Intrigued by his looks and daredevil personality, I took a step forward. The kitten suddenly froze and, spread-eagled against the wire, fixed me with a sapphire gaze. The intensity of his stare shot straight through to my heart. The clamor and noise of the pet shop faded to nothing. I was transfixed.

The kitten refused to unlock his gaze. I couldn't look away. We were caught in a mutual stare. A strange interaction seemed to be happening. Admittedly, hallucinogens were still pumping through me after seven hours of anesthetic ten days earlier. Yet as the kitten bored his electric blue eyes through me, I could feel him insisting, no *demanding*, we become part of each other's lives.

I'd experienced love at first sight once before. When I'd first clapped eyes on Philip, I'd practically turned to pancake mixture. But he was—still is—an incredibly handsome man. That magic evening, standing at the top of the museum steps in an impeccably cut suit, he'd resembled an action hero on his day off. Who wouldn't have fallen for him?

I'd always assumed love at first sight was a human-to-human thing, and not something that could occur between a middle-aged woman and a Siamese kitten. But in those few seconds I'd become enraptured. At some sub-cellular level that kitten and I belonged together.

"See? I told you he's cute," Mary said. "Shall we get you home now?" she added, probably sensing the danger and trying to get me out of the place.

When I tried to turn away the kitten slid his paw between the wire, reached out to me, opened his mouth, and emitted an adorable squeak. I'd always thought Siamese had loud, ugly voices. This little fellow had just proved me wrong. Despite the warning notice with its ridiculous apostrophe, I couldn't resist. I took the kitten's paw and rested it between my fingers and thumb.

The kitten gazed into my eyes and purred ecstatically. All resistance crumbled.

"Look at that!" said Lydia. "He wants to come home with us."

"Didn't you read the sign?" came a disapproving voice, slicing through our romantic tableau.

"I'm sorry," I said, tearing my eyes away from the kitten to address a spotty young man in tortoiseshell glasses. My first reaction was to dislike this pet shop policeman. Yet behind the tortoiseshell glasses his expression was protective. Thin and shabbily dressed, the youth was almost certainly underpaid. He was probably trying to look after the animals as best he could.

"The kitten reached out to me and I . . ."

The kitten withdrew his paw and continued scaling the cage wall.

"If you knew how many people come in this shop every day," the youth continued. "They all want to touch the animals and every one of them has germs on their hands. They pass on all sorts of diseases to the animals."

I nodded reluctantly and put my hand in my pocket.

As the kitten reached the top of the cage wall I wondered what would happen next. Climbing down back feet first would've been the most sensible option, but the kitten had no interest in predictability. Like Tarzan, he swung himself sideways, gripping the wire ceiling with one set of claws after the other. In an instant he was hanging upside down from all fours and, after making sure his audience was still enthralled, let out a triumphant mew. He was more circus performer than feline.

"Is this kitten available?" I asked, hardly able to believe the words bouncing off my lips. The kitten's upside-down gaze swiveled from me to the shop assistant, as if waiting for the answer.

"Oh, that one," he said with the slightest ripple on his lips. "He's had conjunctivitis so he was in isolation at the back of the shop for a few weeks. That's why he's so much older than the other kittens."

"Older? I'd thought he was just bigger," I gabbled. "But of course bigger *means* older . . ."

"Shouldn't we go home and think about it?" Mary asked. "You'll blame me if it turns out to be a disaster."

Once a big sister, always a big sister. The kitten released its grip from the cage ceiling and dropped rapidly earthward. Lydia, Mary, and I drew a breath in unison as he sailed past us only to land safely on top of a ball of brown fluff curled up beside the feeding bowls.

"He always does that," said the shop assistant. "Uses that other kitten for a landing pad. Sleeps on her, too. I don't know how she puts up with it."

Unhurt, the brown kitten seemed almost grateful to have provided a mattress for her hyperactive friend. The Siamese shook himself, and after a few quick licks to check his legs and spine were still in place, swaggered over to the wire again to continue his charm offensive.

Even in my infatuated condition, I could hear faint warning bells. This kitten had so much personality he was on the verge of egotistical. He had potential to be a handful, possibly even a little dysfunctional. That only made me love him more. Like every woman who's been a sucker for a charmer, I didn't care. They weren't warning bells, they were wedding bells! Whatever erratic behavior he didn't grow out of, I'd cure. Hadn't I raised three children successfully, more or less? A four-legged animal would be a pushover.

"Would you like to hold him?" the youth asked.

I nodded vigorously. It felt uncomfortable having my future happiness dependent on a spotty young man who was so offhand about my attachment to the kitten. He hadn't even answered my question properly about whether the little thing was available or not. He seemed quite fond of the creature. Maybe he was planning to keep the kitten for himself.

When I asked the young man what his name was, he seemed embarrassed, perplexed even. Nathan, he said, turning pink and examining the shelves of dog food. I was beginning to get his measure. Nathan was a shy person who, disappointed or intimidated by the human race, felt more comfortable with animals.

Nathan opened the cage door and lunged for the Siamese, who sprang nimbly out of his grasp into a pile of shredded newspaper. The kitten remained motionless inside his hiding place, confident he couldn't be seen. He was betrayed by a small dark tail protruding from the spaghetti of paper.

"He thinks it's a game," Nathan sighed, reaching into the

papery nest and lifting the creature out by the scruff of his neck. I'd never believed people who said that was a humane way to handle kittens, but the little fellow didn't seem to mind.

Nathan lowered his prisoner into my hands. Gazing up at me, the kitten purred like a lawnmower. He was so silky and warm. For the first time in what seemed ages, something inside my chest softened. Liquid honey streamed through my arteries. My breathing suddenly came from a softer, deeper place. Weeks of worry and pain melted away.

"Is he for sale?" I asked.

Nathan nodded, adding that a free vet's checkup and reduced price for neutering would be included. I knew there were all sorts of questions people are supposed to ask before buying a pet. They flew out of my head. Nathan confirmed the kitten was purebred Siamese.

"Does he have papers?"

Nathan shot me a defensive look.

"None of our animals have papers," he said. "If we bothered with that sort of thing they'd be way too expensive."

It made perfect sense. I had no intention of putting him in cat shows, or using him for breeding purposes.

Lydia asked if she could hold the kitten. Reluctantly, I passed him over. He rolled on his back and writhed playfully in her hands. Mary, Lydia, and I chuckled together. After such an anxious time, the relief of laughter was immeasurable.

"What will we call him?" Lydia asked.

"You mean what *would* we call him?" I corrected in my old voice, the sane one that knew getting another kitten would be preposterous.

I'd learned from our experience with goldfish, years earlier, that bestowing an animal with a name creates a bond that sets you up for heartbreak. After Finny, Swimmer, and Jaws had been lowered tearfully into what was becoming a mass grave in our back garden, I'd insisted any new goldfish we acquired would be nameless. They'd simply have numbers. As it turned out, One, Two, and Three survived for biblical years by goldfish standards, creating hundreds of descendants in their backyard pool.

As I contemplated buying the kitten, I thought of Philip. When he'd moved in with us all those years ago, we'd been a ready-made family complete with Cleo. It's one thing to take on a cat as part of a bulk deal, and something quite different to have a kitten land uninvited in your life.

Gender was something the kitten had in its favor. After Rob left home, Philip often complained half-jokingly about being the only male in a household full of women. ("Even the cat's female," he used to grumble.) If we took this little clown home, Philip might form a man-to-kitten bromance.

I'd never been a fan of rugby, but it was Philip's obsession. As the kitten dived from Lydia's arms onto the pet shop floor and sprinted furiously toward the wall of birdcages, I was reminded of the fluid athleticism of one of the most famous rugby All Blacks of all time—Jonah Lomu.

"Jonah," I said, over the budgies' shrieks of alarm. "Let's call him Jonah."

Disenchantment

Beware of charm in cats and men.

A pair of sapphire eyes glinted through slits of the pet carrier as Lydia bore Jonah gently up the front path. Mary followed behind with the food and litter bags, and a leopard-skin cat bed. I was in charge of the kitten's entertainment center—a bag containing balls, fake mice, and a "fishing rod" stick with an imitation bird and a bell attached to the end of an elastic line. It seemed incredible that one small creature required so much equipment.

A royal retinue, we escorted the carrier and its inhabitant respectfully down the hallway to the family room. Lydia lowered the box gently to the floor. It emitted a squeak.

"Shall we let him out?" Lydia asked.

"Maybe just open the cage door and see how he feels," I replied. "He might want to stay in there until he's used to us."

As Lydia bent to slide the carrier's latch open, its door bulged, then burst onto the floor in an explosion of paws and fur. Jonah bounced onto the carpet, looked around, and shook himself.

With pale fur and huge dark ears overshadowing his arresting eyes, he was cuteness personified. The only things that set him apart from classical beauty were his stubby tail and his back feet, which were several sizes too large for him.

He was much bigger than Cleo had been when she'd entered our lives so soon after Sam's death in 1983. Cleo had arrived when our family was torn apart by tragedy. I wondered if Jonah might play a similarly vital role, taking our minds off cancer and focusing us on the future.

After giving us a brief inspection, Jonah dived straight under the cane chair and peered out at us through the bamboo bars.

"Oh the poor thing's terrified," said Mary. "Let him stay there till he's more comfortable. I'll put the kettle on."

I'd never imagined we'd end up with another cat, let alone a Siamese. It's such a presumptuous breed with so many overblown stories in its background. According to legend, only the King of Siam (modern-day Thailand) and members of the royal family were permitted to own a Siamese cat. Whenever a high-ranking person died, one of these felines was chosen to receive the dead person's soul. The cat would then be taken to live in a temple where monks and priests fed it the finest food off solid gold plates. The dead person's relatives provided cushions made of exquisite silks for the creature to lounge around on. Apart from eating, lounging, and looking beautiful, the only other responsibility the cat had was to attend ceremonies. I hoped Jonah wasn't expecting that kind of life with us.

We tried to ignore him nestling under the chair, but it was like ignoring a peacock in a henhouse. As Mary walked past with her mug of tea a paw shot out and batted her ankle.

"He wants to play," she said. "Where's that fishing line?"

The plastic bag rustled as she reached into it and removed the rod with impudent bird attached. As she trailed the bird in front of the cane chair, a paw sprang out and batted it . . . once, twice. The bell jingled a protest every time the bird was hit.

Lydia lifted the two front chair legs off the floor. Mary trailed the fishing rod bird into the center of the room—and boom! Jonah surged out from under the chair and sprang on the hapless bird, grabbing it between his teeth and kicking it with his oversized back feet.

I'd been nervous of laughing since the operation. So many everyday activities—sometimes even just the challenge of sitting in an upright chair—caused jabs of pain so sharp they could take my breath away. But watching a kitten hammering the life out of a toy bird made me chortle so much I spilled my tea. It was a relief to know I could laugh again with no physical pain. In fact, it seemed to haul me back from fear and illness into a vibrant world in which life was continually renewed. Laughing at the kitten freed me up to laugh about everything else that'd been happening lately. It shook off the stale hospital air and brought me back to life.

Jonah sat back on his haunches and looked up at us appraisingly.

"Do you think Cleo would approve?" Lydia asked.

With his lanky limbs and masculine swagger, Jonah was the opposite of Cleo in almost every way. He was twice her size at the same age. His fur was pale as the moon, while Cleo had been black all over. While his coat was soft, his fur was coarser than Cleo's. He was a thoroughbred from a pet shop. Cleo had been an unashamed half-breed from a friend with an excess of kittens. There was no way Cleo could mistake Jonah for a replacement cat.

"How could she not?" I smiled. "Do you know what Cleo would want just now? A saucer of milk."

Lydia hurried to the kitchen, emerging seconds later and placing a bowl of milk in front of the kitten. Intrigued, he sniffed it, then dipped a front paw in the liquid, forming a succession of pale circles on the surface. Jonah raised the damp paw to his nose, sniffed again, and shook his head in disgust. With a swoop of his long back leg, he toppled the bowl over, sending milk gushing over the rug.

Mary stood up to get a cloth from the kitchen. Lydia moved to rescue Jonah from the flood, but before she could get near him he galloped across the floor and shimmied straight up the curtains.

"Here, kitty!" I called.

Jonah hesitated for a moment, as if considering the invitation. But he narrowed his eyes and took flight like a trapeze artist, launching himself through the air to land on top of the kitchen dresser.

Knocked together by an amateur craftsman in the depths of
the New Zealand bush in the mid 1800s, the kauri dresser had
since become a live-in restaurant for generations of borer. Every
time I opened a drawer, piles of sawdust were a reminder the
dresser was another day closer to total collapse. I'd tried to get
it renovated once by a "restorer" who'd left a flier in the letter-
box. He'd returned the dresser reeking of cigarette smoke and
booze, and in even wonkier condition than it'd been to begin
with. Photo albums went in the lower cupboards to keep it
stable. Our best wineglasses went in the upper cabinet because
they didn't weigh much and would therefore be less likely to
cause structural failure.

What I hadn't counted on was a berserk kitten hurling himself
on top of the upper cabinet. The glasses trembled ominously as
he struggled to find his balance.

Lydia climbed a kitchen chair and pleaded with him to jump
into her arms. He glared down at her and refused to budge.
Sighing, Lydia headed off to the garden shed to get the ladder.
Jonah watched intrigued as she gingerly climbed the ladder and
reached out to him.

Just as it seemed she might catch him, he flew off the dresser,
sending champagne flutes toppling over red wine glasses, which
smashed into white wine glasses, shattering the sherry glasses
nobody had used since 1970.

"It's a shame I'm leaving tomorrow," said Mary as Jonah
plummeted toward the kitchen counter, her tone not entirely
sincere.

The kitten, combined with the broken glasses and postopera-
tive exhaustion, was suddenly more than I could handle. How
stupid I'd been to fall for him, let alone give him a name. I hobbled off to the bedroom, shut the door, crawled into bed, and
slept.

I woke to the sound of bells jingling and an unfamiliar squeak-
ing sound. Lydia opened the bedroom door and Jonah burst in
with the fishing rod between his teeth. He leaped on the covers,

narrowly missing the most painful parts of my body, and dropped the fishing rod in my hand.

"He wants to play," said Lydia. "And I need to help Mary with dinner. Can I leave him with you?"

Using my stronger left arm, I lifted the fishing rod and flicked it across my thighs. The bell jingled as Jonah lunged at the fake bird and snared it between his teeth. His reactions were incredibly fast. I flicked the fishing rod in the opposite direction. Impressive and beautiful to watch, he leaped and caught the bird midair. The more rapidly I flicked the rod, the faster Jonah went. When I made the bird fly a few feet into the air he jumped and pirouetted midair like a ballerina. A wind-up kitten on fast-forward, he caught the bird every time.

I was worn out in minutes, but not Jonah. He wanted the game to go on. When I put the fishing rod down, he picked it up between his teeth and pressed it into my hand. Fortunately, Katharine arrived home from school and succumbed immediately.

"Oooooh, Mum! He's *adorable!*" she cooed. "Can I take him for a while?"

Could she ever! Lifting him into her arms and carrying him out of the room, she swore to take on feeding and litter-changing duties for eternity.

To celebrate her last night with us, Mary was preparing a sumptuous meal of casseroled chicken legs and sponge-top pudding from the same Edmonds recipe book our grandmother used. Nostalgic cooking smells lured me out of the bedroom to lie on one of the green sofas and watch my sister and daughter at work. Side by side, they moved in easy rhythm, Lydia peeling vegetables while Mary whipped a sponge-top batter. Dinner would be forty minutes away, precisely timed for Philip's arrival home from work.

Jonah amused himself by running nonstop up and down the stairs. Presumably he'd decided to take a rest from shredding the freshly laid carpet, after galloping around the hall, scaling the family room blinds, and diving into the toilet.

As she folded the pudding batter over a dish of stewed plums, Mary asked if we remembered Cleo being this active. I had hazy memories of Cleo being a handful as a kitten. Maybe it was because I was physically weak this time, but Jonah seemed worse. Much worse. By the time Cleo was Jonah's age, she'd morphed into a calm and reasonable young cat. I'd have no hope of keeping up, let alone catching him if I was alone in the house with him. Just watching him was exhausting. If we'd worked out a way of attaching him to the national grid he'd have kept an entire suburb alight. Maybe it wouldn't be such a tragedy if Philip refused to keep him.

Lydia smoothed a white cloth over the table. Once the plates, glasses, and cutlery were in place, she rearranged a bowl of flowers and lit a candle in my favorite candlestick—Mexican, lime-green pottery and covered with decorative flowers.

"Oh Lydia," I said. "It looks gorg—"

Suddenly, Jonah sprang onto the tabletop, sending forks and plates flying. The candlestick toppled and smashed to pieces. The only thing that stopped the tablecloth from bursting into flames was the water from the flower bowl that was now weeping on its side, its floral contents scattered.

My normal, robust self would have laughed it off.

"Can't somebody calm him down?!" I whined.

Registering my distress, Lydia scooped our vandal off the floor and carried him to an armchair. Mary resurrected what she could of the table arrangement while Lydia held Jonah on her knees, gently resisting his twists and kicks until he stopped struggling. Closing her eyes, she began to chant. Jonah pricked his ears forward, listened intensely, and accompanied her with a gravelly purr. Tuned into an unseen world, cat and daughter drifted into a state of serenity . . .

Minutes later, the eyes snapped open and he was off bouncing down the hall toward my study. We soon heard the eerie harmonies of paws on a computer keyboard.

"Stop him!" I called to Katharine, who'd been lured downstairs by the cacophony.

As Katharine hurried toward my study, Jonah emerged looking thoughtful.

"It's okay," Katharine called. "He's jammed your keyboard but I can fix that. Oh, and he's knocked over the jar you keep rubber bands in but that's nothing."

Jonah trotted toward me, let out a mournful groan, and vomited a coil of rubber bands on the rug.

"Oh dear . . . !"

But he'd just heard the toilet flush. Nothing was more exciting for him than trying to bat the torrent of water with his paw. Turbocharged, he was off to the bathroom.

Watching his tail disappear, I tallied his score. Two champagne flutes and one red wine glass—smashed. One Mexican candlestick—beheaded. Carpet shredded on stairs, plus damp patch where rubber bands were vomited up. Merino beanie (brand new)—chewed and holey. Computer keyboard—jammed.

The dream of owning a kitten had become a nightmare. We'd been hit by a feline tornado that left nothing but destruction in his wake. If Cleo had in any way sent us this creature, it was as a cruel trick to remind us what a perfect family pet and guardian she'd been.

I convulsed with tears. Lydia protested and Katharine cried while Mary looked guilty, but there was no alternative.

The kitten would have to go back.

As I crept off the sofa and down the hall to find the pet carrier, I heard the front door key turn in its lock. Philip appeared with the ravenous look of a man who's smelled chicken casserole at the end of a twelve-hour day.

"Who's this?" he asked as Jonah trotted forward to greet him.

"My biggest mistake," I said. "Would you mind taking him back to the pet shop in the morning?"

Jonah sat neatly in front of Philip, examined him closely, then stretched up a long front paw to pat his knee.

"What's wrong with him?" Philip asked, as Jonah put his head to one side and mewed politely.

"Hyperactive, neurotic, destructive, dysfunctional, vain . . ."

"Vain?"

"He's like one of those fashion models. He knows he's beautiful, and he uses it to manipulate people . . . just look at him . . ."

Jonah stared innocently at a spider on the ceiling. He was so perfectly colored, and those eyes beaming out from behind their robber's mask were exquisite.

"What do the girls think?"

"They want to keep him, but that's easy for them to say. They'll be moving out before we know it."

"You're very dashing, aren't you boy?" said Philip, lifting Jonah into his arms. Jonah lay passively on his back for a few seconds, his outsized kangaroo feet pointing skyward while Philip tickled him behind his ears. Jonah returned the favor by licking his hand. "And affectionate."

"He's exhausting."

"He's just a boy," said Philip. "Let's see how everyone feels after dinner."

"That's the other thing. Remember how Cleo loved food? We could get her to do anything for a piece of chicken. This one refuses to eat."

Philip carried him through to the laundry room, where a bowl full of dry food sat beside another filled with wet food, both untouched. He lowered Jonah in front of the wet food. The kitten sniffed the mound of fishy goo, licked it tentatively, and began bolting it down.

Philip told me to go back to bed and he'd sort things out with "Fur Man." Pet names already? He was bonding dangerously with the intruder. Nevertheless, I was too tired to do anything other than retreat to the bedroom. Lydia tapped on the door and brought in a tray bearing dinner.

There were only three sleeping pills left inside my bedside cabinet. I swallowed two with a swig of water and signed out for the night.

Before dawn next morning we woke to the sound of regular thudding accompanied by jingling bells—a noise that might accompany an invasion of Morris dancers. Philip climbed out of bed. As he turned the door handle, the door swung open and in burst Jonah, fishing rod firmly snared between his teeth. He hurled himself on the duvet, placed the rod on my hand and stepped back expectantly. Philip smiled and disappeared off to the kitchen to make tea and toast.

Nestled on the blankets, Jonah purred like a machine, waiting patiently for the game to begin. I wasn't in the mood to play, especially as he was going back to the pet shop in an hour or two. Jonah looked quizzically at me, then moved forward and touched my hand with a soft paw, its claws diplomatically sheathed. In the most gentlemanly manner, he was issuing an invitation. To wrap my hand around the rod and swing it through the air would involve minimal effort. Surely I wasn't so mean-spirited I'd turn him down?

Sighing, I started swinging the rod with my good left arm, setting the pesky bird and its bell in motion. Jonah watched mesmerized for a few seconds, before adjusting his legs into the ideal lunging position. Anticipating his victim's flight path, he quivered from side to side.

Watching the bird, his focus became intense, as though he was imagining himself inside the body of his prey, and was at one with its every swoop. Then with the grace of Rudolf Nureyev in his prime, Jonah launched himself into the air, catching the bird and bell between his teeth and front paws.

Once we'd started we couldn't stop. Every lunge was balletic. There was no challenge the young kitten wouldn't accept. Higher and higher he leaped until sometimes he seemed to pause midair in a single pose reaching for the bird. A study in cappuccino shades, with those flashing blue eyes, he was so beautiful. And so full of life.

I was falling for Jonah's charms again.

"Still going back to the pet shop, are we?" Philip laughed when he returned laden with mugs of tea and marmalade toast. Easing into his favorite chair, Philip sank his teeth into his toast. But Jonah had no intention of letting him enjoy breakfast in peace. With the bird between his teeth, the kitten jumped off the bed and laid the fishing rod at Philip's feet before dipping his head and stepping backwards. He gazed steadily up at Philip.

"You can't turn him down," I said.

Feigning reluctance, Philip sighed and picked up the fishing rod. But he had no intention of going easy on Jonah. Philip had been an army officer trainer before I met him. Summoning up old skills, he flicked and spun the fishing rod at twice the speed I'd managed. Jonah rose to the challenge, leaping higher, running faster, springing on and off the bed so fast he became a blur of pale fur. Sometimes Jonah caught the bird, other times it was too fast for him.

"Go easy on him," I said.

Philip held the rod still and smiled down at the kitten, whose only signs of exertion were his heaving sides. Once more, they charged into battle.

Philip stood up and twirled the bird in a circle around his legs with Jonah chasing a whisker's length behind.

It was the raucous rough and tumble Philip had missed out on since Rob had left home. Man and cat made quite a pair. Whenever Philip tried to finish the game and put the fishing rod down Jonah picked it up and pressed it into Philip's hand.

"Someone's got to work around here," he sighed, collecting Jonah off the floor and curling him around the blankets over my knees. Jonah emitted a strange sound through his nose—a cross between a cluck and a sneeze, a sort of "snitch." A condescending noise we'd soon become familiar with, the "snitch" was Jonah's way of expressing disappointment or disgust. He hadn't wanted the game to end.

"Never mind, boy," I said. "You can have a rest with me now."

Jonah looked at me with eyes that could melt an ice shelf. Purring, he stepped over the covers, carefully avoiding my sensitive abdomen and torso. He seemed to know exactly where he needed to be, nestled into my neck with his head on the pillow. Heaving a sigh, he sounded like a traveler who, after an epic journey, had finally arrived home. Who was I to argue?

★ ★ ★

When I heard Mary bringing her suitcase down the stairs, I felt a moist lump in my throat. It had been wonderful having her stay for the week. Philip was taking her to the airport. As he stowed her bag in his car, I burrowed in the comforting curve of her shoulder and thanked her for everything.

"Take care," she said. "And good luck with that kitten."

Outside Cat

A cat improves a relationship.

As I grew stronger, Lydia took me for drives into the country. Bare paddocks stretched under relentless blue sky. Skeletal farm animals trudged through craters of cracked mud that had once sparkled with drinking water. It made me yearn for the neon green grass and fat Friesian cows of childhood.

Wherever we went, Lydia opened doors for me and walked half a step behind as though I was worthy of respect. She was so deferential I hardly knew how to respond. I certainly hadn't raised her to treat me that way.

Still, as she massaged oil into my feet I wasn't about to complain. Through all my weeks of recovery, Lydia couldn't have been kinder—cooking, doing laundry, cleaning, even mopping up after I threw up over the blue dachshund slippers. Her regular abdominal massages reduced the swelling and saved me from going back into the hospital to have the fluid drained.

Jonah was a soothing presence for the two of us. Whenever we spoke to him gently, running our hands through his fur, it was only natural to use softer tones with each other. Lydia and I became closer than we'd ever been.

While we didn't have direct discussions about if and when she might return to Sri Lanka, I continued forwarding travel warnings and reports of the civil war to her. The response from Lydia's laptop was zero. When I asked if she'd read my e-mails, or even opened them, she was vague. The information I had was *important*, I'd tell her, aware the accusatory edge was slipping back into my voice.

Incense continued to waft indifferently through the house as she strolled downstairs wearing the pale colors of a monastic student. If I asked if she was still considering becoming a nun, perhaps in some nice local monastery, she shut me down.

While I was willing to accept Lydia could do whatever she liked as a legal adult, I was terrified at the thought of her putting her life at risk.

People could meditate on a bus or a beach . . . just about *any*where, I told her whenever I had the chance. They didn't have to go to . . . I could hardly bear to say the name of the place anymore.

Meanwhile, my efforts to cultivate friends who belonged to "nice local Buddhist" groups fell flat. Beards and hand-made sandals weren't her style. Gazing at the wall above their heads, Lydia demonstrated a lack of interest bordering on rudeness.

One day her old school friend Angelique came for lunch and to see the kitten. Lydia and Angelique had both been top students at school, as well as a year younger than most of their classmates.

Jonah romped toward our visitor, pouncing on her shoe buckles.

"He's adorable!" Angelique cried, lifting him up and pressing him to her cheek.

Angelique's blond highlights made her look like Marilyn Monroe. Her designer clothes contrasted starkly with Lydia's monastic chic. Angelique was halfway through a medical degree and hoping to specialize in pediatrics, so she had a long path ahead.

Picking through their salads, the girls caught up on each others' news. Angelique's boyfriend had just joined a legal firm, and obviously worshiped her. The girls giggled about teachers they'd had, and nodded respectfully about some others. When Lydia mentioned her spiritual ambitions Angelique's eyes glazed.

She kissed Lydia good-bye and clicked down the hall in a cloud of perfume. Anything I said was bound to come out badly. But drying the dishes, I *had* to open my mouth . . .

"Angelique's looking pretty."

Lydia dusted crumbs off the table and changed the subject. "I was just wondering," she said in a tone that was controlled, but somehow dangerous, "if you'd mind knitting me a scarf?"

I'm always flattered when someone requests a sample of my terrible handiwork.

"I'd love to! What color would you like?"

As she shook the duster into the bin, crumbs scattered on the floor.

"Maroon," she replied, shooting me a look of defiance.

My heart lurched. Maroon was the color of monastic robes.

"It can get quite cold in the monastery at night," Lydia added.

I put the tea towel down on the counter. "My daughter the doctor" had such a different ring to it than "my daughter the nun."

Regardless, it was clear I needed to get my head around the probability that Lydia would head back to the monastery in Sri Lanka before long. My illness had brought us closer than ever. I was going to miss her enormously. But she'd been so generous with me it was time to respect her spirituality, and accept how important it was to her. She had certainly never promised to stay indefinitely. Though I still creaked about inside my body, I was able to get around by myself now.

I'd even been bold enough to stand naked in front of the mirror a couple of times. While it was still the same old body, I felt oddly separated from it. My heart went out to the imperfect, wonderful conglomeration of cells that had carried me around for more than five decades. It bore the scars of a military campaign.

The wound across my abdomen was still raw and brutal looking. The swelling hadn't completely subsided. While my new uplifted breasts had a youthful profile, the artificial one drooped slightly lower than its partner. Most of Greg's needlework had been concealed as promised under the breasts or around the sides of them, but my one remaining nipple was circled with red suture lines. On my fake breast, where the nipple should've been, a circle of pale skin stared back at me like a giant eye.

I made an effort to keep this strange new body out of sight most of the time, lifting the sheets to cover my breasts when Philip brought tea into the bedroom each morning. He was invariably tactful, assuring me I looked better than before. But I was far from a *Playboy* centerfold. I wondered what he really thought. Deep down I didn't want to know in case the truth was devastating.

The tiredness was overwhelming at times. I'd collapse on the bed to sleep and sleep. Too much effort went into getting through each day to worry about the future. Every moment felt precious. I could spend an unfathomable amount of time examining dust particles in a shaft of light, or the painting of a poppy on the wall beyond the end of our bed. Enfolding myself in the flower's petals, I savored the miracle of being in a living, breathing body.

Compared to the enormous physical changes I'd been through, the decision to give up thirty years of column writing was minuscule. I felt miraculously free without the burden of Monday morning deadlines. While I missed contact with readers, many stayed in touch. They'd sent floods of e-mails while I'd been in the hospital. Some wrote that after reading me for so many years they felt like friends. A couple even invited me to recuperate at their houses. The generosity of these so-called strangers was overwhelming.

Messages also arrived from women who'd successfully recovered from breast cancer. Most were reassuring, though a few e-mails were edged with terror. They were from women who'd been recently diagnosed with uncertain futures. One had small children she was dreading leaving. I hoped my attempts to reply to these anguished women weren't inadequate. They were a painful reminder not to take anything for granted.

Maybe there was more wisdom in Lydia's request for a maroon scarf than I realized. Knitting was probably an ideal way to sit back, regain my health, and reassess for a while.

I'd just hoped something might've triggered her to change her mind about leaving. Maybe even the kitten . . .

"When are you leaving?" I asked, trying to sound strong.

Jonah danced across the kitchen floor and squeaked up at her. Lydia broke into a smile as she picked him up.

"Oh boy!" she said, kissing his forehead. "We'd better get you settled as an outdoor cat first."

Like Lydia, Jonah had a distinct aversion to being trapped at home. He waited by doors and windows hoping to slither out the moment they were opened. And he took the adage of cats never coming when called to an extreme. Whenever anyone mentioned his name, he sprinted in the opposite direction.

Even "Kitty" had a similar effect. He'd turn, scowl, raise his tail and bolt. Some days all I seemed to see of Jonah were the backs of his outsized hind legs and his tail swaying over the pleated circle of his anus as he galloped away.

Possibly Lydia understood his desire to wander the neighborhood because of her own longing to roam. Living at home, shackled to us (financially anyway) for the foreseeable future, she craved freedom. I couldn't completely blame her. At the same age I'd been married with two kids. That was imprisonment of a different kind, but it presented a mirage of adult independence. Perhaps she regarded the Sri Lankan monastery as an escape route.

According to the vet, the first step to independence for Jonah was getting him "fixed."

I had no idea Philip would take the procedure so personally.

"How can removing an animal's testicles extend his life?" he growled.

Men are supposed to be the logical species, but on the subject of balls rationality flies straight into the trash bin.

I assured Philip that neutering reduced the risk of infection and cancer and that desexed male cats didn't get into fights so often so were less prone to injury. They were also less inclined to wander or spray urine (though that, I imagined, was something only feral cats would do).

Putting it like that made me quietly wonder if the vet mightn't be interested in a two-for-one deal.

"Can't he just have a vasectomy?"

"Neutering only takes five minutes. The operation's much worse for female cats," I said, wondering why it always seemed to be that way for females of any species.

The day Jonah was due to get fixed, Philip had an early start. Katharine had an appointment with her math teacher ("And I get upset when he meows inside his carry box") which left Lydia and me official Breakers of the Balls.

When we collected Jonah from the vet clinic later in the day, he didn't seem diminished. By the look of things, his testicles hadn't been removed so much as deflated.

"Make sure he doesn't lick his stitches too much," the vet nurse said as a playful paw protruded from his carry box to grapple with her belt. "Goodness, he's got personality, hasn't he?"

Jonah bounced back from the operation quickly. To Philip's relief, the "fixing" had left Jonah largely intact. Suffice to say that while the testicles had been flattened, the Eiffel Tower remained. Jonah enjoyed shocking female visitors by coaxing his glistening pink pencil out of its case and licking it with affection and attention to detail.

Any "Ewww! Jonah! Don't be disgusting!" responses only made him lick with more enthusiasm.

One day, when we judged Jonah fully recovered from his "fixing," we decided to give him a trial run as an outside cat in the back garden.

I wasn't strong enough to chase him yet, but wasn't too concerned. Once he associated the tap of a spoon on a tuna can with us calling his name, I was sure we'd get him sorted.

Stepping outside, Philip lowered Jonah onto the deck. Our

kitten sat there cute as Christmas and blinked inquisitively at the sky.

"Look at that!" I said. "No problem at all. He's a sensible boy, aren't you, Fur Man?"

A blast of wind rushed through the olive bushes. Jonah raised his nostrils and tensed. His legs stiffened. His tail puffed. The sound of wind was new to him—and utterly terrifying. Philip bent to pick him up, but the kitten shot across the yard straight up the tree trunk. We hadn't counted on Jonah knowing how to climb trees.

Perched above us, he flattened his ears against the wind as the branches heaved up and down like a raft on a storm at sea. Clinging to the decks, the kitten looked vaguely seasick.

Lydia hurried inside to retrieve the kitchen stepladder. Philip planted it in the earth and ascended toward the escapee. Just as he touched Jonah's fur, the kitten slithered out of his grasp and clambered higher. Paw over milk chocolate paw, Jonah scrambled toward the top branches. A nearby pigeon tut-tutted and evacuated the tree in a huff.

"Let him stay up there!" said Philip.

"But what if he doesn't know how to get down?" Katharine whined. "Or if he climbs down on the neighbor's side of the fence and gets lost."

Exasperated, Philip leaped off the stepladder and, with surprising agility, swung himself up on a branch. The girls and I watched breathless. For every bough Philip climbed, Jonah scaled one higher. The loftier their ascent, the thinner and less reliable-looking their footing became. If Philip trusted the wrong piece of wood he'd crash to the ground.

"Got him!" he called.

The girls and I heaved a collective sigh of relief as Philip rappelled down the trunk with Jonah in the crook of his arm. But just as Philip's shoe touched the earth, the kitten launched himself in the air.

"Block the escape routes!" Philip yelled. "He's going to run for it!"

The girls bounded to their positions along the left side of the house while I stood on the back deck nursing my abdominal stitches.

Jonah became a pale tornado circling the patch of grass in wider and accelerating curves. Philip made a lunge for him, but the kitten was too fast, deftly side-stepping Philip, who plummeted empty-handed to the ground.

"Look out!" he called to the girls, brushing dirt off his elbows. "He's coming your way!"

The girls bent their knees and stretched their arms out, creating a human shield as the kitten sprinted toward them. Then, spinning on his hind legs, he veered away from them . . . and disappeared down the side of the house.

The scene was vaguely familiar. The chase, the attempt at blocking, the fancy footwork followed by unexpected escape. I'd tried to stay awake next to Philip through countless rugby games on television, understanding nothing. That was it! They were playing rugby. Jonah was worthy of his name.

We peered down the side of the house where no living thing, apart from spiders and air-conditioning repairmen, ventured. There was no sight or sound of Jonah.

Philip whispered to the girls to stay where they were while he ran around to the front to wait at the other end of the canyon. I followed him at a sedate pace to give moral support.

"Can you see him?" he called to the girls.

"No! Can you?"

Silence, except for the wind. Jonah had evaporated like a genie.

Out the front by now, I was beginning to wonder if the kitten had slipped out of our lives forever when a silver bullet shot out from the side of the house into the front garden. Philip dived sideways and, in what seemed slow motion, twisted gracefully through the air. He extended his arms, his hands curving around the missile, lifting it an inch or two.

For an instant, man and furry ball hovered midair . . . then time sped up and they collapsed on the soil. Philip landed on his stomach with his arms outstretched around the unharmed kitten. The perfect rugby tackle.

"Poor Jonah!" I cried. But as Philip brushed the blood off his knees and handed me the kitten, it seemed Jonah was unhurt and not at all shaken. He purred ecstatically and stretched a sportsmanlike paw towards Philip.

Inside Cat

*The only thing more worrying than holding cats
and daughters close is setting them free.*

Our daughter and our cat still craved freedom. Lydia clearly
longed to return to her monastery. Jonah wanted to run away
down the street. Both were oblivious to danger. I wasn't ready
to give either of them what they wanted—or not just yet.

I'd hoped Jonah might demonstrate some of the streetwise
savvy Cleo had been born with. Cleo had lived near busy roads
her entire life and had possessed a second sense about keeping
away from traffic. Jonah's idea of a safe haven was hiding under
the wheels of parked cars.

During his trial weeks as an outdoor cat, Jonah proved a
nuisance to others and a danger to himself. He could scramble
up anything, from trees to lampposts, but coming down he
always got into trouble.

One day, a neighbor tapped on the door to report our cat was
stuck up on his roof. He kindly offered the girls a ladder so they
could reclaim him.

Another time a different neighbor brought him home trembling in her arms after he'd tried to take on her two black
tomcats. I'd seen those two monsters patrolling the street. The
size of small panthers, they were cat mafia. She told us the pair
of them had cornered Jonah before she'd rescued him. He was,
she said, lucky to have escaped with both eyes intact.

Jonah's attempts at bird stalking were tragic. The moment he
saw a pigeon he'd freeze and crouch close to the ground.

Homing in on his victim he shadowed every little waddle and peck until he almost merged with his prey.

His camouflage coloring gave Jonah potential to terrorize the bird world—until he curled his lips back and emitted a loud "Heh! Heh!" giving the pigeon time to rearrange its feathers and deliver some reprimanding "tut-tuts" before flapping up onto the fence.

As for the usual cat business of gliding effortlessly along fence tops, it was beyond Jonah. Birds laughed at him whenever he tried it. With the front and back feet of one side of his body limping along the top of the palings, and the other two feet trailing behind on the crossbeam below, he hobbled along looking like a two-legged mutant.

Jonah's nerves were made of crystal. He jumped and cowered at the slightest noise. The slam of a rubbish bin lid sent him scuttling for cover.

The sound of dogs barking, on the other hand, was a battle cry. No matter how big or brutal-looking the dog was, Jonah would charge toward it, tail flying, confident he'd crush the thing with a flash of his eyes.

He had no idea how to fight, adhering to courtly ideals of warfare. Much yowling and posturing was involved but he always kept his claws sheathed. To him, battles were largely psychological, staring the enemy down until they realized how unworthy they were and skulked away.

We were constantly on Jonah safaris, running down the street past the WANTED signs for missing cats, calling his name or rummaging uninvited through neighbors' gardens. Occasionally, he'd allow us to catch him without much fuss but most of the time he'd refuse to return to the loving arms of his family until we'd all had a good sprint around the street for half an hour or so.

Despite his escapist ways, he was hopelessly dependent. He always stood in the window waiting for us to come home, and was first at the door to greet Philip and the girls. When we put him in a cattery for a weekend while we checked out Rob and

Chantelle's wedding venue, he was miserable. One of the cattery workers, Vivienne, had taken a shine to Jonah. She said she'd played with him for an hour each day, and he made her laugh. She was soft-spoken and gentle. I liked her straight away. A flicker of concern crossed her face when she mentioned Jonah had been very needy and thrown up twice. She said catteries mightn't suit him. If we went away again, she'd be more than happy to cat sit him at our place.

I returned to the pet shop and asked Nathan for advice about our would-be runaway. He sold me a red cat harness with a bell and lead attached. Cats love them, he said. Imagining how smart the red would look against Jonah's coloring, I bought the optional brass disc and had it etched with his name and phone number.

Jonah detested his harness to begin with. He considered doggy-style walks beneath his dignity. It took him months to understand the harness was offering him a form of freedom.

Soon after the name tag was attached, he managed to wriggle Houdini-like out of the red straps, forcing Philip to play rugby again. One morning when I left Jonah in his harness in the back garden for a few minutes, he managed to entangle himself almost to the point of crucifixion on the olive tree stakes.

The ongoing struggles with our cat were nerve jangling. A peaceful diversion was required. I went to the wool shop and purchased some maroon yarn. When Lydia saw me clicking needles in front of *Deal or No Deal* she was delighted, acting as if my knitting her a maroon scarf symbolized acceptance of her religious ambitions. I was trying. Even though I had an open-door approach to spirituality, I couldn't help worrying about how much she'd be giving up if she shut herself away as a nun in Sri Lanka. There was enough wool left over to make the world's ugliest beanie, which I duly did.

Tying both my daughter and cat up in red threads, I hoped to stop them both ruining their lives. Nonetheless, I was happy to support Lydia in her efforts to help Jonah become an outdoor cat.

Until Geoffrey turned up.

Our friend Geoffrey's an expert on almost everything. If you want to know how to make wine out of shoe leather, or ice cream from rainwater, he's your man.

When he heard we had a new kitten, he was quick to drop over.

"Jonah," he said, casting an appraising eye over our kitten. "Isn't that an unlucky name?"

"What do you mean?" Lydia asked.

"You know, the old superstition," Geoffrey answered. "Jonah was the sailors' demon."

I assured him we weren't taking Jonah on a sea voyage in the near future.

"He'll have to be an indoor cat," said Geoffrey. "The average life span of an inner-city cat is eighteen months. If you let him outside he'll get run over, poisoned, mauled by dogs, or stolen."

Our cream and chocolate kitten was too mesmerized by a housefly circling his head to notice the cloud of gloom hovering over Geoffrey.

"It's even worse for males," Geoffrey added, sinking his teeth into a slice of banana cake. "They're territorial. They get into fights. If they don't get killed the vets' bills are horrendous. And they can catch AIDS off other cats."

"Cats get AIDS?" Philip asked. "You're joking!"

"I certainly am not. They have their own form of it, different from human AIDS. It's endemic among city cats."

Lydia's mouth dropped. It was difficult to argue with Geoff's prognosis.

Jonah's head spun faster and faster as he kept pace with the fly. He was going cross-eyed. Listing slightly, he was liable to topple over with dizziness. But a fly was a dragon with wings as far as Jonah was concerned. Self-appointed World's Number One Domestic Dragon Slayer, he was immune to minor irritations like giddiness.

"Shame you didn't get a female," Geoffrey sighed, licking the crumbs off his fingers. "They're easier to manage."

"That's a bit sexist," said Lydia.

"True though," said Geoffrey, sounding unattractively smug.

Jonah launched into the air and snapped the fly between his teeth at least three feet above the ground. The maneuver was swift and entirely elegant. Who wouldn't want to share their home with such a magnificent creature? I could only think Geoffrey was envious.

"I'm just giving you the facts," he added, draining his second cup of coffee.

"You live close to town and your cat's ancient, isn't it?" I asked.

"Yes, but she's female and she hates going outside. When I open the door she refuses to go out. And she's the size of a tiger, pretty much."

Jonah's fur glistened in the sunlight as he tried to prod the fly back to life. It lay on its back wiggling its legs halfheartedly in the air, reminding me of a yoga pose I'm not particularly fond of.

"So we'll have to keep Jonah inside all the time if he's to have any chance of reaching the age of two?" I asked.

"It's illegal to let him out at night anyway," Geoffrey replied, glancing at the time on his phone. "Cats destroy wildlife. And kill possums."

Here we go again, I thought. If there's ever going to be a war between Australia and New Zealand it'll be over possums. Native to Australia, possums were introduced into New Zealand in the 1830s with hopes of setting up a fur trade. With no natural predators in New Zealand, and hardly any socialites wanting to envelop themselves in possum fur, the animals ran rampant. They continue to decimate New Zealand's native bush.

In short, while Australians swerve to avoid possums on the road, New Zealanders tighten their grip on the wheel and accelerate straight at them. Killing a possum in Australia is breaking the law. Doing the same thing in New Zealand is an excuse to open another can of beer. Not that Philip or I have had anything to do with the demise of a marsupial. Getting into a shouting match with Geoffrey over possums was pointless.

Jonah had no interest in destroying anything other than his house dragon anyway. Pulling his lips back in case it might bite or sting, he crunched it loudly—glancing around the room to ensure he had an audience.

"It's cruel to keep cats inside all the time," Lydia said, standing to clear the cups off the table. Even though my last drain tube and its ugly bottle had been removed, I still wasn't too steady on my feet. Lydia insisted I sit down while she cleared up. I couldn't believe I'd produced such a domesticated daughter.

"Crueler than letting them get run over?" Geoffrey shot back.

I was almost relieved when Geoffrey slid into his parka and trudged down the path.

Lydia and I exchanged glances.

"He was right," I sighed. "Jonah will live longer if he's an indoor cat."

"But that's imprisonment!" she retorted. "Imagine what it'd be like for him never feeling grass under his paws."

It was beginning to sound like another of our Sri Lanka debates.

"We'll take him out on his lead," I said.

"He hates it!" Lydia retorted.

The girls and I went back to the pet shop and bought a cat tunnel for running through, a scratching post, table tennis balls that could be patted through a maze of plastic channels ("for mental development"), little balls with bells in them, big balls with batteries making them roll around mysteriously inside paper bags, toy mice steeped in catnip, and a full range of fishing rods. The house was a cat playground.

Though I felt burdened with guilt and failure at Jonah being an indoor cat, he loved barrelling through his tunnel and pouncing on unsuspecting passersby. It had a hole in the middle for an extra element of surprise. Katharine found the tunnel doubled as a submarine. When she dragged it down the hall with Jonah on board, he popped his head out of a hole to enjoy the passing scenery.

"I guess that's it," Lydia sighed one day, twirling her new

maroon scarf around her neck. "There's nothing more for me to do here."

We both knew the hidden meaning of what she was saying. Not only was she unhappy with Jonah's household arrest, it was six weeks since I'd had the surgery and she'd been the most wonderful nurse and daughter.

I could manage without her now.

A week later, packed and ready to set off again for Sri Lanka, she floated downstairs in a cloud of white. The color of purity and—a far less comforting thought for the anguished parent— martyrdom. Her fisherman's pants and shawl gave her a *Vogue*-meets-ashram look. I had to respect her courage, however misguided it might be.

Sensing she was leaving, Jonah ran figure eights around her ankles, meowing constantly. She picked him up and kissed his nose while Philip carried her backpack to the car. It wasn't an arduous task. She wasn't taking much more than her maroon scarf, a scented candle for the monk, and gifts for the nuns and orphans. I slid sideways like a crab into the front seat. Getting in and out of cars was still problematic.

Lydia sat in the back while we drove her to the airport. For the umpteenth time, she assured us that the monk and nuns would be meeting her at Colombo airport and driving her straight to the monastery. There would be military checkpoints, she said, but monks and nuns were treated with respect in Sri Lanka. They were protected in their tiny community in the hills. She would be safe.

"Don't worry," she added. "I'll be back for Rob's wedding."

Rob and Chantelle's wedding was now three months away. It seemed a long time to sit on a rock meditating.

The car was silent, not from anger or resentment. For better or for worse, I'd come to accept my influence was minimal, though I was more than anxious about the dangers she seemed so blithely unaware of.

Lydia had shown no interest in the background of Sri Lanka's civil war or the plight of the Tamil separatists. The few books I'd been able to find on the subject had been set aside and left unread. The old video show ran through my head—Lydia getting kidnapped or caught in a terrorist attack. I struggled to press the pause button. There was no point fighting it or telling her the Sri Lankan military had just announced it had captured the important Tamil Tiger naval base of Vidattaltivu in the North.

The one good thing about breast cancer and the rows we'd had was Lydia had proved mother-daughter love was a two-way thing.

I'd said a lot of stupid things over the years, mostly about minutiae that weren't important. Mum had done the same to me, and it'd worn into my self-esteem. I still couldn't look in the mirror without hearing her words—"You should get a corset," "Whatever happened to your lovely curls?" Her last words to me were: "What would you know?" Admittedly, I'd asked for it.

Watching Mum ride terrible waves of agony in her last hours, I'd tried to summon up appropriate words: "You're doing well," I said stupidly. Even though she'd lost her false teeth and control over almost all her bodily functions, there was still enough of Mum left to shoot a bull's-eye. She was right. I knew nothing of what she was going through.

Driving to the airport, I hoped Lydia understood how deeply my love for her was woven into every inappropriate thing I'd ever said to her. It was just a case of Mother's Tourette's Syndrome:

"That shirt's too short. You'll catch cold." (*I wish you good health always.*)

"You're too thin." (*No need to compare yourself with magazine scarecrows. You're beautiful as you are.*)

"Your eyebrows could do with waxing." (*Enjoy your sensuality. Make the most of your beauty and youth while it lasts.*)

"There's a hole in your tights." (*I'm on your side.*)

"Have fun!" (*Fill your room with flowers. Drink champagne. Open your heart to others. Dream huge. You can do anything you choose with your life.*)

"Take care." (*Love yourself for the wonderful woman you are. Don't stand in a man's shadow. Protect yourself. You are precious beyond words.*)

At the check-in counter, Philip reached for a name tag on top of the desk, took a pen from his pocket, and filled in Lydia's details. He attached the label protectively to her backpack.

I kissed her cheeks, pink and warm, and thanked her for looking after me so wonderfully after my surgery.

Smiling, she promised to phone and text and write more often.

As we watched her float away like a snowflake toward the departure gate, the mother in me thought, *White's a dreadful color for stains. I hope she doesn't spill tomato sauce over herself.*

She turned and waved, then vanished through the doors.

Jealousy

Inside every angel cat lurks a demon.

The apple tree outside my study window slept through winter. Stripped of leaves, it was a skeleton of gnarled wood, a patchwork of scars where branches had been lopped off. The tree and I were both familiar with the bite of the surgeon's scalpel.

A gardening friend reckoned the tree was close to a hundred years old, probably the same as the house. She pointed out potentially fatal growths and fungi on its limbs and offered to bring her saw around to hack them off. Winter, she said, was the best time for pruning. I sympathized with the tree. It'd been through enough. I thanked her and suggested we wait another year before putting it through more surgery.

Just as I was giving up on the tree and wondering who to call to cut it down, it sucked deep into the earth and sprouted a leaf. Fresh and vulnerable, the leaf clung to its ancient branch. As it unfurled against the pastel sky, I marveled at the rhythms of nature.

Life manifests in waves—a gathering of energy, followed by letting go. It happens in childbirth as contractions surge and subside. The same goes for the sea with its ceaseless rising and falling of the tide. Human breath follows an identical pattern, filling and emptying. Even the universe expands and contracts.

As superficial creatures, we value the obvious. The surge has more appeal than the withdrawal. We favor summer over cold months, daytime over night. More growth happens in winter than anyone imagines, though. Creativity lurks in darkness.

Not long after the first brave leaf, hundreds of others burst impudently out of the wood. Against all predictions, the apple tree was willing itself back to life.

Likewise, I was creaking my way back into the world. Though my lungs still puffed like bagpipes, a walk to the end of the street no longer felt like a marathon, and I didn't need to lie down for a rest after the Herculean effort of putting my trousers on any more.

I was incredibly grateful to Lydia, who kept her promise and made regular calls from her jungle monastery. In these conversations we both avoided the contentious topic of taking robes.

While Lydia embraced freedom in Sri Lanka, Jonah was under house arrest. We had security screens fitted on some windows so they could be opened without him escaping. The French doors stayed permanently shut. Philip, Katharine, and I slowly adjusted to being jailers imprisoned with their inmate.

Jonah took on some of Lydia's nursing responsibilities, following me about the house, making impatient clucking noises, urging me to lie down and rest.

When I finally obeyed his instructions he'd leap onto the bed and snuggle into my abdomen as if to say, "See? This is what we should be doing! Let's have a nap now."

Feeling his purr vibrate through my body, I knew I'd finally found the friend I'd been missing. Listener, healer, the companion who never judged. All I'd ever needed was a feline. Maybe our old neighbor had been right, and Cleo had sent an angel cat.

Jonah improved the look of the house by simply gliding through it. There wasn't a carpet or cushion his coloring didn't enhance. He'd grown into such a magnificent-looking cat he seemed too glamorous to belong to us. His fur had darkened from cappuccino to shades of *café latte* over winter. Whiskers stood out like pale nylon thread against an espresso-colored face. His eyes, which were blue as Sri Lankan sapphires, gazed out from the depths of their darkened mask. Improbably large ears hovered like bat wings over his narrow face. A long nose gave him the profile of an Egyptian pharaoh.

He had only one flaw—two upper teeth protruding fang-like over his lower lip.

Jonah was so lanky I wouldn't have been surprised if his ancestors had been squeezed out of a pipe. Tiptoeing about on his long legs, he seemed a couple of inches taller than a cat should be.

Our feline spent hours preening his tail, a twitchy serpent with a separate identity. He carried it like a pennant so it doubled as a location device for us. We followed its tip as he glided behind a chair. When he crouched on all fours to doze in the sun, he snaked it around his front feet and back in between his legs.

Even though he was a devoted companion, he was constantly on the lookout for escape routes—a window left open, or a crack in a door. Every afternoon Katharine and I clicked him into his harness so he could prowl the backyard for bugs. He strained against the harness, always pushing to go farther than it allowed.

Philip assured us that Jonah would get used to being an inside cat. Of the 200 million pet cats in the world, heaps lived happily in apartments, he pointed out.

Jonah's squeak morphed to a deep-throated yowl that said, "*This isn't good enough! Do what I want!! Now!!! Neeeowww!!!!*"

Our young cat seemed to feel, see, and hear everything a hundred times more acutely than the rest of us. Even when curled up on a lap with his eyes closed, he was only one quarter asleep. Muscles twitched under his silky fur. A creak in the eaves or the distant sigh of a tram gliding down High Street was enough to jolt him awake.

With Lydia away, the house was quiet during the day. Jonah scratched at my study door one morning, so I lifted him onto my shoulder and carried him in. He purred a liquid song as I eased into the chair and switched on the computer.

"This is where we should be now," he seemed to say. *"Let's take a look at that old Cleo manuscript."*

Reading over what I'd written before my cancer surgery, I was crestfallen. Even though my prognosis was good, there was a possibility this could be the last book I'd have the chance to write. The manuscript was too self-pitying and depressing. I wanted to celebrate the wonder of being alive more than ever. With Jonah nestled on my knee, I drew a breath and reached for the delete button. Thousands of words, half a book, evaporated into cyberspace.

That done, I stared into the cavern of the computer screen. And started again.

I was beginning to wonder if Jonah was a born writer's cat. Every morning, he tapped on the study door until I opened it and sat at the desk. Heavy on my lap, he'd purr himself to sleep and lie there motionless for hours. Whenever I stood up to stretch my legs, he'd shake himself awake and deliver me a good snitching off.

By mid afternoon, my brain would be too tired to do anything but watch crap television, which Jonah also enjoyed. He preferred wildlife programs, and for some inexplicable reason, modern dance. But his favorite show was *Inspector Rex*. One glimpse of the German shepherd detective and Jonah would jump onto the ledge in front of the television and follow the dog across the screen. When I watched game shows or *Antiques Road Show*, he'd yawn as if to say "Purrrrlease change the channel!"

Male to the core, Jonah adored mechanics. The only thing that interested him more than a flushing toilet was the printer. Whenever the machine clattered to life, he jumped on top of it and patted the pages as they shuffled out.

In between shredding the stair carpet and rappelling down the curtains, he enjoyed his role as chief editorial adviser. We were getting along well.

I should've known it was too good to last.

Most days my only human contact was with Bronte, Stevan, or whoever was making takeaway coffees across the road. They'd ask how the book was coming along and hand me a polystyrene cup of writer's jet fuel.

I returned to the house one morning, coffee in hand, to find my study had been trashed. The wastepaper basket was upended. Photos on top of the bookshelf were sprawled on their faces. Mum's framed 1949 reference from a newspaper editor claiming she was nearly as good as a man had toppled onto the floor.

But the worst damage was to my computer keyboard. Four letters had been torn off and strewn over the floor. One by one I picked up the letters and examined them—Z, F, P. The fourth, and most damaged, tile was E—the most commonly used letter in the English language.

"*Jonah!*" I roared.

A small furry face appeared around the edge of the study door. It looked up at me with a cobalt glare—and roared right back.

The message was clear. I'd been spending too much time at the computer. He needed attention more than that stupid machine.

Our angel cat had morphed into a little devil.

Deception

The velvet dictator.

After Jonah's act of vandalism, I no longer trusted him in my study. But he cried outside the door while I worked, which was unbearable.

On the hypothesis that his need for attention had to be finite, I devised a plan. If I gave him enough pampering in one hit at the start of the day he'd calm down and be a regular, undemanding cat for the remaining hours.

Jonah adored having his back stroked. I was generous. The optimum number of strokes, I decided, was 200. Jonah shuddered with pleasure, crouching deep in my lap while I delivered his portion for the day.

"There you go, boy," I'd say, placing him back on the floor when I'd finished.

Except 200 wasn't enough. He jumped back on my lap and demanded more.

And he knew exactly what I was up to. When I put him back down again he would sprint down the hall to the study door and try to slide in before I got there.

My life was being ruled by a cat. If only Lydia were here she'd know what to do with such a willful animal.

Even though my days were busy with writing, wedding planning, and preparing meals for Philip and Katharine, I missed incense wafting down the stairs. I half expected Lydia to appear and say "Ha! April Fool!" Except it wasn't April. It was November.

Over the weeks we'd grown accustomed to the unpredictable nature of the phone calls from Sri Lanka. When the line went dead, it didn't necessarily mean Lydia had taken offense and hung up. Her calls were intermittent because the monastery phone was often out of action for days, especially if there'd been rain.

I wished there was a way of pumping Sri Lanka's water surplus into tanks and shipping it to Australia. The drought was getting worse with the terrifying threat of bushfires in summer.

When Lydia was able to get through on the phone, I asked her about what she'd been up to. It was the usual round of teaching monks English, visiting hospital patients and orphans, and, of course, meditating. Though I tried to picture her doing all these things, it was impossible to conjure up anything that made it real. What did the land smell like there? Did the people love her, or were they exploiting her? Or, alternatively, was she exploiting them? She assured me she was paying rent.

"It's really beautiful here," she said. "You should come and visit."

My snort of laughter bounced off the kitchen walls. I'd seen enough of the Third World through rims of various toilet seats to last a lifetime. The names of several exotic destinations summon memories for me not of swaying palm trees but of intense physical misery.

If I was to be doing any traveling in the future, especially after my brush with breast cancer, I'd decided it was going to involve gleaming bathrooms, haute cuisine, and beds soft as cupcakes.

"How many steps did you say there are up to the monastery?" I asked, playing her along.

"A few, but we'd carry your luggage."

"Kath told me you saw a rat in your room," I added. Katharine was an excellent source of subversive information.

"It mightn't even be a rat!" said Lydia defensively. "It was just a shadow. It didn't come anywhere near me."

By this time I was counting the days till Lydia would be home. By my reckoning, I only had three more weeks of trying to get to sleep at night without imagining her kidnapped, caught up in unspeakable violence, or seriously ill from food poisoning, malaria, or some other tropical disease. Not to mention the possibility of her being bitten by one of the ninety-eight snake varieties in Sri Lanka, or attacked by a scorpion, rogue elephant, leopard, water buffalo, mongoose, or jackal.

As for monkeys, which are everywhere in Sri Lanka, after listening to a doctor friend giving me a rundown on the deadliness of monkey bites, I no longer regarded them as harmless pseudo-humans.

On top of all the physical dangers, I worried what was happening inside Lydia's head. I wondered if hours of meditation had tipped her over the edge into religious fervor. My questions were deflected with silence followed by, "It's hard to explain." I didn't dare ask if she was still thinking of turning her back on the West and all its meat-eating, shallow commercialism.

A sparkle would invariably come into her voice when we talked about Rob's wedding. For a few moments, I would hear traces of the old Lydia—the little girl dressed as a fairy jumping on a trampoline; the toddler waddling through a park in red shoes insisting swans were ducks. She'd had strong opinions even then.

Whenever Lydia talked as though she was still part of our family, I gulped back tears. Maybe spending three months at the monastery would be like Jonah's 200 strokes and get the whole thing out of her system. Then again, considering Jonah's 200 strokes had been a failure, I decided to steer clear of amateur behavioral science.

Replacing the receiver after a call one day, I glanced around the kitchen. Compared to the colorful world I imagined Lydia was living in, we inhabited shades of beige. Shirley's colors looked tired both inside and out. Rob's wedding was only a month and a half away and we were planning a pre-wedding barbecue for thirty or forty people under the tree in the back desert. The house needed sprucing up.

Looking around, I wondered what Mum would've done to give the house a bit of a lift. Like me, she'd hated cleaning. When layers of grime formed on her kitchen shelves, rather than scrubbing them she painted. Her favorite paint was pastel blue enamel, probably imbued with enough lead to account for several family eccentricities. She thought the color looked "hygienic" and she liked it being high gloss. She said it "covered well." Tears of blue paint dripped from the edges of the kitchen shelves and set hard.

Running my eye over Shirley's shabbiness, my mind naturally turned to paint. I phoned David the designer, who knew just the people who could help us out in a hurry.

I wasn't looking forward to the arrival of the painters. The smell would disrupt my writing, not to mention the inevitable prattle of talk radio on their ghetto-blasters.

Their clattering ladders and stomping boots were bound to terrify Jonah. They'd leave doors and windows open for him to escape through so that precious hours I needed to work on the book would be spent scouring the neighborhood.

On their first day, the painters rattled on the door just after 7 a.m. I had a contract with the Universe not to get up before 7:30, but Philip had gone for a run so there was no choice but to climb out of bed. Still in my nightie, hair uncombed, I scooped Jonah into my arms before opening the front door a crack.

"I'm sorry but our cat is Siamese and very highly strung," I said. "We have to keep him inside. I'll just shut him in whichever rooms you're not working in, if that's okay."

The boss painter nodded, no doubt used to people making unreasonable requests. He seemed oblivious to the fact I wasn't dressed yet and my hair appeared to have been through an electrical storm.

"Beautiful cat," he said, casting an appraising eye over Jonah through the crack. "But he's not Siamese. He's Tonkinese."

"Really?" I said, backing down the hallway to make way for

him and his two assistants, all dressed in white overalls, to come
in. "The pet shop man told us he's Siamese."

I could feel Jonah coiling every muscle as the painters
arranged their pots and brushes and drop cloths on the floor.
Any moment now he was going to explode out of my arms and
go berserk.

"No way!" said the painter, stroking Jonah's forehead. "He's
Tonkinese. Swear my life on it. I've got two cats just like him at
home and they're both Tonks. Your cat's too dark for a Siamese.
He's definitely a Tonk."

To my relief, Jonah purred at the painter's touch. Maybe
they were going to get along all right. If the painter was correct,
Jonah was not only a nutcase, he was an imposter. Smiling down
at our cat, I didn't care a thing about his pedigree. His personality was enormous enough to warrant an entire new breed of his
own. But it was intriguing to imagine his background might be
even murkier than we'd thought.

I went to the computer and Googled Tonkinese. Half Siamese,
half Burmese, Tonkinese cats are said to encompass the best of
both breeds. Interestingly, the name stems back to Mum's
favorite musical, *South Pacific*. The character she played,
Bloody Mary, was supposed to be Tonkinese, from an island
free from prejudice against half-breeds.

If the painter wanted Jonah to be Tonkinese that was fine by
me, especially as Tonkinese were supposed to be "less demanding and highly strung" than Siamese. Maybe while he was
working on his Tonkinese-ness, Jonah could learn to have a
"softer voice," and be "playful rather than hyperactive."

Jonah adored the painters to the point of worshiping them. He
waited for them beside the front door every morning. If they
were working at ground level, he sat alongside them, peering
into their pots and teasing their brushes. When they climbed
ladders, he sat anxiously below, or leaped up onto a window
ledge to keep them company.

With their white overalls, stealthy movements, and penchant

for climbing, the painters must've seemed like human cats to Jonah. When they had morning coffee in the kitchen, our cat sprang up onto the table and batted his eyes at them, mewing seductively and stretching an elongated paw to pat their faces. Fortunately, they loved him back.

Painters have gone upmarket. Instant coffee isn't good enough for them anymore. They prefer plunger coffee or, better still, takeaway lattes from Spoonful. They like china mugs on a pretty tray. If the cookies don't look homemade they leave them on the plate to go soft in the sun. Those who don't like coffee favor freshly squeezed orange juice in a glass (not plastic) with ice.

Painters see and hear everything in a house. They peered curiously through the study window as I struggled to complete the final chapters of the Cleo book. I steeled myself against the certainty that at least one of them would also be writing a book, or have a friend or relation who was. Everyone in the world was writing a book, or (more patronizingly) planning to do it when they retired.

"Is it a children's book?" one of them asked.

By this stage my confidence was seeping through the floor-boards. Maybe it *was* a children's book, which wasn't a bad thing because I have enormous respect for people who write for children. Then again the aftermath of a child's death was surely too dark a theme for a children's book. Maybe the agents and publishers who'd turned it down had been right. When I finally wrote the last sentence and then typed those longed-for words "The End" they didn't seem right. Life goes in cycles. Cleo's departure was the start of a new phase. I deleted "The End," replaced it with "The Beginning"—and, with huge trepidation, pressed Send.

As the painters worked through the house, I helped reorganize rooms they'd finished painting and tidied the ones they planned to work on next. I wasn't physically capable of lifting and moving much, so Philip did most of the donkey work after he got home at night.

Just as one mound of books, paintings, and furniture was put back in place, another roomful was dismantled and shuffled into corners under drop cloths. It was like shifting the sea.

In the laundry room near Jonah's food bowls, I noticed faint streaks dribbling in roughly parallel lines down the wall. I asked the painters to put an extra coat over them.

A few days later, the marks mysteriously reappeared. Bending, I examined them more closely. Free-form in shape, they resembled something Jackson Pollock might've painted. They spoke of the jungle, too, as if some wild creature had thrown his art against the wall as an insult. There was something sinister about them. Symbolic, almost. I wondered what they could mean.

Romance

Cats and daughters come home when they please.

Two weeks before the wedding, Chantelle appeared glowing with excitement at the front door. Her gown was finally ready. It was in her car. She didn't want to store it at their place. Even if she tried to hide it in their spare room, she was sure Rob would find it. I was thrilled when she asked me to guard the precious garment at our place.

Under the watchful eyes of the painters, we carried the gown, sheathed in protective covering, up the front path. From his viewpoint in the living room window, Jonah's ears pricked with interest. He ran to meet us at the door, glued himself to our heels, and trotted after us into my study. I was too engrossed to shut him out. Chantelle unzipped the cover to reveal a wedding gown fit for a princess. Pearls on the bodice shimmered against the soft pink silk. It was simply the most . . .

"*Jonah!*" Chantelle cried.

We'd been too engrossed in the gown to notice the effect it was having on our cat. With his ears pointed forward and blue ray eyes, he lunged forward and buried himself under the hem of the garment. We were too nervous to grab him in case he dug his claws into the silk.

"Jonah, come out!" I called. But he only wriggled deeper into the folds of the tulle under-layer.

Enraptured by the softness and glitz of the wedding gown, Jonah refused to budge. One careless scratch would cause untold emotional and financial damage. Chantelle had proved herself an incredibly level-headed bride-to-be so far, but if Jonah ruined her dress she'd have every reason to become Bridezilla.

I fetched one of his fishing rod toys and managed to divert his attention long enough for Chantelle to lift the gown off him and zip it safely back in its bag. I scribbled "NO PEEKING!!!" on a scrap of paper and Scotch-taped it to the cover.

Not every writer gets to store a bridal dress in her study cupboard. I was honored Chantelle had trusted me with its keeping, especially with our live-in feline formal-wear fetishist.

Every day, once I'd made sure Jonah was safely shut out of the study, I'd open the cupboard door to ogle the gown. A couple of times I disobeyed my own instructions and unzipped the cover to admire the garment folded like a butterfly inside its chrysalis.

A symbol of love and hope for the future, the wedding dress shimmered with expectation. It felt like a lucky charm. Especially when an e-mail arrived from Louise at Allen & Unwin saying she loved *Cleo*. I naturally assumed Louise was being polite and protecting my fragile writer's ego. Jude, who was to edit *Cleo*, sent an e-mail echoing Louise's enthusiasm—and the anxiety lifted. Maybe the book wasn't so bad after all.

When fifteen pages of editorial suggestions arrived from Jude soon after, my heart muscles contracted. But once I understood what a sensitive and thorough editing job she had done, I was more than willing to follow her guidelines. She was asking me to delve into the dark emotional corners I'd obliterated from the first version of *Cleo*.

As I revised, reliving the painful days after Sam's death wasn't easy, though I was surprised how much detail I remembered. But remembered pain isn't as bad as it is first time round.

I hoped maybe now the book would have a better chance of reaching out to other parents who'd suffered loss—and that *Cleo* might find a few readers not just in New Zealand, but Australia as well.

As the wedding day drew closer, the house hummed with excitement. Every phone call and early wedding present delivered to our doorstep brought more happiness. The fact that six months earlier I'd worried I mightn't be around to be part of this made it all the more wonderful. Nevertheless, I still had to be careful. While my body was stronger, I still wasn't entirely back to normal. Whenever I pushed myself too hard, I'd crash in a heap of exhaustion. Occasionally I'd collapse in tearful frustration, wondering if I'd ever feel strong again. During these low moments, malevolent thoughts crept into my mind. What if this extraordinary tiredness was abnormal, and cancer was still swirling inside me?

It was hard to believe Rob was getting married. I still thought of him as a six-year-old playing hide-and-seek with Cleo, or as the young Sea Scout who loved sailing. Then there was the fourteen-year-old hurrumphing home in his blue school uniform through a cloud of teenage hormones. We were all thrilled when the boy who'd had "learning difficulties" won a scholarship to engineering school. Then devastated when at the age of nineteen he was struck by serious illness.

Rob and I had been through so much together. The day I'd had to phone him to say Cleo had died, he'd sighed and said, "There goes the last link with Sam." Our grief would always be an invisible bond between us. Even these days, when we had a moment alone, we'd thumb through old photos and talk fondly about Sam.

Rob always says bad times help you appreciate the good. Casting my mind back over the uncertainty and pain of recent months made these joyous days leading up to the wedding so precious.

In quieter, somber moments I'd Google the latest events in Sri Lanka. The month before Rob's wedding a suicide bombing in the town of Anuradhapura claimed the lives of twenty-seven people, including a former general. While Lydia insisted the monastery was a million miles from these atrocities, my maternal heart still fretted.

With the wedding only two weeks away, we were just about ready for visitors. Ahead of them all was one very important arrival. When I phoned the airport an automated voice said the flight would be arriving ten minutes early. That couldn't be right. Planes are never early.

Philip and I bustled into the car and hurtled down the motorway.

"She'll have lost weight," I said. "Two vegetarian curries a day must be incredibly purging. I'm not going to say a word."

Philip smiled tactfully, but remained silent. He dropped me outside the Arrivals area and went to park the car. There was no sign of her among the passengers spilling in from Singapore. Maybe she'd missed her connection. The trip from the monastery to Colombo airport would've taken more than four hours. There could've been all sorts of holdups—elephants, potholes, terrorists. Alternatively, the flight from Sri Lanka to Singapore could have been delayed.

There's nothing like an airport Arrivals area to reinstate faith in human nature. A young Indian man clutched a cellophane-encased rose. A Chinese family stared intensely at the automatic doors. The atmosphere crackled with expectancy. The doors snapped open to reveal a tired-looking man in a suit. A woman ran forward trailing a child. They embraced in a pyramid of joy. All those stories about smiling being good for people's health must be true. He looked suddenly younger and relieved of his jet lag.

Calls from Lydia over recent weeks had been sporadic—either she was in silent retreat or the monastery's electricity supply was disabled. Once she'd written a letter but the post office had run out of stamps.

The doors opened again. My chest lurched. But I could tell from the luggage trolley it wasn't her. Expensive suitcases and duty-free booze weren't her style.

"No sign of her yet?" Philip asked, slightly breathless after jogging from the parking garage.

The doors weren't being cooperative. They spat out a beautiful young Indian woman who was swept away by her rose-toting lover, followed by an ancient Chinese woman to be mobbed by her family. Maybe customs officials were giving Lydia a hard time. I'd watched *Border Patrol* enough times to know how they operate, always on the lookout for weirdos. Maybe they'd mistaken a lingering aroma of incense on her clothes for something else.

Even if Lydia hadn't become a nun, she'd certainly been living as one, sleeping in a cell and meditating more than twelve hours a day. I steeled myself for the possibility she'd decided to surprise us with a shaved head and maroon robes.

Years of waiting at airport barriers have taught me one thing. The only way to get people to walk through those doors is to go to the café and buy a polystyrene cup, preferably two, full of unbearably hot tea. Staggering back through the crowd, with splashes of tea scalding my hands, I heard a shout of delight from Philip. She'd arrived.

Thinner, yes. Almost worryingly so. Yet there was beautiful warmth in her eyes. Her clothes were reasonably normal, thank goodness. White pants and an ethnic-looking jacket. I was relieved to see her hair was still all there. The expensive color job I'd booked her before she'd left had given her several inches of regrowth. The overall effect was unkempt or possibly rock star, depending on your perspective.

Thrusting the teas in a rubbish bin, I ran toward her and wrapped her in my arms.

"You look . . ." I said, *way too skinny but I'll fatten you up in no time.*

". . . wonderful!"

Allure

A house is happy when a daughter knows she is beautiful.

Instead of getting more independent with age the way Cleo had, Jonah became more needy. He missed the painters terribly, waiting by the door for them in the mornings. When they didn't show up, he followed me around the house meowing and meowing, reminding me of the children when they were unsettled as babies. When they couldn't stop crying, I'd carry them around in a shoulder sling. It always worked. The warmth and closeness calmed them down.

Using the same technique with our unhappy cat, I put him in a cloth supermarket bag and slid the handles up one arm to my shoulder. Cocooned in the bag, he stopped meowing and started purring. The rhythm of my footsteps soothed him. With his head peering over the top of the bag, he saw everything that was going on and was comforted.

Jonah would've stayed that way for hours, but he was getting heavy these days. My arms still tired easily. Even when I lowered him gently back on the floor, he'd stay curled inside the bag hoping someone might take over nursing duties. Jonah needed attendants—lots of them. It was just as well Shirley was filling up with people again.

He romped tail aloft down the hall to greet Lydia, but refrained from throwing himself at her. Most people who left the house for more than twenty-four hours were treated as traitors and snubbed for at least two days. After three months' absence, Lydia clearly deserved serious punishment. He sniffed her sandals. The aroma intrigued him. He ran his nose over her fisherman's pants, her backpack, and, when she lifted him up off the floor, her hair. He seemed to be reading her perfumes the way a person would absorb the contents of a book. I wondered if the scents whispered tales of snakes and temples, incense and elephants. Even my dull human senses had detected wafts of spice, smoke, and dust combined with something vaguely floral.

Once Jonah had sniffed and dabbed his nose into the folds of Lydia's bags and clothes to his satisfaction, all was forgiven. He buried his head in her neck and purred like a tuk-tuk. He then bestowed a rare and generous gift—a lick on the back of her hand. After that, he refused to let her out of his sight. Wherever she went, Jonah was a whisker behind. When she sat, he burrowed into her lap as though trying to anchor her down. If she meditated, he sat, eyes closed like an ancient statue, between the candle and the photo of her guru on the "altar" in her bedroom.

Wonderful as it was to hear Lydia's footsteps padding lightly up the stairs again, she seemed to be floating around on her own separate cloud, physically with us, but mentally in some other world. While she beamed benevolence, she seemed disconnected. I couldn't help feeling she was regarding her meat-eating, fun-loving, non-Buddhist family as a let-down.

Once again, I resented the monk who'd used his charisma to lure her away from us.

It's not uncommon for a mother to lose touch with who her daughter really is. It happens from time to time either by accident or on purpose. I'd distanced myself from Mum, selfishly and sometimes callously, in favor of my independence, sanity, identity. Those were my excuses. Most strong young women toy with the notion of rejecting their roots. Especially if the voice of their mother resounds inside their heads, passing judgment on everything they do. A daughter needs to find out if her strength is real or borrowed.

I'd managed to get my head around Lydia turning her back on us and our values for a while. But the prospect of her losing touch with herself was more concerning. This floaty, spiritual being didn't feel like the real Lydia. But if she was determined to turn herself into somebody else, I had no power to argue with her.

Besides, I felt responsible to a certain extent. If her father and I hadn't divorced maybe things would be different. As a little girl she'd been so anxious not to hurt anyone she'd counted the days she spent in each household meticulously to ensure she gave each family equal time. Nothing like a broken home to turn children into diplomats.

But then not everything about her upbringing had been terrible. Both families, parents and step-parents, brother Rob, and half-sisters adored her with all their hearts.

If she found us offensive or inferior after her time in the jungle, I wished she'd talk about it. Instead, she just smiled enigmatically with that out-of-focus look in her eyes, answering my questions with, "It's hard to explain."

Now she'd become a semi-saintly being, I didn't know how to reach her. I wanted to reintroduce her to the delights of being a beautiful young woman in the society she belonged to.

Katharine suggested that an all-girl shopping expedition to find outfits for Rob's wedding might do the trick. Lydia was reluctant to accompany us at first, but we dragged her along.

Katharine fell in love with a purple dress in a boutique window. With a billowing skirt and ruffled neck, we agreed it was a perfect fit. The shop assistant wrapped it in tissue and slid it in a bag. Katharine beamed with the triumph of the successful shopper-gatherer as we left the store.

Lydia appeared dazzled by the colors and styles on offer. She was drawn to demure outfits in muted shades. Whenever Katharine and I persuaded her to try on dresses with low necklines that made the most of her perfect figure, she shook her head, embarrassed. If the style exposed her arms, she reached for her shawl to cover them.

Finding an outfit I felt comfortable in also presented

challenges. With my tummy tuck and new boobs, my body was a different shape from the last time I'd been shopping for evening wear. I felt like a teenager, not knowing what clothes might suit my altered body.

While the reconstruction had been harrowing, I was pleased I'd gone through with it. Because of Greg's handiwork, I could go for days without being reminded I'd faced a deadly disease. From a personal perspective, it'd been good to have reconstruction simultaneously with the mastectomy. I'm too much of a coward to have volunteered to go back to hospital for another round of major surgery.

Fully dressed, I actually had a better shape than before breast cancer. In my bra and knickers I gave a pretty good imitation of normality. Finding a good bra had been problematic, though. In the weeks and months after surgery, I'd had to wear soft bras with minimal shape. Now I was willing to be more adventurous I was disappointed how limited the options were. Underwire bras seemed foolhardy considering their reputation, deserved or otherwise, for upping the risk of breast cancer. Yet finding an attractive bra with no underwire was almost impossible. Every lingerie department was packed with underwire bras. I'd have to seek out the most mature-looking assistant available and explain my circumstances while she apologetically produced a few dowdy options. Underwear manufacturers hadn't seemed to realize women still want to feel sexy after cancer.

Once my underwear was removed, there was the giant abdominal scar and the missing nipple to contend with. Whenever I expressed doubt about the wisdom of putting myself through hours of extra surgery, Philip would put his arms around me and reassure me. How he always managed to say the right thing is beyond me.

Accepting reassurance wasn't one of my strong points, however. I couldn't quite believe him when he said I looked great. I'd seen his diplomatic skills in action with other people too many times.

Feeling vulnerable, my radar was on high alert to catch him

admiring other women with unscarred bodies. Either he's a saint, or too quick for me. I never caught him out.

While my breasts may have looked the part, they were hardly a source of erotic sensation any more. It took a while to adjust to having no feeling at all in my fake breast, and very little in the left uplifted one. I'd learned to check my upper chest was covered before going out in freezing weather. Because of the numbness in that region it was easy to expose myself to the elements inadvertently and catch cold—or worse, flash some innocent passerby.

The girls encouraged me to slide into a full-length silvery dress. With a low neckline and no sleeves, it wasn't my usual style. Cleavage! A victory statement against disease. With a black shoulder wrap and a few yards of Hollywood tape, I felt safely tucked in . . . and, surprisingly, almost glamorous.

After days trawling the shops with Lydia, we ended up back in the same boutique Katharine's dress had come from.

"There is *that one . . .*" said Lydia, tentatively indicating a rack near the front of the shop.

"You mean this?" I said, lifting an ivory linen suit into the light. It was safe to the point of being invisible.

"No, *this* one," Lydia said, pointing at a riot of silk and lace. "Do you think it's too colorful?"

"Not at all!" Katharine and I chorused in unison. "Try it on!"

Waiting outside the changing room, Katharine and I bubbled with anticipation. We heard feet shuffling and the swish of fabric. Lydia was taking forever. Katharine bent to look under the door, but said all she could see was bare feet. We called through the door asking if the size was okay. She wasn't sure.

The changing room door opened to reveal something amazing. Not Lydia the saint and caregiver, nor Lydia the charity-shop university student. This was a new Lydia, an alluring young woman swathed in swirls of vibrant color. The full skirt swung sensually from her hips as she stepped forward. The tight-fitting bodice emphasized her waist. Narrow shoulder straps and black lace across the, well, it was more a chest-line than a neckline, gave the dress form and femininity.

"You look stunning!" I breathed.

Lydia's smile filled the shop with sunshine.

"I'd need a shawl," she said. "But this dress is too expensive."

Glimpsing the price tag, I gulped. Nevertheless, a gown that enhanced her beauty and brought her back to the core of her own culture was beyond price. We bought the dress and took it home, where, much to Jonah's delight, the girls spent the afternoon rifling through my jewelry drawer.

I'd offered to buy them earrings and necklaces, but they insisted on choosing pieces from our family's past. Katharine opted for a cameo necklace that had belonged to Great Aunt Myrtle, who like many of the women in our family had (by the standards of her generation) been oversexed and overadventurous.

Lydia opted for flamboyant drop earrings I used to wear in the 1980s, along with Mum's diamanté necklace. Mum had loved that necklace, especially during the 1960s, when it sparkled against her skin on special occasions.

Their rebel daughter ancestors would've felt honored to have their trinkets aired on such a special family occasion in the twenty-first century.

Jonah was thrilled when he unearthed a single peacock feather earring from the depths of the jewelry drawer. He was even more pleased when Katharine attached it to a ribbon he could wear around his neck.

Decked out in his customized designer necklace, Jonah preened himself on the kitchen table where he *knew* he wasn't supposed to sit. Raising his front foot, he pretended to be engrossed in the task of giving himself a manicure. Licking the gaps between his claws, he cast sideways glances, watching and waiting for his favorite words: "Jonah you *are* beautiful!"

I wasn't sure it was a good idea to feed his vanity, but at the core of every vain person there's usually a soft-centered blob of insecurity. Perhaps if we flattered him he'd grow into a confident cat who didn't have to bother impressing others.

Smart as he looked, Jonah wouldn't be attending the wedding. I phoned the cattery but they were fully booked. Fortunately, I still had Vivienne's number. She remembered Jonah and when asked if she'd visit him at home during the wedding weekend quickly said yes.

There was one other small problem. Rob and Chantelle's cat Ferdie had nowhere to go, either. Vivienne said she'd be more than willing to look after both cats at our place. A cat bachelor pad. It sounded a breeze.

Dysfunction

A taste of liberty is better than none.

"He eats rubber bands? *And* merino wool?" said Vivienne.

Jonah arched his back sensually as she ran her hand over his spine. She was the first female visitor he'd really approved of. Watching how she handled him, allowing him to make the advances and give affection on his own terms, I liked her even more than the first time we'd met. Her hair was dyed purple and scraped back in a ponytail—not a look that would suit many women over thirty-five, but purple was her color, and a perfect match for her brown eyes. There was softness in those eyes, especially when discussing animals—a sparkle of humor, too.

"He likes alpaca wool as well, but more for sleeping on than eating," I replied. "Though come to think of it, he did chew holes in my alpaca cardigan."

"That's pica," said Vivienne.

"Like what pregnant women get when they want to eat lumps of coal and stuff?"

Vivienne nodded.

Uncertain I could trust her diagnosis, I asked if she had a cat. Her eyes lit up. She had nine.

"*Nine?!*" I echoed, barely able to conceal the fact that my opinion of Vivienne had just changed from "unusual" to "mad cat lady." I'd seen a television program about women who couldn't stop collecting cats. It's a psychological disorder.

She asked if I'd like to see photos. While I had no desire to inspect pictures of poor mangy things clambering all over her house, I didn't want to cause offense. Vivienne reached into her surprisingly organized purple handbag to retrieve a pocket-sized photo album.

"These are your cats?" I asked, turning page after page of glossy coated, well-fed felines. Every one of them was a supreme example of a loved and pampered animal. "How do you do it?"

"Not always easily," Vivienne laughed. "They're all rescue animals. Zoe was left on the side of the road when she was a kitten. Igor lost one eye and his owners didn't want him anymore. Sally was abused. They've all had a rough time."

I felt humbled. Any frustrations we had wrestling with one cat's lion-sized ego evaporated alongside the challenges of nine live-in felines. Vivienne might be mad about cats, but she was no mad cat lady. No wonder she hadn't been perturbed when asked if she thought she could look after Jonah and Ferdie at our place for the wedding weekend.

Intrigued, I poured Vivienne a glass of wine and delved discreetly into her background. Not only was she a qualified cat behaviorist, she was an animal activist. Having never met someone who fought for animal rights before, I realized my prejudices were just as inaccurate as they'd been about mad cat ladies. I'd always imagined animal activists were on the loony side. But when I learned about the work Vivienne and her friends did, I was abashed.

One of Vivienne's friends had recently received a tip-off that the council was planning to trap some wild cats in an old bus depot and take them away to be destroyed. In what sounded like an action movie adventure, Vivienne and her friends broke into the depot around midnight and collected the cats themselves.

"A lot of the cats weren't feral at all," she said. "They were quite friendly. They were just family pets who'd been abandoned there."

She and her friends transported the felines to a no-kill shelter, where efforts would be made to find good homes for them. Rescuing animals from death row required enormous commitment and funding. It was heartwarming to learn that animals had human guardians like Vivienne and her friends.

While she was talking, Jonah crept along the back of the sofa behind her and toyed idly with her ponytail. The game soon became vigorous. He rolled on his back, snared a bunch of purple curls between his front paws and ran them like dental floss through his teeth.

Apologizing, I untangled him from the nest he'd made of her hair. As I lowered him back onto the rug, I became aware of Vivienne's watchful gaze. I waited for the usual "Isn't he cute!?" comment, but her expression was serious.

"It's the breed," she said. "Orientals are high-maintenance. How old did you say he was when you got him?"

"I'm not sure. At least a couple of months, possibly older. He was certainly the largest kitten in the shop."

"Hmmm, that would figure," Vivienne said as Jonah scampered off to claw the stair carpet. "He was probably a reject."

"What do you mean reject?" I asked, affronted on Jonah's behalf.

"Because he was older than the other cats, somebody could've bought him before you did. They probably decided they didn't like him for some reason and took him back to the shop. Do you have any idea why they might've done that?"

I wasn't sure how to answer.

"The pet shop man said he'd had conjunctivitis, so they'd had to keep him a bit longer."

"You shouldn't believe everything a pet shop man tells you," said Vivienne as a streak of chocolate and cream sprinted between us meowing loudly.

"Well, he is a full-on cat . . ." I said, as Jonah bounced onto the window ledge and promptly fell off in a muddle of legs and paws. "But he's very affectionate. And he helped me recover from a mastectomy and write a book. He's just so . . . funny."

"He is funny," she said, smiling warmly as Jonah tugged at the lace of her purple shoe. "But he's also dysfunctional."

"How do you mean?"

"Well, there's the pica, the separation anxiety, and he strikes me as obsessive compulsive, too," said Vivienne. "Did you notice when you opened the front door he ran to greet me, then went straight down the hall to scratch the stair carpet?"

"In all honesty, no," I said, thinking that I hadn't experienced such defensiveness since crouching on a dwarf-sized chair at parent-teacher interviews ("My child is not disruptive/a slow reader/hopeless at handwriting. You just *think* he is"). No way was I going to tell Vivienne the really deranged things Jonah got up to: stealing hats and gloves from people's wardrobes, collecting socks and key rings, hiding in the rubbish bin cupboard.

"We're all a bit crazy here," I added. "Jonah fits in."

Vivienne suggested some of his problems stemmed from boredom. I asked if she meant we should let him be an outdoor cat, but she was quick to say no. With Jonah's jumpiness, an encounter with a dog, let alone a car, could be disastrous.

She asked if the scratching post in the corner was the only one we had. If we wanted him to stop destroying the stair carpet, she said, he needed more scratching poles, and taller ones.

"Isn't that one tall enough?" I asked, worrying that the house already resembled a pet shop.

"See how long his body is?" Vivienne said. "That pole isn't nearly tall enough for him to stretch out properly against and have a good scratch. And have you thought about getting an outside enclosure for him?"

"You mean a *cage*?" I asked, even more dispirited.

"I've seen some amazing cat runs," Vivienne said, scribbling phone numbers on our kitchen notepad. "Take a look on the web, or try some of these people."

Which is how, a week before the wedding, Jonah became the luckiest cat in the neighborhood. A fresh delivery of scratchers, balls, puzzles, and an infrared torch for chasing red dots made us look even more overrun by a cat.

When the world's tallest cat scratcher was delivered, Jonah circled it first with curiosity, then delight.

Vivienne's assessment had been spot-on. Not only did he

relish stretching his body out against the length of the ridiculously tall pole, he loved sitting on the platform at the top, which put him at the perfect height to preside over family meals. When the girls were cooking or doing dishes, they slid Jonah on his pole into the kitchen where he inspected their activities with the authority of an Egyptian slave-driver overseeing the construction of the pyramids.

Soon after (and despite Philip's fear it was going to be ugly) an elaborate cat run was erected in the back garden. From a cat door inside a laundry cupboard, Jonah emerged into a wire mesh tower that led him through several yards of tunnel above the iceberg roses which ended up in a larger tower near the olive trees. The second tower was a substantial enclosure containing several wooden ledges and two cat hammocks. To complete the luxury lodge, the girls and I planted bunches of cat grass under the hammocks.

I was relieved Mum was no longer around to witness this spectacle of feline worship.

Joy

A mother's greatest moment is to see her child happy.

Enamel sky arched over the pre-wedding barbecue in our back garden. With Jonah safely inside his run, we threw open the French doors. It was a perfect evening, if a little hot. The drought remained so severe I didn't bother apologizing about the dusty patch where grass should be.

Guests gazed curiously at the new cat run and its handsome inmate while Philip cooked up mountains of prawns, steak, and designer sausages. The girls labored over salads in the kitchen. I was secretly proud of Lydia's skill in the kitchen these days. Like all top chefs, she could rustle up a curry or a batch of melting moments without any signs of effort. She was practically a domestic goddess, apart from a tendency to leave the countertop in a mess. But that was a minor quibble.

It was great to see Mary again, along with her husband Barry and their grown-up children. Our old friends and neighbors from Wellington, Ginny and Rick de Silva, arrived in a blaze of laughter. Ginny, Rick, and their son Jason had been such a source of strength to Rob and I after Sam's death, having them at Rob's wedding brought a sense of completion—and a reminder to open another bottle of champagne.

When Rob and Lydia's father Steve arrived with his wife Amanda and their daughter Hannah, it was good to be reminded my ex-husband had moved on and found contentment. His response was offhand when I thanked him again for paying for

Lydia's return to Australia while I was in hospital. He probably thought it an inappropriate subject to mention just now.

Sitting alongside his lovely fiancée on the circular seat under the tree, Rob looked so happy. I was touched, too, that so many of his school friends had traveled thousands of miles for the occasion. Among them were the boys Rob had gone on a road trip into the outback with not long after his surgery. Most of them were grown-up now and married to goodhearted women. From that group, Rob had chosen his oldest friend, Andrew, to be his best man.

Music, laughter, dreams, and reminiscences. As the sky faded to pink, only one individual made it clear he wasn't enjoying the celebration. Standing on the top ledge inside his five-star cabana, Jonah yowled to be let out.

We rose early next morning and hurled clothes into suitcases. A country wedding sounds simple. We'd been so intoxicated by the notion of celebrating in a hilltop convent, we hadn't realized how obsessive we'd need to be about details.

A lot of overseas guests had arrived crazed with jet lag and with no idea how to get to Daylesford. Philip did the math and allocated them into available cars. Lydia opted to travel with Steve and Amanda. Katharine squeezed in with the de Silvas and us. Rob and Chantelle had made arrangements with their friends.

The responsibility of transporting the bridal gown from my study cupboard to the country was so great only the bride herself was willing to take it on. When she arrived to collect her gown, she deposited a cat-carrying case on the family room floor. There wasn't a sound from the carry case, or from Jonah, who was casting a steely eye over it from his tallest scratching post.

All of a sudden the carry case burst open and a silvery creature rose into the air. We watched open-mouthed as Ferdie flew like a genie out of a bottle, straight at Jonah's face. Jonah sprang back, locking wiry limbs around the invader. The young cats tumbled to the floor and rolled over each other.

We didn't have time to work out if they were playing or fighting. Ferdie was the larger and stockier of the two. If they were enemies, Jonah was bound to come off worse. I hoped Vivienne would sort them out.

Just when it looked as if everything else was under control, the wedding cake was delivered. We'd assumed it would be in three separate tiers that could be farmed out to sit on obliging passengers' laps. But the cake's tiers were firmly glued together with icing roses. There was no room for such a lofty creation in any of the cars.

After several panicky phone calls we found out Chantelle's aunt, Trudy, had space in the back of her station wagon. It was fitting for Trudy to be bearer of the wedding cake since she was the one who'd arranged Rob and Chantelle's first date to a "footy" (soccer) game nearly a decade earlier.

Ginny and Rick squeezed into our car and we joined a convoy of vehicles packed with wedding guests heading to the country. Wedged in the back with Katharine between us, Ginny and I reverted to the outrageous banter that'd sealed our friendship all those years ago while our men gazed good-naturedly at the scenery.

We stopped at Mount Macedon, where we'd arranged to rendezvous for lunch with other wedding cars. Dry wind blasted like a furnace through the tree-lined street. There were extreme fire warnings throughout Victoria and the temperature in Daylesford was predicted to be in the high 80s. When we first moved to Australia, hot weather had distressed me. Though it didn't worry me much anymore, I did wonder how anyone survived before air-conditioning. Maybe those who weren't tough simply melted. I hoped our visitors from temperate climates weren't going to faint inside the chapel tomorrow.

We scurried in from the furnace to arrange ourselves around a long café table. Rick wondered aloud if it was always this hot in Australia, and ordered a bottle of cooling white wine. Alcohol intensifies its effects in hot weather—a fact some guests seemed aware of. While they sipped juice and mineral water, Ginny and

I became shamelessly louder. We anointed ourselves the noisy end of the table. Some things never change.

Tumbling back into the car, we laughed and gabbled the last leg of the journey away.

If ever a town was designed for romance, it must be Daylesford. Sprinkled over volcanic hills and basins, it has a delightfully colonial atmosphere. A history of gold digging and mineral spas add a touch of glitz. Shops, shaded by deep verandahs, specialize in everything from handmade chocolates to alpaca wear.

With its clear country air, Daylesford's pleasures are simple and sensuous. If there isn't a wedding to attend, you can stroll around the lake and have a soak in the hot pools. Good food and wine plentiful. The coffee's passable, too.

A large group of us met for dinner that evening at the Farmers Arms. Tables full of happy faces prepared for a boisterous night ahead. Much as I wanted to join them, the words on the menu started dancing in a sickening blur. A rockslide of exhaustion, combined with a reaction to our lunchtime excesses, rumbled in.

These black holes of tiredness were a new thing. I used to be able to dig deep and push through weariness. But this time, when I'd most wanted it, the energy reserves were empty. I simply had to retreat. It was a reminder that it takes more than five months to recover fully from major surgery. I made embarrassed excuses and retired to the cottage, where I filled the spa bath and watched the hills turn purple, then suddenly indigo.

Next morning, a roll of thunder startled us awake. Dark clouds clustered malevolently around the hills. While the landscape was parched, and local farmers would be praying for rain, I hoped Rob and Chantelle's day wasn't going to be marred by it. I needn't have worried. The clouds quickly evaporated into transparent blue and the thermometer started sprinting upward.

Sharing the cottage with Ginnie and Rick turned out to be a bonus. Ginnie had packed an array of fashion accessories to solve every imaginable style crisis. When Katharine realized she'd forgotten the belt to her purple dress, Ginnie whipped a black sash from her suitcase and tied it so expertly around Katharine's waist that it looked better than the original.

Rob and Andrew, freshly shaved and nervous, knocked on the cottage door. They needed somewhere to iron their shirts.

My throat went dry as the momentousness of the occasion set in. Nobody *has* to get married any more. When wedding vows were invented, people didn't expect to live much past their thirties. Staying together for a lifetime probably meant only ten or twenty years. Today's couples, even those who marry in their thirties, can realistically hope to celebrate a fiftieth wedding anniversary. To promise fifty years of love and loyalty to one person in today's world is beyond daring.

"Do you know how to do this?" Rob asked, handing me an ivory rose with its stem encased in green tape, and a long pin.

Attaching a rose to my son's wedding jacket was the last thing he was going to ask of me as a single man. While we'd always be close, I was officially stepping back. It was time for him to carve a future of his own making with Chantelle.

None of the surge of jealousies and insecurities mothers are supposed to experience at times like this surfaced. All I could feel was immense happiness for Rob. For a man in his early thirties, he'd had a lifetime's heartache after losing his older brother. With help from loving friends and family, not to mention Cleo, he'd grown into a fine man. Having recovered from the mire of debilitating illness, he was a successful engineer. More important, he had loyal friends—and now love. This day deserved to be celebrated in style.

The only hint of sadness came from Sam's absence. If he'd lived and grown to adulthood, he'd have been in the cottage with us too. Sam the extrovert, the joker, would be reveling in the fun. He'd be ribbing his brother, throwing his head back in laughter and later on giving a toast designed to cause his brother monumental embarrassment. If he'd lived, perhaps by now Sam would have been married with a family of his own—though it was hard to imagine he would have succumbed to conventional patterns.

I thought of my parents, too, and how much they'd loved a party. Dad, his eyes twinkling, would be raiding the fridge. Mum, ravishing in some outfit she'd thrown together for the occasion, would be waving her hands about and enthralling a circle of admirers with an outrageous yarn.

They were all with us anyway, curling around us like shimmering ribbons. They were in our laughter, our mannerisms, our physical features. They'd always be part of us. Narrowing my eyes, I could almost see a small black cat weaving around Rob's ankles. Yes, Cleo was with us, too.

As Lydia, gorgeous in her floral dress and makeup, stepped through the door, she brought some of Mum's glamour. Watching Katharine bounce her freshly tonged curls as she twirled in her purple dress recalled Mum's theatricality.

Wandering past the bathroom and glimpsing Rob adjusting his gold wedding tie in the mirror, I saw Dad's style and sensitivity. Past and present merged in celebration.

Handsome as a prince, Rob planted a damp kiss on my cheek. Our son was too grounded to be aware of his movie star looks. He and Andrew climbed into a car to arrive traditionally early at the chapel.

"Are we ready?" asked Philip, taking my hand. The girls weren't quite. Even though they were perfect as summer flowers, they needed one more coat of lip gloss each. Tissues, lipsticks, and powder compacts were tucked away in evening bags. I checked my waterproof mascara. The cottage door finally clicked shut behind us.

Celebration

Blessings take many forms.

A skylark's melody pierced the summer air as Philip, the girls, and I climbed a grassy lane to the convent, its domed tower looming over us as we reached its gates. Bees bustled in lavender bushes. Petunias dazzled red and white. The rooftops of Daylesford spread below us, melting into golden fields and blue hills.

Rob and Andrew pulled up in their car seconds after we'd arrived. It would've been quicker for them to walk. Guests waved from an upstairs veranda. They'd arrived early. We weren't the only ones excited about this wedding.

The photographer greeted us and arranged us in family groups. He pretended not to be irked by the enthusiastic amateurs clicking away at his elbow, stealing his shots. His photos were going to turn out better anyway, he said.

I'd wondered how a hundred people were going to fit inside the tiny chapel, but they squeezed in four or five to a plain wooden bench. With bare floorboards and lofty ceilings, it was a simple space. More than a century of prayer had seeped into its honey-colored walls. A trio of candles glowed at the altar alongside a splurge of ivory roses.

Thank goodness there were no windows apart from the stained-glass images above the altar. We were insulated from the heat. With luck our more delicate guests would survive the ceremony.

A pair of guitarists plucked out Cole Porter while the room buzzed with anticipation. Standing at the altar in his well-cut suit, hands behind his back, Rob could've been mistaken for European royalty. His teeth flashed as he exchanged small talk with his best man.

"I never thought I'd get married," Lydia whispered, taking a tissue from her evening bag and dabbing her eyes. "Or if I did I wouldn't bother with any of this fuss. But weddings are lovely."

Something inside my rib cage melted. The joy of seeing Rob about to be married was surpassed for a second by the possibility that Lydia hadn't turned her back on finding fulfilment by conventional means. I toyed with an image of her sitting in front of a flat-screen television with a couple of kids and an adoring husband—but that was possibly taking things too far. Choosing furniture with an architect spouse for a flat in Montmartre, maybe? Or sipping prosecco with a devoted doctor of philosophy in an attic in Berlin? Anything was possible.

I'd been continuing to monitor the news in Sri Lanka, of course. Government troops had just captured the northern town of Kilinochchi, held for ten years by the Tamil Tigers as their administrative headquarters. Sri Lanka's president was hailing it as an unparalleled victory and was urging the rebels to surrender.

Frisson rippled through the chapel when the musicians struck up the unmistakable notes of "Pachelbel's Canon." The stately piece that often features trumpets and other "serious" instruments sounded more laid back played by a pair of guitars. Everyone knew what it meant. Heads swiveled. Eager glances were made toward the door at the back of the chapel. The door's amber glass radiated a gold halo. There was movement behind the glass. The musicians charged into a second, more vigorous round of "Pachelbel's Canon." Guests fell silent in expectation. The door stayed closed.

The congregation became restless as the temperature edged up from pleasantly warm to stifling. Even Rob, his back to us, started twitching his left leg. Had the bride discovered some awful damage to her gown inflicted by our renegade cat?

Another round of "Pachelbel's Canon" started up, the notes wavering in confidence. The guests started whispering, then chattering among themselves. They'd almost given up hope the modern-day wedding march was going to produce anything. And if the bride *was* going to appear it would surely be at the start of yet another round of . . .

The door glided open. A dark-haired bridesmaid dressed in scarlet strode forward, her lips as red as her dress. Her legs, tanned and athletic, paced toward the altar. She was a ravishing young woman, but all eyes were on the vision several yards behind her.

We drew a single breath as Chantelle drifted past on her father's arm. The gown Jonah had been so fascinated by shimmered pink and peach on her lovely body. Pearls and crystals on the gown's bodice glistened in the soft light. It was as though the gown had been specially designed for this chapel. With her hair swept up and adorned by a single rose, she was perfection.

Unable to wait any longer, Rob turned to admire his bride. His smile trampolined off the walls as Chantelle's blue eyes beamed back at him. No sonnet could've done justice to that moment—an electric nanosecond, gone in a flash but eternal as the sun. Everyone in the room felt the chemistry between the couple.

My vision blurred. Whoever invented waterproof mascara was a genius. The paper tissue guy runs a close second. Gallons of fluid must have leaked out of my eyes over the years. This time they were tears of happiness.

After the ceremony, guests poured into the reception area and found their seats. Doors were flung open on to the terrace. The warm evening breeze was gentle as a kiss. Food, champagne, and laughter were followed by more food, champagne, and laughter. And the speeches.

While I'd known Andrew, the best man, since he was about fourteen, he'd seldom said more than two sentences to me. He seemed such a reserved character, I'd wondered how he'd handle best man status. But when Andrew rose to give the traditional toast, he became Seinfeld of the Southern Hemisphere.

Andrew enlightened us about a few things Rob would've preferred kept secret—including the illegal removal of a neon strip light from a gentlemen's convenience. Chantelle's brother gave a speech on behalf of her family. Philip stood and said a few words, followed by Steve.

With the speeches over, people lifted their forks and spoons to dig into their desserts, but Chantelle's uncle, who was MC, called a halt. There was to be one more speech, he said.

We examined the room curiously to see who the unexpected orator was. A chair was scraped back and Lydia stepped forward as gracefully as her unaccustomed heels would allow.

Smiling at us all, Lydia announced she didn't want to make a speech so much as give a blessing. It would be a chant to invite celestial beings to take part in the celebration, and to share our happiness with those who had departed. Guests fell silent as the unfamiliar language rolled over them. It was the same singsongy chanting I'd heard in hospital.

As it died away and Lydia returned to her seat, there was a pause while people wondered what to do next. My cheeks turned hot with embarrassment. Chanting in private was one thing. If she'd asked me beforehand, I'd have said inflicting it on a group of revelers was inappropriate. Fortunately, the musicians took charge. Joined by a drummer, they morphed into a dance band. The new Mr. and Mrs. Brown, who'd rejected the idea of a bridal waltz, invited everyone to join them on the floor.

Fueled by champagne and romance, couples surrendered to impulse. A silver-haired pair circled cautiously, creeping like crabs in a half-remembered quickstep. The bridesmaid crossed the room and took the hand of a teenage boy. His embarrassment was quickly surpassed by delight at being chosen by the second most beautiful woman in the room.

Self-consciousness melted away as teenagers shimmied, and strangers asked each other to dance. Looking around, I realized almost every living person we loved was there in one room, dancing, kissing . . . and, oh no, the bride grabbed me, turned around and slapped my hands on either side of her waist— forming a conga line! A pair of hands grabbed my waist from behind. Glancing over my shoulder, I saw Lydia beaming back at me. I couldn't remember the last time I'd seen her dance.

I thought conga lines belonged to 1950s movies. But as more and more people joined the human snake, all of us stamping and swaying to the same rhythm, a primal sense of belonging took over. Any separateness we'd felt as individuals evaporated. On this night, for this incredibly joyous occasion, we were one pulsating creature, a tribe. I never wanted the conga line to end.

After the cake was cut and feet turned numb, people retreated to a bar downstairs. Reclining in a beanbag chair, I was joined by a relative who's a devout Catholic and just the sort of person to be offended by our nonconformist occasion.

"Do you know what I thought was the most special part of tonight?" she asked, sipping a bright green cocktail. "It was that blessing Lydia gave. She changed the atmosphere of the entire room. Did you feel it?"

Several others echoed my relative's sentiment throughout the night. I was relieved our guests had taken Lydia's blessing in the spirit it had been given. I should have trusted her more.

The clock had run out of numbers by the time we collapsed on our bed in the holiday cottage. Philip and I agreed it had been a wonderful wedding, possibly the best we'd been to— apart from our own.

I'd hardly been able to believe my luck that day I walked down a medieval aisle in Switzerland to see my handsome husband-to-be waiting at the altar. "Till death us do part" had rolled lightly off our tongues. The idea of having to part some-day was the last thing on our minds. But the mastectomy had made us both run through the scenario—one of us trying to sleep in an empty bed while the other floated away into stardust. Such a powerful reminder of the fragility of our relationship had made us appreciate each other more; made us less afraid to express affection. It was strange to think cancer could enhance a marriage.

Rob and Chantelle delayed their honeymoon to take a trip to Vietnam later in the year. We put on brunch at the convent café next morning for guests who were reluctant to leave. A surprising number showed up, competing for the shadiest corners in which to devour croissants and coffee. The sun scorched a hole in the sky while the air buzzed with stories from the night before.

One by one, they kissed our cheeks and crunched down the gravel path. As our guests turned and waved good-bye I felt a touch of sadness . . . but only because one of the happiest twenty-four hours of my life was over.

Hostage

The glower can be mightier than the claw.

We pulled up outside Shirley in the late afternoon, anxious to learn if Jonah and Ferdie had survived their honeymoon weekend. Rob and Chantelle, eager to collect their beloved cat baby, were only ten minutes behind. We wanted to present a picture of feline harmony by the time they arrived.

As we climbed the path we heard insistent meowing from behind the front door. *Good,* I thought, *at least one cat's alive.* Philip turned the key and opened the door cautiously. Jonah thrust his head through the crack and glared up at us. (*"You took your time!"* he seemed to be saying.)

The house felt oddly tense and silent, as if it'd been the scene of unspeakable drama. Lydia gathered Jonah in her arms and inspected him for signs of damage. Eyes, ears, nose, and feet were all intact. Not bad after two days with a cat double his weight. We called for Ferdie. No reply.

Vivienne had probably separated the boys and put Ferdie in the cat run, I thought. We went outside and peered into the towers and through the tunnel. No sign of silver fur.

The floor was littered with unfamiliar cat toys, along with some handmade contraptions including six empty toilet rolls Scotch-taped together in the shape of a pyramid.

Lydia found a note under a house key on the kitchen table:

Hi there. Hope you had a great wedding. The boys got along fine, though Ferdie tried to eat Jonah's food as well as his own! Jonah still thinks he's boss. He wanted me to spend all my time with him. Whenever I tried to cuddle Ferdie he got jealous, so I had to give Ferdie hugs when Jonah wasn't looking. I lent them some toys, and made a few as well. Hope you don't mind.

Vx

P.S. Jonah loves playing hide-and-seek for cat treats inside the toilet rolls.

Ferdie had obviously been in residence while Vivienne was staying. But where was he now? The girls searched for him upstairs while I scoured downstairs, calling his name. Jonah sat like a prince on top of his scratching pole, nonchalantly licking his paws.

"What have you done with Ferdie, boy?" I asked.

Jonah swished his tail and narrowed his eyes as if to say it was none of my business.

"Do you think he ran out the front door when we opened it and nobody saw?" asked Lydia.

Impossible. One of us would've noticed. Besides, Jonah had filled the entire entrance hall both physically and personality-wise.

"Rob and Chantelle will be here soon," said Katharine. "What are we going to tell them—Ferdie's got an invisibility cloak?"

If their beloved cat had disappeared it was going to be their worst wedding present. And I'd spend the rest of my life feeling responsible. No, worse. Guilty.

"Did you hear that?" asked Philip, whose ears are differently tuned to mine.

"No. What?"

"Meowing. It was coming from . . . over there," he said, pointing at the fireplace.

"You mean that muffled . . ."

"There he is!" said Philip, crouching on all fours and peering up the chimney. "He's hiding up here!"

I'd heard of Santas up chimneys, and the occasional bird and chimney sweep. But never a cat.

The girls and I watched, astonished as Philip reached into the void. After a few grunts and groans, Ferdie emerged. His fur was daubed with soot. His pride had taken a bashing. Apart from that he was unharmed.

Jonah was a lightweight compared to Ferdie, and a failure as a fighter. We were amazed he'd managed to frighten his week-end housemate up the chimney.

Ferdie was ecstatic when the newlyweds arrived to collect him. We weren't going to say anything, but Chantelle noticed the soot marks on his fur. Her eyes widened as Philip described the chimney rescue. For all our good intentions, Ferdie was desperate to escape Jonah's psychological torture. I'd never seen a cat spring so gratefully into his carry case.

Rob and his bride climbed into their car with their precious cargo on board. We stood with the girls on the veranda and waved good-bye.

"What a great weekend!" I sighed, as Philip put his arm around me and we turned to go back inside.

"Apart from the finale," he added.

Heroes in Wheelchairs

Cats don't understand the meaning of self-pity.

I'd hoped Rob's wedding might have proved a turning point for Lydia. Like any beautiful young woman, she'd basked in the admiring looks and flattering comments she'd received that night. But to my disappointment she was soon back in her white pants and pale tops, complete with shoulder-hugging shawl.

Three days after the wedding I could stand it no longer and asked if she was returning to Sri Lanka. To my relief, she announced she'd decided to stay in Australia for a while and change her study course to psychology.

Seizing the chance to update her looks, I dragged her around some shops. But my attempts to interest her in hairdressers and clothes nearly always failed. Whenever I tried to bully her into letting me buy a dress that showed off her figure, Lydia would examine herself in the shop mirror and put her head to one side. It's lovely, she'd say, but she really didn't want me spending money on her.

Shop assistants would shake their heads as we left empty-handed. Some said they'd never seen a mother begging her daughter to let her buy her things, and not the other way around.

She often went out to meditation sessions or Buddhist society meetings at night, never to anything requiring lipstick and heels. The absence of men, suitable or otherwise, was noticeable at first but then we grew used to it. When I asked what'd happened to Ned, Lydia said he'd fallen in love with an actress.

I scanned her face for signs of emotion, but could find none.

Sometimes I peeked through her door to see her sitting cross-legged, eyes closed, in front of her homemade altar, Jonah looking at her quizzically under the gaze of the laughing monk.

Desperate for a hint of what was going on inside her head, I took the sneak's option and interrogated her sister. Katharine's response wasn't entirely satisfactory. She said Lydia was still thinking about becoming a nun. Or writing a book, or opening a retreat center. While I'd always encouraged Lydia to dream, her ideas seemed as floaty as a Chagall painting.

As well as going back to university, Lydia resumed her work with disabled people, graduating to a wider range of clients. The bus she drove turned up regularly outside the house. One day she called me out to meet a group of teenage boys. Preparing for some masculine banter, I followed her out to the vehicle where she slid the door open. Three wasted figures swayed like plants on the seats, their mouths open, their hands locked into claws.

"Say hello to my mum," she said so naturally she could've been talking to friends. One boy responded by rocking violently backwards and forwards. Another rolled his eyes back in his skull. I felt proud of her.

When I asked how she was able to do the work, she said her clients reminded her how to live. They hardly ever felt sorry for themselves, and they existed totally in the now. Unshackled by the burdens of keeping up appearances and worrying about the future, they were free to be authentic. Being in their presence made her happy—though lifting them sometimes hurt her back. While she didn't mind drool or feeding people through tubes, she wasn't always so keen on changing adult nappies.

The more saintly my vegetarian, meditating, caring daughter became, the more tainted and self-centered I felt by comparison. Sometimes when she sat with us at dinner, carefully skirting the Bolognese sauce (traces of meat), for the salad and spaghetti, spikes of tension radiated from both sides of the table.

Philip and I felt judged for not selling our house and donating the funds to an African village. He shifted uncomfortably when Lydia suggested he might have a more rewarding career working for a nonprofit organization. I felt equally awkward when it was hinted I could do more charity work.

She wasn't the only one doing the judging, of course. Sometimes we thought she'd set herself apart on a throne of untouchable purity. On other occasions Lydia and I seemed engaged in a game of chess—with her three moves ahead. Her selfless behavior made her invulnerable to criticism. Her ideals were impeccable. The work she did was invaluable, underpaid, and hardly recognized by society.

And yet in my darker moments—and this puts me in such unflattering light I hesitate to commit it to print—watching her with the wheelchair-ridden, wiping and wheeling, carrying and cajoling, I couldn't help wondering if looking after the weak gave her a power kick.

"Where shall we go today?" she'd ask brightly, aware most of the unfortunate souls in her care had no hope of answering. "I know a place where they sell the best custard tarts in the state. It's just a two-hour drive away. Let's go!"

Her disabled charges were in no position to argue. They had to comply with being wheeled into the bus and carted off. But who was I to have an opinion? If the only alternative was to be shut away in front of television all day, a custard tart odyssey would've been fantastic.

Some of Lydia's clients unnerved me, but their courage and, in many cases, intense love of life were inspirational. Compared to them I felt pathetic worrying about shortness of breath and whether cancer cells were still lurking inside my late-middle-aged body. They were superheroes on wheels. Meeting her younger clients, I felt heartache for their parents.

That said, I sometimes begrudged the way I'd get lassoed into Lydia's good works. On a searing hot Saturday two week-ends after Rob's wedding, she asked if she could bring a group of elderly clients around for morning tea.

"How many?" I asked.

"Five or six. We'll bring our own food and drink, so don't go to any trouble," she said brightly. "We can go to a park and have a picnic there if you're busy," she added, tuning into my reluctance.

They couldn't possibly eat outside when the temperature was predicted to reach 40 plus degrees.

Katharine rolled her eyes. Visits from Lydia's clients could be very draining.

I made a pancake mix. The pancakes curled in the pan, transforming into something previously unknown to mankind. The doorbell rattled. I opened the door. Heat exfoliated my face.

When I saw the broken humanity huddled on the front porch my chest lurched. I hurried them inside where the air-conditioning labored ineffectually. Lydia introduced them one by one. Lawrence's body was so stiff and shrunken he could barely walk. Agatha's matronly form was mobile, but her eyes were devoid of life. Ellie, white-haired in a wheelchair, was eerily talkative. Sofia didn't talk, but nodded and smiled too much for comfort. Bert introduced himself erroneously as the boss.

Jonah bolted upstairs.

I was relieved Lydia had an assistant, Emma. Together with Katharine, they helped the visitors hobble down the hall, where cake and sandwiches were set out on plates. The pancakes were surprisingly successful. Aware that some of the women would've been consummate homemakers in their day, I apologized about forgetting the baking powder, but nobody seemed to mind.

Conversation didn't exactly crackle. Ellie chattered away, but her subject matter scattered like torn-up pieces of paper. She changed mid-sentence from knitting to tram timetables.

I nudged Katharine and told her to fetch her violin. She reluctantly complied.

Lawrence touched his hearing aid when he saw the violin. Music hurt his ears. Katharine moved her music stand to the other end of the hall.

"*Music!*" cried Sofia, hurrying to join her. Patting the music stand, she pointed at Katharine and said, "Play 'Silent Night.'"

It was two months since Christmas, but nobody was counting.

As the first notes floated down the hall, ancient voices warbled tentatively around the melody they'd known since birth.

The ghosts of close to 500 years of Christmas memories hovered around the table. Promises of Christmases to come were severely limited. I reached for a paper towel to dab the tears.

After they'd sung more carols and stayed on for lunch (because it was in the picnic basket anyway) our visitors became restless. Bert wanted Katharine to improvise some jazz on her violin. He jiggled with irritation when she explained her training was classical. Lydia and Emma escorted the others one by one to the bathroom.

"Do we have a bucket and mop?" Lydia whispered. "Agatha's had an accident."

When it was time to leave, Lydia assembled her clients inside the front door. They needed to get down the path and into the van as quickly as possible. The wind had come up and it was unbearable outside. There was an ominous tang of smoke on the breeze.

Lydia assured me she'd be dropping her clients home to shelter from the heat straight away. Before opening the front door, she conducted a swift search of Agatha's handbag to discover one of our candlesticks and a tube of my Lancôme face wash. Lydia laughed and said we'd got off lightly. Whenever they went to town, Agatha had a habit of snatching food off people's plates.

Waving our visitors good-bye, I clutched the paper towel. Lydia's clients always gave more than they took.

Embracing the Enemy

A cat is not always a reliable host.

"Guess what?" said Lydia, her tone unusually bright.

I was wary of this particular tone. It usually meant I was about to be bullied into something and I wasn't in a very obliging mood.

"What?" I asked distractedly. A "general knowledge" crossword puzzle was driving me nuts, asking for the Christian names of rock singers I'd never heard of.

"My Teacher's coming to stay."

"That's nice," I said. "Who's he staying with?"

I hate it when I have to look up crossword answers in the back of the book. But how else was I going to get "Metal with atomic number 22"? Ah yes. Titanium.

"Us."

My pen rattled to the floor. Jonah snared it between his teeth and disappeared.

Her monk? That man! *Staying* with us?! My mouth opened. No words came out . . .

"He can't," I said at last. "We don't have room."

"He can have my bedroom," she replied. "I'll sleep on the couch."

It was our home, not a religious retreat house.

But then it was Lydia's home, too.

"How long do you want him here?"

"I was thinking a month," she said matter-of-factly.

A *month* taking care of a man who thinks he's a god?

"Too long," I said.

Assuming the subject was closed, I went in search of Jonah and my pen.

"Three weeks?" she called after me.

If Lydia knew anything at all about me, it's that I'm a reluctant hostess. If anyone was coming to stay for an entire month, I could think of several thousand others I'd feel more comfortable with than the man beaming from the photo frame in her bedroom.

"Don't monks stay in monasteries?" I asked.

"Well, he *has* been invited to stay at a big house in the country where they've built a house specifically for him, but he says he'd rather be close to town."

If the guru stayed with us, his hold over Lydia would tighten. He might even start trying to convert the rest of us. Besides, I was still angry at him for luring her away to Sri Lanka when I'd been unwell.

"He can't come here," I said.

"But I *want* him to!" said Lydia, her eyes round and moist like Bambi's. "He won't be any trouble. I'll look after him and I'll cook all his meals. Not that he eats much. Can't he stay for at least a night or two?"

Taking a stand against my Taurus daughter is useless. Refusing to let the monk over our threshold would only drive her more defiantly into the folds of his robes.

"I suppose he can stay one night," I sighed.

"Two."

"Oh all right," I muttered, hardly believing what I was saying.

Having a monk to stay, even for two nights, is a daunting prospect. A monk is too holy to share a bathroom with mere mortals. He needs a bath, shower, and toilet all to himself. While Lydia was more than happy to donate the upstairs bathroom to the cause, her sister wasn't so keen.

"I thought monks were all for the simple life," grumbled Katharine, transferring her towel and toiletries to the downstairs bathroom. "What makes this one so special?"

Jonah, always sensitive to change, was on high alert. Like a clockwork toy on steroids, he bolted up and down the hall, meowing nonstop. Shadowing Lydia, he leaped on and off her bed while she smoothed fresh sheets over the mattress and laid out clean towels. I checked her room for items with potential to offend our ethereal visitor. A photo of Lydia and her school friends laughing in bikinis at the beach, a print of a bare-breasted woman, copies of *Madam Bovary* and *Anna Karenina* left over from school.

The monk's dining needs were specific. He would eat two vegetarian meals a day—alone in his room. And due to religious requirements, nothing would pass his lips after midday.

It was also important we refrained from touching him. Handshaking, arm-around-the-shouldering, and hugging were out of the question. The robed one hadn't even arrived yet but was already proving to be more high-maintenance than our lunatic cat.

I'm not proud of my inability to stick to rules. The harder I try not to cause offense the worse it gets. Whenever I'm introduced to a devout Christian, for instance, "Jesus!" and "Christ!" spring out of my mouth every second sentence. It would've been safer if Lydia hadn't told me not to touch the monk. My hands were already itching, begging to wrap themselves around him.

I began to wonder if it mightn't be easier for us to move into a hotel while he was in residence. But Philip was adamant. He wasn't shifting out of his house for anyone. I suggested Rob and Chantelle might like to cancel their usual Sunday lunchtime visit, but they were curious to meet the man who had rearranged Lydia's head.

Even our more broad-minded friends raised their eyebrows. A daughter converting to Buddhism was on the verge of inter-esting. Having a monk come to stay in the house was weird. Dusting and (much to Jonah's distaste) vacuuming, I started to get nervous.

"Are cats okay?" I asked Lydia.

"He doesn't particularly like cats."

Jonah shot her a disdainful glower from the top of his scratching pole.

"But don't Buddhists love all living creatures?" I asked. "Isn't that why they're vegetarian?"

She was too busy unloading packets of tofu and noodles to answer.

The monk arrived that evening in a flurry of charisma. Locking my hands together safely behind my back, I stood in the doorway smiling and nodding like those toys people used to put in the back windows of their cars.

Philip was behind me, so I couldn't see what he was doing—something noncommittal, no doubt. Katharine stood to one side, smiling warily. Jonah pushed forward, flung himself at the monk and emitted an ear-shattering yowl.

To my astonishment, Lydia bowed deeply. I hadn't imagined my willful, stroppy daughter possessed the appropriate muscle sets to perform such an exaggerated gesture of respect. In this man's presence her back straightened and her demeanor became demure and subservient.

The monk beamed benevolently through his gold-rimmed spectacles. He was as smooth-faced as he'd been the last time we'd met five years ago. While he claimed to be in his sixties, he could just as easily have been thirty-five. As a de-aging program, religious life was clearly more effective than plastic surgery.

As our guest sailed down the corridor, Jonah and the rest of us followed. I was keen to understand this man who was so important to my daughter. I would've liked to ask his views on the war in his country, and what, if any, plans he had for Lydia.

After sinking into a chair by the fireplace, the monk chatted about his travels. He was charming, self-assured and, in every sense, untouchable. A man from another world, he unnervingly referred to Lydia as his disciple. I worried we weren't treating him with the reverence he was accustomed to. Still, since Lydia was kneeling on the floor beside him, hands passively resting on her lap, she was undoubtedly making up for the rest of us. Jonah, too, seemed enthralled.

I was relieved it was after dark, so we wouldn't have to worry what to feed our guest. As the monk told us about the fund-raising programs and lectures he was giving while he was in Melbourne, Jonah circled his chair, meowing and trying to snare his attention. Whether it was the glamorous drape of his robes or the exotic smells from far-off countries, Jonah was fascinated—and appeared to be attempting a charm offensive. I watched uneasily as he disappeared under our visitor's maroon hemline.

"Shooooo!" the monk hissed, delivering a well-aimed kick.

Jonah flew out from under the robe. Astonished, he blinked and shook himself. Once he'd regained composure, Jonah sprang on top of his scratching post, and with loud clicking sounds proceeded to lick his private parts.

When people don't eat or drink there isn't much to keep them up late. Lydia escorted her Teacher upstairs while we put ourselves nervously to bed. With any luck Lydia's room was monastic enough to make him feel at home—though not too at home, hopefully.

I woke early next morning to find Lydia rummaging through the fridge. She'd arranged a plate of rice and vegetables on a tray to take upstairs to the guru, and was now placing a separate bowl of food beside the plate.

"Who's that for?" I asked.

"That's for the Buddha," she replied solemnly.

"The Buddha's going to eat that?" I asked, incredulous.

"It's an *offering*," she said, looking at me sternly.

There it was again. That feeling of being lowly, and somehow wrong. Yet I wasn't trying to make fun of her or her newfound belief system. I was more than willing to confess ignorance. Having a monk under the roof was just a case of too much too soon.

A stream of disciples, mostly Westerners, flowed through the house to sit in his presence while he regaled them with updates on the monastery-building program. A new kitchen was keeping the nuns happy, but his plans were much grander. He hoped someday to erect an enormous statue on top of the hill above the monastery.

In between visitors, I asked the monk about his background. He told me that after growing up poor in a village, he'd become attached to a great teacher. He showed me photos of the man, a dignified-looking monk who he said had lived well into his nineties.

As a young monk, our visitor had spent several years meditating in a cave, the entrance of which was ultimately transformed into a cottage. He'd since moved to more comfortable accommodation farther up the hill. The cave cottage was currently occupied by a younger monk, an equally fervent meditator. It remained the central point of the monastery.

We took the monk to the botanic gardens that afternoon. As we stared out over the lake, I asked him about differences between Buddhism in Sri Lanka and Tibet. The answer was long and convoluted, and included unflattering asides about Philip's potential for Enlightenment, which I hoped could be put down to the language barrier. Philip was mercifully out of earshot, engrossed in conversation with a black swan.

Changing the topic, I told the monk how I'd seen him sitting on the end of my bed not long after my surgery. He threw his head back and laughed with delight.

"I did that thing!" he declared, waving a hand in the air. "Yes! I did that!"

So, global self-transportation was in his repertoire. I wasn't sure who was crazier—him for thinking he'd done it, or me for having seen him.

On the second day, a rare diversion from normal practice was announced. The monk would be willing to do us the honor of having lunch with us downstairs at the oak table providing, of course, it was fully vegetarian and occurred before midday.

Being Sunday, Rob and Chantelle were due to come over. I sent them a text, warning them to show up early if they wanted to be fed.

I have to say it wasn't one of our more relaxed family get-togethers. Having a monk at the end of the table did change the ambience somewhat. Nevertheless, everyone did their best, politely offering plates of salad, bread, and stir-fried beans to each other. At one point I caught Rob looking longingly at a plate of ham in the fridge.

Jonah, thank heavens, seemed to have recovered from his previous night's obsession and was behaving semi-normally.

With our plates filled we raised our forks and were about to tuck in, when the monk reminded us it was time to give a blessing. Our forks clattered to the table and we lowered our heads.

"Does he mean he wants to say grace?" I whispered to Lydia, who was embarrassed by our crassness. But honestly, who were we to know whether Buddhists said grace? Though, come to think of it, the blessing of food is probably a universal religious practice.

The monk's blessing was particularly elaborate. He blessed the earth our food had come from this day, the rain and the sun and the farmers who'd grown it. We nodded agreement and lifted our forks, but the blessing hadn't finished. We lowered our forks and studied our plates as he blessed the people who'd transported the food to the city . . .

Awkward silence hovered over the table. The silence ballooned into a presence that filled the room and pressed against the French windows. Rob flashed a glance at me from across the table. Philip, on his right, appeared to be engrossed in some complicated mathematical equation. Katharine, sitting next to me, rested her chin on her chest and looked neither left nor right. Only Lydia and the monk seemed entirely at ease with the impenetrable absence of noise.

Then it started. A scuffling sound from the laundry room followed by a slam. I caught Katharine's eye. We both knew what it was. Jonah had chosen this sacred moment to use his litter box. The scuffling grew louder until it became determined scratching. Jonah was digging deep in his litter box and reveling in the sensation of his claws against the plastic base.

Sccccrrrrrrich, scccccccrrrrach, he went, faster and faster, until it sounded like a ditchdigger was working away in the next room.

The monk drew a breath and started blessing the people who'd stored our food, and the shopkeepers who'd put it on their shelves. Sccccrrich, scccccrrrrrach. Jonah was letting us know exactly what he thought. Katharine's chest started heaving in schoolgirl giggles. Immature, yet unstoppable . . . and, under the circumstances, extremely contagious.

I don't know what it was—a reaction to stressful circumstances—but before I knew it, I was exploding with giggles, too. I glanced sideways at Rob and Chantelle's poker faces. Philip, too, was as solemn as a funeral director. They were so studiously controlled I only wanted to laugh more. The effort of trying to stop myself made my ribs ache. The more I tried to repress the giggles the louder they became, morphing into donkey-like hoots. It must've been at least thirty years since I'd been afflicted like this. I tried to disguise them as coughs but nobody was fooled, least of all Lydia, whose cheeks turned as crimson as her Teacher's robes.

Once the meal was mercifully over, the monk excused himself to rest upstairs. Clattering with the dishes over the kitchen sink, Lydia shot Katharine and I a look that could have frozen the tropics.

Next morning as we bobbed and bowed and waved the monk good-bye, parting was such sweet . . . relief.

Yearning

Happiness is a new pink ribbon.

Soon after the monk's stay, Lydia drove me to the hospital to get a new nipple. Greg had assured me it was a simple forty-minute "tidy up" that would be nothing compared to the massive bodywork he'd done seven months earlier in August. With a new nipple, he said, I'd be able to wear flimsy summer tops. We were obviously on different planets.

I could understand why some women who have a breast reconstruction don't bother getting a new nipple. I'd only experienced a flicker of self-consciousness about having a miniature helicopter pad where the old nipple used to be twice—once when a woman walked in on me in a changing room, and another time when I caught Philip's eye sliding sideways while I was stepping out of the shower. Still, seeing as I'd gone to all the trouble of getting a new boob, it seemed logical to add the final touch. And Greg was eager to put the final twirl of icing on the cake he'd created.

If there's one way to stop a conversation, it's announcing you're about to acquire a new nipple. If you said you were getting a new earlobe or a new little toe, people might take polite interest. Mention the N word and they don't know what to say. Nipples are sexual.

To those strong enough to ask, I'd explain Greg was going to cut a couple of centimeters of skin from my left areola and graft it to the helicopter pad, at the same time bunching up a knob of skin in the center to create the new nipple's dome. While he was at it he was going to "review" a small flap that looked like a dog's ear at one end of my abdominal scar.

What was a simple morning's work for Greg was a whole other matter from my end of the scalpel. Those in the know say there's no such thing as minor surgery. A slip of the knife or a tube put in the wrong place and . . .

I embarked on the now familiar routine of shedding clothes and jewelry, along with my dignity and everything else connecting me to the outside world, to stow them in a locker. Hospitals are like that. You succumb to them. It helps to remind yourself that surgeons and nurses are highly educated. They know your life sits quivering like a sparrow in their palms.

If a surgical team was a rock band, the surgeon would be lead guitarist with backup vocals from the nurses. The guy who pushes the trolley would be on drums. And the anesthetist? He'd be bass guitarist. Like all good bass guitarists, the anesthetist tends to have a modest ego, compared to the surgeon anyway. The anesthetist knows he's important but feels undervalued. It's worth trying to flatter him and form a bond in the few seconds you're awake with him since he's the one with the most potential to kill you.

Flat on my back in a blue shower cap, I tried to work my charms but the nipple anesthetist wasn't interested.

"That was quick," I said when he asked only three questions and signalled for me to be wheeled into surgery.

"You survived seven hours last time," he replied rather coldly. "You'll get through forty minutes."

Needle stab. Cold fluid up my arm. Good night.

Waking up was slow. Pain in my abdomen. Headache. Nausea. Sore throat. Worse, a sign on a door saying "Leave X Ray's Here." A nurse asked if I was comfortable. Not with that rogue apostrophe in the room. I'd never have put my life in their hands if I'd known they couldn't do apostrophes.

Back home I winced with pain changing blood-soaked bandages. Resembling a "proper" woman again involved an inordinate amount of trouble.

I sometimes wondered what Mum would have done if she'd been in my situation. For a woman of her generation, she was extremely image conscious. She'd had an innate sense of style that could turn heads even in her seventies. She'd tried to pass that glamour on to me. Shopping for my first bra with her, I was surprised how the garment pulled and dug into my flesh. Soon after, she squeezed me into a garter belt and stockings, a sanitary belt with huge safety pins and a surfboard-size pad, *plus* a corset (*"It's just a light one, dear"*). The effort involved in being a "real" woman was onerous beyond belief.

In my circumstances, there was no doubt Mum would've gone for the full reconstruction gig, plus nipple. Besides, there was Philip to consider. Not to mention a vestige of my own vanity.

Recovery was longer and slower than "simple day procedure" implied. Lydia slid into nursing mode again, providing ceaseless tides of takeaway coffees from Spoonful and cooking meals. Likewise, Jonah seemed to understand I was in pain and snuggled up to me on the bed as if to say, *"Let's settle in for a good rest now, shall we?"* I took comfort in the knowledge that once it was healed, all that remained was to have the nipple tattooed a darker color in a few months' time.

The sight of Philip appearing in the hallway with a bunch of flowers sent an electrical force through our cat. His eyes became a pair of opalescent saucers, his ears pointed forward, his whiskers tense as fencing wire.

Meowing feverishly, Jonah sprang up on his back feet and stretched the length of his body up Philip's thighs. With his front paws he dabbed Philip's hips, begging incessantly.

Jonah wasn't interested in the flowers themselves, or the paper and cellophane they were wrapped in. He wanted the florist's ribbon.

Jonah's obsession with ribbons was by no means indiscriminate. It had to be the *right* sort of ribbon from the *right* florist, meaning a particular type of satiny string from a shop called Say It With Flowers near our old house. Whenever someone appeared with flowers wrapped in the wrong sort of ribbon,

Jonah put on an operatic display. After the initial surge of excitement, he'd examine the flowers to discover they were wrapped in crisp polyester ribbon, a broad band of silk, or some other unacceptable tie. His eyes would narrow with disgust, his tail would sink, and he'd skulk away.

If, however, they were flowers from the *right* florist using the *right* ribbon, Jonah became ecstatic. The instant the flowers were lowered onto the table he assailed them, gnawing and digging at the string. A human would usually try and shoo him off, and then—to Jonah's great joy—unravel the bouquet. The instant the ribbon was detached from the flowers, Jonah pounced on it, snaring it between his teeth and carrying it away like a gambler who'd just beaten the casino.

With ceaseless pride and enthusiasm, he'd carry the string around with him day and night, begging people to engage in Jonah-and-the-Ribbon games. The alternatives were boundless. The ribbon could be a snake winding across the carpet, a bird gliding through the air, a mouse hiding under the rock of a cushion. He even circled chair legs with it until they were tied up.

Jonah and his ribbon would be inseparable for weeks until the object of his passion frayed at both ends and shredded. Even then, our cat refused to forsake his treasure.

Concerned that the disheveled strands might be a danger to his digestion, I'd wait until his attention was diverted by a real-life moth or a shadow on the kitchen floor and dispose of the beloved object in the rubbish bin.

Watching Jonah searching for his lost love afterward was heart-wrenching. I visited the florist shop and furtively asked for lengths of ribbon, no flowers attached. The woman behind the counter thought I was a rose short of a bouquet. Once I explained Jonah's addiction, she was vaguely amused.

"Does your cat have a favorite color?" she asked, fingering the stash of ribbons gleaming seductively from a hook on the wall. If Jonah could see them he'd have experienced religious ecstasy.

"Pink," I replied. "Even though he's a boy. He is Siamese,

which might go some of the way to explaining it. Though some say he's Tonkinese . . ."

The woman was starting to look wary. I'd given her too much information. Still, she was kind enough to let me have the stuff, and supply it on a regular basis. I tried to keep Jonah's habit under control, supplying one string at a time until he'd destroyed it.

Discipline soon slipped. Ribbons at all stages of the life cycle sprawled over the house, particularly in our bedroom, where they were draped over the floor, bed, and tables. I wondered what the cleaners made of it. They probably thought we used them for kinky sex.

While he was still hugely affectionate, and adored his morning routine playing fishing rod and ribbons with Philip, Jonah gave the impression his world was far from perfect. Even his exclusive outdoor run carpeted with cat grass and catnip didn't do it for him anymore. After half an hour lying in one of the hammocks and being tortured by fat pigeons on the fence, he'd trot inside and demand to be stroked or carried.

When he wasn't getting enough attention from his human subjects, he'd patrol the house like a shark, slinking from one room to the next, sniffing out escape routes. I felt hurt Jonah still wanted to run away. And some of the escapades he sent us on chasing him around the neighborhood were humiliating.

One evening, after he'd squeezed out of a crack in the front door and the girls and I were forced on yet another Jonah hunt, we saw him trotting away halfway down the street. Plowing toward him from the other end of the street was a large black dog, attached to its owner by a leash. Confident he could take the dog with a single swipe, Jonah accelerated toward his foe. The girls and I cried out as the animals drew closer together. Confrontation was inevitable. Jonah was about to become dog food.

Not for the first time, I wondered how such an intelligent animal could lack common sense. What made Jonah imagine he could take on a dog seventeen times his size? Dreading what was going to happen next, I closed my eyes.

A baritone bark stabbed the air. It was the joyous, confident sound hunting dogs make when they know they've run down a fox.

Suddenly I felt a rush of wind between my ankles. Opening my eyes, I saw a cream and brown streak scoot between my feet. It shot straight behind us to hide under my car. Hot on its heels gamboled over 200 pounds of eager canine, closely followed by a bemused owner. After trying to follow its prey through my legs, the dog nearly knocked me backwards. It then took a detour and charged around me toward my car.

"That your cat?" the dog owner asked, panting slightly. "Spike just wants to be friendly. See? He's wagging his tail."

The dog's bark rose to a staccato tenor as it tried to lure Jonah out from his hiding place for a tête-à-tête. But Jonah wasn't tempted. He emitted a dark, throaty yowl from under the car.

The dog lurched back on its haunches in surprise.

"I've never heard a cat sound like a cow before," said his owner.

Jonah's yearning for broader horizons continued to be mirrored in our older daughter. The monk's visit had made her restless.

My heart jarred when she talked of returning to Sri Lanka. I kept an anxious ear out when she phoned the monastery. Whenever she spoke to the strangers at the end of the line, I was intrigued to hear her lapsing into the musical talk she used for chanting.

She'd always had a good ear for languages, but it seemed incredible she could have picked up Sinhalese so quickly. Her sentences ran smoothly and whoever she was speaking to had no trouble understanding her. The more I eavesdropped on Lydia's secret life, the more mysterious it became.

If she was taking the trouble to learn the language, she obviously believed she had some kind of future in Sri Lanka. I continued monitoring the news. Though the country was still awash with violence, twenty-five years of war was dragging to a bloody conclusion. On May 16, 2009, the Sri Lankan president claimed victory over the Tamil Tigers. A silence rather than a truce, some said. But I hoped it might mean that if Lydia decided to go there in the future it mightn't be such a source of worry.

When the phone shrieked to life close to midnight one night, I fumbled for the receiver. Since Sam's accident, my nerves had been permanently rearranged and completely lacked resilience around unexpected phone calls. Whenever anyone asked what I'd like for my birthday I'd say anything except a surprise.

To my astonishment, the caller was my Sydney publisher, Louise. Her tone was urgent. I took a breath and waited for terrible news.

Louise said her colleagues had taken *Cleo* to the London Book Fair—and it was a huge hit. At this very moment, five British publishers were bidding for the UK rights, and publishers from at least ten other countries were keen to translate the book into their own languages.

I'd developed a technique for dealing with bad news—stepping back, slowing thought processes down, trying not to say anything stupid. But good news? *Incredibly* good news? It was almost impossible to believe our quirky story about loss, love, and a small black kitten was being launched into the world.

Now I was fully awake, my mouth was capable of shaping only two words and repeating them again and again. Wow and thanks.

"You've written an international bestseller," said Louise. "It'll change your life."

After I got off the phone, the bedroom shadows seemed to fill with the presence of those I'd tried to honor through the book. Sam and Mum enveloped me with loving warmth, along with Cleo herself. I'd finally found a way to acknowledge the parents, strangers, and friends who'd helped us through our loss—along with the man who'd sat with Sam during his final minutes on the roadside. The book had also given me a way to let the driver of the car that had killed our son know that I forgave her at a deep and truthful level.

Stardust

A cat takes on the world.

The book *Cleo* padded softly onto the scene with a launch in a Melbourne bookstore. Among the fifty or so people there, it was wonderful to see some of our dearest friends smiling and generously asking for their copies to be signed. Julie, my yoga teacher, Dave the interior designer, Katharine's violin teacher . . .

Not so close friends had also dragged themselves away from the early evening news to be there—the shrink who'd helped me through breast cancer; Robert who'd designed my website, though we'd never met.

A wonderful woman I'd made friends with through Lydia's school, Professor Deirdre Coleman, gave a speech that was so thoughtful and kind I was almost overcome.

Most important was having Philip and our nearly grown-up family there. Rob and Chantelle carried that special glow lovers have. Lydia and Katharine had invited some of their friends along, and were looking especially beautiful.

People sometimes ask how the members of my family feel about featuring in so much of my writing. All I can say is they're incredibly generous and tolerant about it. Rob, Lydia, and Katharine grew up knowing nothing different. They were written about even before they were born, through almost all our ups and downs until the present. I was helped by the fact that for most of their lives they were convinced no one could possibly want to read Mum's ramblings.

It probably hasn't been so easy for Philip. It took him a while to adjust to being writer's fodder, on the understanding he read anything he featured in before it was published.

A week after the Melbourne signing, I flew across to New Zealand for another even more moving launch in Wellington, where much of the book had been set. I was honored that Louise traveled from Sydney for the event. Both she and Roderick Deane, who'd first encouraged me to write the book several years earlier, gave terrific speeches that were followed by tearful reunions with old friends and neighbors.

With invitations to appear on television and give talks in Australia and New Zealand, it looked like I was no longer destined to live under the middle-aged woman's invisibility shroud. Maybe I wouldn't be doing crosswords and watching *The Weakest Link* until I was carried out of the house in my recliner rocker.

I was half expecting the family to show signs of resentment, but their eyes shone whenever good news about the book came in. And there was plenty of it.

Hurrying to the computer every morning, I could track where the book had just been released by the foreign-language e-mails that had flooded in from readers overnight. Russia and Taiwan one week, Italy the next. I hadn't realized the Translate function on a computer could be so handy. *Cleo*'s success was teaching me that people are similar the world over. We cherish our pets and we'd give our lives for our children. Given that humans care so much about the same things, it's tragic that so much energy is wasted concentrating on our differences.

Lydia rolled her sleeves up and took over instinctually when dishes piled up in the sink or I'd inadvertently forgotten to cook dinner. Following her lead, Katharine became equally helpful. I never had to ask for a table to be set or cleared.

Cancer had taught our daughters to shoulder responsibility and flourish as young women. Watching them laughing and talking together, I sometimes felt overwhelmed with gratitude. If things had unfolded differently and I'd delayed the mammogram, I'd have been present only as a memory.

Countless e-mails flashed up on the computer screen. Many
of them were incredibly touching, a tribute to cats and their
importance in people's lives. One woman whose husband had
committed suicide wrote saying their cat (who was usually terrified of strangers) had stayed by her husband's side while
paramedics worked to save him. Another was from a woman
whose clinical depression after a miscarriage seemed incurable—
until a cat called Cleo stepped into her life. Then there was
Wilson, the cat who refused to leave the bedside of a four-year-
old stricken by leukemia. The night the boy died, Wilson ran
onto the road and was hit by a car. A vet, understanding the
family's torment, did everything he could to save the cat and
Wilson survived to help them through grief.

These and numerous other stories moved me so deeply I'd
often be in tears in front of the computer. While I responded
to every e-mail as best I could, words often felt inadequate.
Occasionally, when I couldn't string the right response together, I'd ask Lydia or Katharine for assistance. Lydia was
particularly helpful when it came to dealing with unconventional people. She suggested the woman who kept seventy-two
cats, a donkey, an owl, and three peacocks in her house might
need professional guidance. I was beginning to realize her Sri
Lankan experience combined with psychology studies were
giving a breadth of understanding that was rare in a person
of her age.

Cleo was opening the world to me in other ways, too. A movie
deal was signed and I was invited on a global publicity tour. Out
in the world after nearly two years engrossed with illness and
book writing, I was anxious to present a passable public image.
My tracksuit collection went in the bin. The breast cancer John
Wayne uniform went, too.

Being interviewed by foreign journalists was a disconcerting
prospect. Even though I'd worked in media for three decades
and had a pretty good idea how to feed an angle to a reporter,
my homely antipodean style mightn't go down well. I thought
about trying to "improve" my presentation to seem more

sophisticated. But in the end I decided honesty was safer. If the real-life author of *Cleo* was a disappointment, so be it.

Unlike our trips to the airport when we'd seen Lydia off to the monastery, the car hummed with enthusiasm. Amid promises to send postcards and text messages to Philip and both girls, I realized this adventure into the unknown was in some ways a middle-aged version of what Lydia had done.

As I kissed Philip and Katharine good-bye, Lydia stood back. For a moment I thought perhaps she wasn't going to kiss me at all. As I turned to walk through the departure doors, Lydia stepped forward.

"I'm so proud of you," she said, hugging me warmly.

I felt sheepish that Lydia was so generous in her support. My behavior toward her Sri Lankan exploits had been inglorious by comparison.

A Strauss waltz spiraled inside my head as the plane I was on circled Vienna, where I was to do publicity for the German-language edition of the book. I craned my neck for glimpses of Viennese woods. Bare and spiky in their October garb, they seemed to stretch forever over snowy ridges.

Martina, my Austrian-based publisher, had e-mailed extremely clear instructions about finding a taxi from Vienna airport. Turn right straight after Customs, head out the automatic doors, then look for a little red hut. A man in the hut would find a cab.

Everything happened exactly as she predicted. Except easier, quicker. I wished I could speak German. It seemed inadequate, rude even, to rely on the famous reputation German speakers have for fluent English. The taxi driver and I sat in silence while Lady Gaga sang something raunchy on his radio. When I asked what he thought of her, he delivered a professorial analysis of how she combined artistic ability with mainstream appeal. All in perfect English.

Julie Andrews would've been perfectly at home in my hotel room. White as edelweiss, it was crisp as schnitzel without the noodles. My suitcase spilled its contents on the floor and the room suddenly looked more like home.

To walk off the jet lag, I headed to the Mozart museum next door. Said to be the only remaining building in Vienna where Mozart actually lived, it was gracious. Sailing through its light-filled rooms, I could almost imagine the short-lived genius flitting through the doorways in one of his embroidered jackets.

His bronze death mask was mesmerizing. Mozart appeared to have been surprisingly handsome, almost like Elvis with his hair swished back from his forehead.

Just as well I'd written about a champagne-drinking friend in *Cleo*. Every foreign publisher seemed convinced I drank copious amounts of nothing else. I stopped arguing when they poured champagne at 11 a.m. or three in the afternoon.

Martina became my Austrian soul mate. She had two cats and had checked out satellite images of Wellington to see if it matched my descriptions in the book. Over dinner she explained how writers and artists are revered in Austria and Germany.

"You mean like rugby players?" I asked. She didn't seem to understand. I *must* learn German, I thought. Or possibly move to Vienna.

Clopping over cobblestones in the dark on my way to give a reading one night, I was unnerved by the fact I was being shadowed—not by one, but several silhouettes. When I sped up, they accelerated. If I slowed down, they reduced speed. Their breathing was audible. In the end I stopped, turned around and prepared to confront my would-be assailants, my heart pulsing in my ears as they closed in to mug me, or worse.

"Mrs. Brown?" asked a polite voice. "I love your book. Could I possibly have your autograph?"

Reading from my book in an elaborate jewel of a room where Mozart often played had to be one of the greatest honors of my life. It was difficult to know what the audience made of this big-boned antipodean author. Martina later reported someone had remarked I looked like the Queen—a perplexing comment.

Perhaps it was something to do with the way my hair had been concreted into place in a local salon earlier in the day.

Philip was in good hands with Lydia and Katharine looking after him. Nevertheless, I sent messages and photos home whenever I had the chance. Lydia was always quick to respond with a "Fantastic!" or an update on her latest marks, almost always Very High Distinction. I was slowly beginning to understand that any pain she'd given me I'd returned to her with interest. For that I felt deep remorse.

When I reached London, where *Cleo* had hit the *Sunday Times* Bestseller List in its first week, a forest of flowers waited in the hotel room. I assumed there'd been a mistake, but they were from Lisa, my brilliant and generous UK publisher. At the BBC I was sealed inside a booth and given headphones for fielding back-to-back radio interviews. It was easy to tell which jocks had read the book and which were simply filling airtime. Later that day, Lisa threw an afternoon tea in Hodder & Stoughton's office in Euston so I could meet the thirty or so people who'd worked on the UK edition. At least three of them were New Zealanders. This was followed by yet more champagne.

I'd assumed Lisbon would be more restful than London. The Portuguese publisher of *Cleo* was incredibly suave. He met me at the airport and drove me to a funky '60s-style hotel. I loved the way Lisbon gazed out over white cobblestones to the sea.

"U wd love it here," I texted Lydia. "People are casual & friendly. It's like Australasia with history." I hesitated to add the seafood was great in case it offended her vegetarian soul.

Late at night, early morning in Australia, I'd talk to Philip on the phone. He reported that he, the girls, and Jonah were all thriving. I asked if there'd been any more talk of Sri Lanka and was relieved when he said no, though Lydia still meditated a lot and was secretary of the University Buddhist Society. There'd been no sign of the monk, either. We were hopeful she'd stick with her psychology course in Melbourne for another year.

★ ★ ★

The book had sold well to Portuguese teenagers, so I was asked to speak to high school students in a hall for a whole hour. Once I realized they were just like the kids at Katharine's school, we got on well. After I'd convinced them I wasn't really a grown-up, they were a fantastic audience. They mobbed me afterwards, each with a story to tell or some personal pain to share. My throat started burning. I began to worry my health wasn't up to international book tours.

After the school visit it was on to interviews with a national newspaper and a magazine. I had a fantastic time in Portugal, but it was no holiday. Some interviews were easier than others. I was bemused by the intellectual nature of the questions posed by a bespectacled woman journalist in Lisbon, and had been unnerved while subjected to Freudian probing about my relationship with my mother at the Vienna Book Fair.

By the time I reached the concrete canyons of New York, the sore throat felt like a bushfire at the back of my mouth. I struggled to hide my exhaustion from my enthusiastic New York publishers. They took me to lunch at one of the city's smartest restaurants and announced they were putting "Number One International Bestseller" on their cover of *Cleo*. Admiring the sleek fashion sense of my luncheon companions, nothing seemed further away than cancer and the mastectomy. Life had changed radically in less than two years.

Despite the wonderful U.S. welcome, I developed shivers and a persistent cough. I longed to be back home in bed. A doctor visited the hotel room and said my condition was understandable. A book tour would be extremely draining, and cancer lowers the immune system.

Curious about the book, he acknowledged the importance of pets in today's world. Two of his patients had suffered severe clinical depression after the death of their cats. He scribbled a prescription for antibiotics and gave me an inhaler for the plane. I signed a copy of *Cleo* for him and wished I could pack him in my suitcase.

★ ★ ★

Back in Australia, Jonah adored being a celebrity cat. Every morning he trotted behind me into my study. Though I still didn't trust him alone in there, he loved nestling on my lap to inspect the overnight e-mails. He was pumped the day a French television crew arrived at Shirley to make a documentary for a much-loved animal program in France called *30 Millions des Amis* (Thirty Million Friends).

You'd think getting a few shots of a cat behaving naturally around a house would be easy, but Jonah had no intention of making the cameraman's job a breeze. When I tried to hold him on my lap and stroke his fur as a demonstration of cat/human-slave devotion, Jonah flattened his ears, wriggled slippery as a pumpkinseed out of my grasp, and galloped down the hall.

The cameraman wasn't fazed and said he'd like a shot of me carrying Jonah through the front door and outside. My throat tensed. From Jonah's perspective any trip out the front door presented an opportunity to run away and give the black cats down the street the insults they deserved.

I nervously picked our pet off the floor as the cameraman positioned himself outside on the front path. Jonah tensed in my arms as I turned the front door handle and stepped onto the veranda, trying to look relaxed. So far so good. Jonah and I were presenting the perfect picture of bonding across the species.

But then the security door slammed behind us and the highly strung animal jumped two feet in the air. Yelping, I stretched my arms out to grab him. Fortunately, as gravity pulled him back toward me, I was able to gather him up.

I was exasperated and a little embarrassed by our uncooperative cat, but the cameraman was unruffled. He had a background in wildlife filming—quite apt given the circumstances—and just shrugged and moved on to film an interview with Rob, who'd escaped from work for an hour.

Not sure what to do next, I laid lunch out on the table for the camera crew. I imagined their work was probably over for the day. But the cameraman was indefatigable. He spent the after-noon creeping around after Jonah, crawling along the floor recording his exhibitionist antics, bouncing down the hall like a kangaroo, flashing up and down stairs like a lightning bolt.

Even after Jonah was exhausted and collapsed on a sofa cushion, the cameraman kept filming, with the cat opening his eye every so often to check he was still the center of attention.

Admittedly, the wildlife filming approach was suitable for Jonah, but I was dubious how the end product would look. I needn't have worried. When I finally saw the program, it was exquisitely made. The door-slamming incident had been tactfully edited out. Jonah came across as the outlandish creature he is—even though the dubbing was beyond my schoolgirl French.

New Life

Few joys are greater than the arrival of a new generation.

Life had changed since the publication of *Cleo*. It was taking on different shapes and colors at home, too. On one of their Sunday lunch visits, I noticed Chantelle wasn't drinking any wine. There was a possibility she was on a diet, though hardly necessary in her case. The alternative scenario was too exciting to contemplate.

Lydia and Katharine were clearing plates from the table when Chantelle broke the joyous news. Their baby was due early June. Philip, the girls, and I smothered her with kisses while Rob sat back, trying to contain his pride.

Blushing, Chantelle said they hadn't intended it to happen so soon. She'd been to a psychic who'd said they wouldn't have a baby for another three years, so they'd relaxed a bit. It was wonderful news, though I have to confess the concept of Rob, my little boy, becoming a father was mind-bending. Lydia and Katharine were heading into Auntsville. Philip, my toy boy, was morphing into a grandfather. And me—a *grandmother*?!

I suddenly understood why Mum had been so prickly about the dismal range of grandmotherly titles available—Nana (too goat-like), Grandma (too *Little Red Riding Hood*), Granny (well, honestly). A Maori friend said he called his grandmother Kuia, which looked lovely on paper, but processed through an Australian accent would inevitably be pronounced "queer." If I had to be called anything, I decided it might as well be vague and nonthreatening, so I took a leaf out of the Teletubbies' book and opted for Lala.

During the months that followed, Jonah took a special interest in Chantelle's changing body shape. Every Sunday lunchtime he deigned to curve himself around her bulge, his head pressed against her stomach as if listening for a heartbeat.

Months whirled past, and before we knew it the baby was a week overdue. There'd been a few false alarms, but every time it looked like something was happening the contractions faded away. By this time Chantelle was fed up. Rob was on edge. I'd run out of knitting wool.

On Wednesday night, five days after baby Brown was due, the family put in bets for when he/she would arrive. Being an optimist, I opted for Friday. Lydia and Katharine chose Saturday. When Philip put in his bid for Sunday, I told him the poor parents couldn't possibly wait that long.

On Friday morning, Chantelle sent a text saying the contractions were regular and they'd be heading into hospital in a couple of hours. After several hours' silence I sent a text: "?" A reply came back straight away "0. Contractions gone away." Saturday was no better.

In the early hours of Sunday morning, I struggled out of bed for my usual nocturnal visit to the bathroom. The bedside clock was glowing 3:15. As I rolled back into bed, my cell phone bleeped to life. Fingers trembling, I fumbled to get the text message open. It was from Rob. Baby Annie had just been born, weighing nine pounds. Mother and daughter (and father!) all well. Room A24.

Flicking the light on, I shook Philip awake. He'd just become a grandfather. I asked him what he wanted to be called. Not Pop or Grandad, surely? "How about Papa?" I suggested, planting a kiss on his prickly cheek. "Papa and Lala has a ring to it." Philip smiled and nodded sleepy agreement.

Confident I wouldn't be getting any more sleep, I got up and put the kettle on. A stardust baby had arrived on planet earth. She wasn't ours, but with any luck part of her life would be entwined with ours in a dance of parenthood two steps removed. No broken nights or parent-teacher interviews, but plenty of excuses to go to the zoo, see *Disney on Ice*, and act like a kid again.

Lydia and Katharine tumbled out of their beds when they heard the news and scrambled into their clothes. Jonah was wide awake and wired, having been moved off his favorite sleeping pillow—Katharine's arm. If we were off on an early morning mission he was determined to accompany us, thrusting himself at the front door, head-butting the panels, and meowing urgently. Like clowns in a bullfight, we each took turns diverting his attention so that one after the other we could slip outside onto the veranda.

Last one out, I reminded Jonah he had an important job to do looking after the house and closed the door. As the car backed on to the sleeping street, we gazed up at the living room to see an unmistakable silhouette pressing its nose against the window. Two headlamps of eyes glowered annoyance.

Cameras in hand, we strode through gray hospital corridors. I was half expecting to be stopped by a belligerent nursing sister, the type who used to roam maternity wards keeping a stopwatch on visiting hours. But those old girls had long gone, along with their enema bags.

The hospital was in a predawn coma. Not a rattle of a trolley or breakfast tray to be heard. Our pace quickened as we headed for Room A24. Turning a corner we encountered an elderly Indian man sitting on a chair in the corridor, a small boy perched on his knee. The old man's face was deeply creased and his eyes rheumy with age, yet he was smiling like the sun. Well into his eighties, he didn't have many years left but his daughter (or possibly granddaughter) was behind one of the doors tending to a new life that had stripped any sadness from his old age. It struck me then how lovely maternity wards are compared to the other worry-filled floors of a hospital.

Barely able to contain our excitement, we finally found Room

A24 and burst in on a charming nativity scene. Though Chantelle looked tired, as did Rob, their smiles were triumphant and tender as we hovered over the tiny bassinet. Under her pink and white blanket Annie was very pretty, her domed head sprinkled with wisps of brown hair, her starfish hands with tapering fingers.

Holding the comforting weight of my granddaughter for the first time, I studied her face and thought of the hundreds of thousands of people who were part of this little human. Some of her features were familiar: her almond-shaped eyes were not unlike Rob's when he was a newborn, and her Cupid's bow mouth could've been stolen from Mum. There was fortitude in that face, too—an inheritance from a long line of women unafraid of swimming against the tide.

Entranced by the little face, I could have gone on studying her for hours, but Annie had a queue of admirers desperate to embrace her and begin their own story with her. I kissed her little forehead and with great care transferred her to Aunt Lydia.

"Be careful how you hold her," I instructed. "Make sure you support the . . ."

"Yes, I know," said Lydia smiling softly down at her niece. "Neck."

My older daughter never ceased to surprise me. Where had she learned how to hold babies properly? Perhaps it was an extension of her work with disabled people, or the Sri Lankan orphanage.

As Lydia gazed down at the infant, tenderly stroking her head, I was reminded of my favorite work by Leonardo da Vinci, the cartoon painted around 1500 and on display in London's National Gallery. Lydia's expression mirrored the Virgin Mary's and St. Anne's as they admired the Christ child in the painting.

While the subject of Da Vinci's work is divine, he used everyday women for models. It was heartwarming to see the surge of nurture experienced by two beauties 600 years ago echoed by a young woman in a twenty-first century maternity hospital. Underneath all the so-called advances, humans haven't changed.

Flushed with emotion, Lydia rocked and cooed over the bundle. She had such a strong maternal instinct, which was what had driven her to care for the weak and infirm, heal the world. Perhaps one day she'd feel ready to set those impossible ideals aside and settle for a man who understood her and a child of her own.

Just as I was picturing her conventional future, monk and monastery free, Lydia turned to the exhausted parents.

"Would you mind if I chant?" she asked.

Gratitude

Do not judge cats or daughters—if it can be avoided.

As Rob and Chantelle adjusted to the rigorous demands of night feeding and deciphering the needs of their tiny daughter, I marveled at the enormity of parenthood. Impossible to describe to those who haven't "been there," becoming a mum or dad changes people profoundly. While Annie thrived and grew plump, her parents transformed into serious adults, always putting their daughter first.

Well into her second year of psychology, Lydia continued scoring great marks. The gray bus made regular appearances outside the house, and she ran fund-raisers for the University Buddhist Society. Her life seemed too earnest. The countless hours spent meditating in her room upstairs gave her a disconnected, unworldly manner. I sometimes felt we were sharing the house with a phantom rather than a twenty-five-year-old. My anxiety about her throwing herself into religion was dwarfed by my concern that she might lose her identity. I worried our daughter might float away like a balloon while we watched, helpless. Every now and then I'd hear her chatting animatedly in Sinhalese on the phone. She was still in touch with the monastery.

In the meantime, I was due for my two-year breast cancer checkup. The night before it, I lay awake unable to get back to sleep. It was hard to believe so much time had gone by since the mastectomy and Jonah bursting into our lives. Jonah wasn't a kitten anymore. He panted when I flicked the fishing rod too fast these days.

From a health perspective, the past two years had consisted of, among other things, pains and pinches I probably wouldn't have noticed pre-cancer. I'd also endured tiredness that was overwhelming at times. Then again, I'd been fool enough to write a book in the middle of it.

Confronting my own mortality had been more challenging than I'd imagined. Though the thought of my life ending was nowhere near as devastating as the loss of Sam, I was surprised to find a tiny part of me believed, despite all the evidence, I'd live forever. A remnant from youthful days when I never thought about dying, it wasn't particularly helpful. Life was richer now I understood how swiftly it slips away. Cancer had taught me to live like a cat, savoring every moment.

I'd experienced the unbelievable highs of Rob's wedding, finding out my book about Cleo had become an international bestseller, and the joy of welcoming a granddaughter into the world. My glass was overflowing.

Driving off to meet Philip at the clinic, I assured Katharine and Lydia that everything would be fine—though I didn't entirely believe it. With a trusty book of crosswords concealed in my handbag, I parked outside the clinic and caught the lift to the fourth floor. Four's an unlucky number, according to Chinese superstition. Eight, on the other hand, is incredibly lucky. Feeling queasy as the lift sailed skyward, I silently doubled the four and pretended I was going to eight.

The clinic waiting room featured the same *Architectural Digests* as two years earlier: "Marrakesh Meets Malibu." One of the reason people live in glamorous homes is to lull themselves into the fantasy that they're immune from life's harshness.

Courage, I've discovered, isn't my line of expertise. It was easier to be brave about breast cancer two years earlier when I didn't know what I was pretending to be brave about.

I grabbed a paper cup and squeezed hot water out of a tap to make peppermint tea. I was more health conscious these days.

A red-haired woman in full army kit stepped out of the elevator. An old Greek woman with purple legs eased herself cautiously into a chair next to me. A couple of seats along from me was a disgruntled-looking woman with dyed hair chopped so savagely short she resembled a hedgehog. A young Indian woman came in to have her dressings changed. Breast cancer isn't choosy. Last Thursday had taken a hundred years off her life, she told the nurse.

Oblivious to the fact most of the women in the waiting room were staring death in the eye sockets, a bloke shouted into his cell phone. "What're you doin' tonight?" Hot with rage, I wanted to throttle him.

A tall blonde with stooped shoulders strode in and sat down next to the hedgehog haircut woman. Like a couple who'd been married too long, they didn't talk or look at each other, though they were unquestionably together. Maybe they'd had a row.

I'd assumed it was the grumpy one in for a checkup but when the nurse appeared the blonde sprang to her feet and disappeared down the corridor. Her partner seemed self-absorbed for a while, then her mouth turned down and she rubbed a tear away with her knuckle.

A husband buried himself in the sports section of a newspaper. Philip offered to make another peppermint tea. I said yes. Good to keep men busy.

A nurse approached me after a while. "Come through please," she said.

I scurried down the corridor in her wake, grateful for the change of atmosphere.

Stepping into the examination area, I knew the drill. Remove everything from the waist up and put on the white terry-cloth robe that transformed me into a patient. *God, I hate it here*, I thought, as I took off my red coat and dangly earrings.

Running away was an option but it wasn't this place or this particular Tuesday that was to blame. Today was merely a milestone, to record the progress of the past two years. Or not. Greg had said it'd be five years before I was "out of the woods."

Like a dog at the vet's, I was wary of the Chinese mammogram technician, reminding her my right breast was fake so only the left one needed squashing in her machine. Ouch.

Leaving me to ferry the images to the radiologist, the technician said she'd be back in a tick. Five, fifteen, twenty minutes passed. I wondered why she was taking so long. Fear ran a chill through me. Had they found something?

"Oh, you're still there," she said brightly from the doorway. "We found a shadow deep in your chest cavity but it's nothing cynical."

Thank goodness. As a journalist, I'd strived to avoid cynicism. It was a relief to know a residual cynic hadn't set up house in my chest. I moved on to the ultrasound room and after that got dressed to meet up with Philip in the surgeon's office. The surgeon said she liked my blouse and that the mammogram was clear.

Skipping out of the clinic, I kissed Philip good-bye and sent him back to work. Giant meringues of clouds hovered over the park. Voluptuous with moisture, they reminded me of the clouds I grew up with that went dark around the edges before unleashing themselves on dairy paddocks.

The back of my nose tingled. A cool breeze carried the damp, metallic smell of moisture. Finally it rained—and not just the miserable showers we'd made do with for months on end, but proper, wetting rain. It bounced on the street until the gutters chattered with life.

People laughed and lifted their faces to the deluge. The drought had finally broken.

As I turned the ignition key the car radio sprang to life with Three Dog Night's "Joy to the World." I turned it up as loud as my ears could stand and drove home shouting: "Jeremiah was a bullfrog!" The windscreen wipers couldn't slap fast enough to keep up with the downpour. With rain hammering on the car's roof and a clean bill of health, I'd fallen in love with life again.

I should have celebrated with champagne. Instead I went

home, cleaned out the kitchen cupboards, and thought about
making a garden. A Gratitude Garden.

Ever since we'd bought Shirley, the front yard was so sparsely
sprinkled with sand we could've raised camels. Weeds were
things that'd thrived, along with ravenous fingers of sea grass
scrabbling from under the fence.

With poor soil and a harsh climate, the new garden was never
going to be a showstopper. The land wasn't much bigger than
a kitten basket. That didn't mean it couldn't have a spiritual
aspect, though. Lydia was enthusiastic when I shared the idea
of a Gratitude Garden, particularly when I told her I wanted it
to have a focal point for meditation.

We thumbed through a couple of gardening design books
together. Most consisted of flashy barbecue areas and plunge
pools. They aimed to impress rather than inspire connection to
the soul.

At first I thought of creating a spiral hedge that could form a
walking meditation path. But our garden was too small for an
elaborate hedge system. We had to keep it simple—a circle,
perhaps, with carefully chosen plants and a central focus. A ring
shape would symbolize the circle of women. And we needed
water to represent life, purity, and forgiveness.

Lydia and I dragged the old semicircular seat from the backyard and placed it facing outwards under the apple tree. Resting
on the seat, we gazed over power lines and the tiled roofs across
the street. The view could easily be softened with some plants.

"This is exciting!" said Lydia. "Let's go look at fountains."

We drove miles out of town to a place that sold garden statues and water features, many of dubious taste. We strode past
lascivious cherubs relieving themselves into ponds. Lydia
paused at a selection of Buddhas and winged Asian deities. I
steered her away from them.

We were about to give up and go home when a large bowl
beside the checkout counter caught our attention. Filled with
water, it was probably made of concrete, but had been "distressed"

to appear as if it had been dug out of the earth. In the middle of the bowl sat a rough-hewn stone orb, slightly bigger than a soccer ball. Water spouted through a hole in the orb, creating a restful trickle. If the bowl was lifted and set on a stand, we agreed it would be perfect.

"Do you think there's room for goldfish?" Lydia asked.

"You want goldfish?"

"For peace," she said, nodding.

Two days later the water feature was delivered, plonked in pieces beside the front steps. Hoping we hadn't been overambitious, I called Warren, a talented landscape gardener. Tanned and muscular from years working under the sun, Warren isn't the most talkative guy on earth. He looked at the water bowl and nodded. When I described my vision for the front garden, he cast a practiced eye over the concrete paving stones on the sloping path. Finding a place for the feature would be simple compared to everything else that needed doing, he said. Earth needed shifting and flattening, and a retaining wall would have to go in close to the front fence. Three steps and a new front path would also need to go in.

Why did simplicity have to be so complicated?

The size and expense of the project began to balloon, but I trusted Warren. When he and his mates began burrowing like wombats through the front garden, I wasn't so sure. Neighbors paused to stare over the fence. One of them complained that overnight rain had sent mud running from our place down the gutter to his property. Warren trudged down the street and patiently shoveled up the offending residue.

As with the painters, Jonah developed a crush on Warren. He waited in the front window for him every morning and pressed against the screen door, meowing seductively. When Warren and his team had their morning coffee on the back deck, Jonah bolted through the tunnel of his cat run and into his tower to admire them from one of his hammocks. Jonah had a thing for workmen's boots. He adored weaving through a pair of muscular legs and tugging on well-worn shoelaces.

I panicked when I saw the enormous cavity Warren had dug out front, and the seriousness of the retaining wall. My simple Gratitude Garden was turning into something out of *Grand Designs*. Not wanting to be the client from hell, but becoming one anyway, I asked Warren if he knew what he was doing.

Lifting his head from the depths of his excavations, he looked at me and raised an eyebrow.

"Couldn't the changes be a little less . . . dramatic?" I asked.

Warren rested a hand on his shovel, sighed deeply, and assured me everything would be fine. Fools and children should never see things half done.

Once new earth was delivered and pressed into the cavity, the shape of the new garden started to emerge. The levels Warren had gone to such trouble to create turned out to be perfect. The unusable slope leading up to the apple tree had transformed into an inviting terrace to be covered in lawn. Warren also created a beautiful front path with recycled bricks inlaid with small river stones. He built a stand in the center of the flattened soil and cemented the water bowl in place. I felt foolish for having doubted him.

Fortunately, Warren still liked me enough to invite me to climb into his SUV to visit a garden center. Even though the drought was officially over, I wasn't willing to take risks with plants. Our garden had to be able to survive weeks, possibly even months, with no rain or watering. Hardiness was a prerequisite and perfume was desired. I also wanted the plants to have personal meaning.

For years I'd taken olive trees for granted. While I respected their resilience and the relationship they'd had with people through history, I'd always regarded them as straggly, gray plants. Then I saw a painting by van Gogh in which he'd portrayed olive trees as wise, silvery beings. Like the painter himself, these olive trees were no strangers to suffering, but van Gogh depicted them as tough and shimmering with vitality. When I was finally able to visit the olive grove van Gogh painted near Saint-Rémy-de-Provence in France, I almost wept. What greater gift can a genius give than to teach others how to see the world?

Olive branches also symbolize peace. For millennia they've provided succour with their fruit. Peace and nurture: perfect for a Gratitude Garden. Warren ordered several well-developed olive trees to go along the front and side fences to (ultimately) provide privacy.

Rosemary is underrated. Not only is it hardy in Australia, it provides perfume for a garden, food for bees, and flavoring for roast lamb. Also, according to Shakespeare, rosemary symbolizes remembrance. Mum had always kept a vase of rosemary sprigs on her table in homage to those she'd lost. As years went by and more of her friends and relations passed away, the vessel became so crowded she needed a bigger vase. In honor of Mum and many other angels, we planted a rosemary hedge alongside Warren's new path.

Deep red roses went in under the living room window from which Jonah liked to survey his realm. Their perfume would spread sensuously through summer evenings.

Katharine put in a request for lavender, which passed both the perfume and hardiness tests. When Warren planted a couple of large bushes in front of the roses, the bees could hardly wait.

In homage to New Zealand, I bought some bronze flaxes that went in a row along one of the side fences. Sadly, they craved the damp climate of our homeland and didn't thrive as vigorously as the native grasses behind the front fence—or even the gardenia bushes Warren had planted under the semicircular seat. I'd taken Mum a gardenia flower when she was dying and she'd drunk in its perfume as though it was life itself.

The effect was enhanced with pots of spectacular succulents either side of the front door. Exploding in outrageous shapes of mauves, greens, and coppers, they contrasted against Shirley's red bricks.

Only one task remained. The focal point of the new garden had yet to spring to life. Lydia and I watched from my study window as Warren filled the bowl with a hose and connected the pump. We held our breath. Nothing happened. Unperturbed, Warren strode around the side of the house to tweak the electrics.

There was a hum, followed by a gurgle, then water splashed joyfully over the orb.

Our next task was to go to the pet shop and buy some gold-fish. Anyone who says goldfish have a short memory hasn't observed them. Every morning, three orange streaks waited in exactly the same spot to be fed. They grew long and plump in their new home—and adept at avoiding dive-bombing pigeons in need of a bath.

Our Gratitude Garden complete, I'd often look up from my computer screen to see Lydia sitting on the circular seat. Sometimes I'd join her and we'd gaze on the sprouting leaves with the satisfaction of those who've shared an act of creation.

Sitting together in the garden, our conversations weren't as jagged as they used to be, but my daughter still seemed to with-hold her deepest thoughts.

Obsession

Beware the dejected cat. He will seek revenge.

With his designer cat run, a retinue of human groupies, and a house bursting with fishing rods, ribbons, and scratching posts, Jonah was the feline who had everything. When a smart red crib with stainless-steel legs and mesh sides appeared in the living room one afternoon, he naturally assumed it was yet another item for his enjoyment. Raising his tail in a question mark, he put his head to one side, sniffed its new smell, and purred.

"It's not for you, Jonah," I said, watching him circle the crib at increasing speed.

Deaf to my words, he sprang into the bed's squishy depths and pranced over the mattress.

"Come out!" I cried, trying to catch him. But he slithered from my grasp and bounced onto the floor. Just as I was about to praise him for an uncharacteristic display of obedience, he sailed past my nose back into the crib. Into the crib, out of the crib, into the crib . . . Another new game that, as far as Jonah was concerned, could go on for the rest of the year.

"It's the *baby's* crib!" I said, lifting him again and again from his mesh-walled pleasure palace.

The idea that something new and fun could arrive in the house and not be specifically meant for his enjoyment was new to Jonah. Taken aback, he changed his approach. Instead of being designed for jumping in and out of, he decided maybe it was just a bed. He seized every opportunity to jump in and curl up on the mattress. Hauling him out, I remembered how horrified Mum had been when Cleo climbed into Lydia's crib before she was born. Cats, she'd said, could smother babies.

I was pleased to discover the crib had a detachable mesh roof that could be zipped into place—presumably to keep out insects. Even that didn't work. Jonah was almost as happy to sleep on top of the crib as to play in it. The crib, as far as he was concerned, was his.

I started hiding the crib in various rooms, but he always found out where it was and scratched and yowled to be let in.

Jonah sensed a power shift in the household—one that wasn't in his favor. The tension revolved around the red crib.

Then one day it happened. Jonah woke from his afternoon nap on Katharine's bed and ambled downstairs into his worst nightmare. The portable crib—*his* playpen—was inhabited by a strange alien form. The intruder was virtually hairless, a plump blob resembling a pink jellybean. Jonah shuddered in revulsion. Not only had the jellybean taken over his playpen and fallen fast asleep in it, every human in the household, as well as Rob and Chantelle—who'd brought baby Annie over for a visit—were "oooooing" and "aaaahhhing" over the jellybean in tones he hadn't heard since he was a kitten.

Watching Jonah shrink back into his fur, I could tell he was assessing the situation. He could hardly believe his ears when he heard people saying, "Isn't she *beautiful?*" and "Oh, she's so *cute!*"

Beautiful and cute were *his* words. Through disbelieving slits, he examined his humans. They'd gone berserk. Had they forgotten he was the only one who deserved to be oooooed and aaaahed over?

For the first time in his life, Jonah had a rival. The solution was obvious. One swift assault and the jellybean would be dethroned. Quivering on his haunches, he prepared for attack. With parental instincts on high alert, Rob and Chantelle tensed, ready to lunge forward to protect their baby.

"No, Jonah!" I cried, grabbing him and putting him away in the laundry room.

We carried on admiring the new baby, counting her fingers and stroking her head, when the air was split by a terrible sound. Slow and mournful, it was like an air raid siren. Jonah was crying.

"He's got to get used to Annie," Rob said, unable to bear the sound anymore. "Let's see how he goes."

Releasing Jonah from prison, I placed him on the platform on top of his scratching post, where he always felt safe and in control. To keep him amused, I passed him a couple of florist ribbons. But he wasn't interested. Instead, adopting his usual lordly position, he crouched down, eyes glued on the baby.

Conversation reverted to booties and baby food while Jonah gave himself a full-body spa. Paws, pads, wedges between the pads of his paws. Front of the ears, back of the ears, the crevice behind the back of the ears. Not a centimeter was overlooked. Hind leg on high, the cat was giving a good impression of pretending not to care—but his brain was working overtime.

Lydia was passing cookies around when a shadow flew past her, knocking the plate out of her hand. A bird? A plane. No, it was super-Jonah with orange florist ribbon snared between his teeth and trailing behind him like a banner.

"Man!" Lydia cried as the cookies toppled onto the carpet. That was the closest she got to swearing these days. The rest of us watched open-mouthed as Jonah landed clumsily on top of the cookies, a foot or two or so from the crib.

"That's it, Jonah!" I snapped. "Back in the laundry room for you."

"Wait a minute," said Lydia. "I think he's got a plan."

Sighing impatiently, I sat back. With the florist ribbon still in his mouth, Jonah crept cautiously toward Annie asleep in her cot. His ears pricked forward as he moved closer and examined her through the mesh. Raising a paw he tenderly patted the mesh near her head. Then, to my amazement, he stepped back and performed an elegant bow. Head lowered, he placed the orange ribbon in a straight line along the carpet beside the cot and backed away.

"See? It's a gift," whispered Lydia. "He's giving Annie a present."

Our cat and our daughter. Two beings who always took the other way. And never ceased to surprise me with their complexity and willingness to love.

Even though Jonah did his best to appreciate Annie, his obsession with the portable cot remained fierce. No matter which room I hid it in, he sniffed it out and would cry, begging admission. If the door opened even half a crack he'd push his way in and throw himself at the cot, jumping inside it or (if the roof was zipped up) on top of it. He rubbed himself against the sides of it and patted the stainless-steel legs, admiring them as if they were works of art.

Just as Jonah was managing to adjust to the idea of playing undercat to a baby (while she was visiting the house, at least) another unsettling event glistened on the horizon.

One morning Jonah trotted into the Marquis de Sade room to find Philip packing a suitcase. Jonah loathed suitcases. To him they symbolized abandonment. Even the sight of an overnight bag resulted in manic sprinting up and down the hall, refusal to let anyone out of his sight and, of course, persistent meowing that reverberated off the eardrum until it became one discordant note. Jonah's ears pricked like a pair of dark chocolate Toblerones when he saw the dark green suitcase. It was enormous, the largest we possessed and still cobwebby from its time in the attic. Philip was leaving for a six-week study course at Stanford University in the United States.

The world's tidiest packer, Philip patted layers of neatly folded shirts and underpants into the suitcase. Watching him slide gleaming shoes into actual *shoe bags*, I marveled again how we'd ever got together, let alone stayed married. He cried out when Jonah hurled himself into the suitcase on top of his clothes. Coiled like a shell, Jonah dug his claws in and stared up at Philip beseechingly.

"Sorry, Fur Man," he said, lifting him out. "You can't come with me."

The instant his paws touched the carpet Jonah jumped back into the suitcase again, and again, and again . . . Exasperated,

Philip shut Jonah out of the room. A nose and two paws squeezed themselves under the door.

A taxi glided to a halt outside the house. Philip zipped the bag shut and trudged down the hall. Jonah threw himself at the suitcase, trying to glue himself to it. Philip lifted Jonah, kissed his furry forehead, and told him not to worry, he'd be home soon. As Philip held Jonah up to his face, the cat stretched a long front leg toward him and pressed his paw in Philip's chest. It was as if Jonah was leaving an imprint on Philip's heart.

After we'd managed to wedge ourselves and the suitcase through the front door, Philip and I stood at the roadside and kissed good-bye. We glanced guiltily up at the living room window. No sign of Jonah.

"He's not even missing you," I said.

"Yes, he is," said Philip, pointing at an upstairs window from which a lonely feline stared down at us.

Jonah suffered the extrovert's curse. He needed people. When they weren't around to dazzle with his exuberant personality, he crumbled. He thrived on admiration, fishing rod and ribbon games, languorous hours draped over human laps, and the sport of being chased whenever he went on illegal rampages around the neighborhood. Separation anxiety, Vivienne called it.

I could relate to some of his insecurity. Earlier in our marriage, I'd have kicked up a fuss if Philip had absented himself for six whole weeks. In the broader canvas of life, however, a month and a half's a mere speck of paint. It's not that many airings of *The Daily Show* (my latest addiction) or six episodes of *My Life on the D-List* (though Kathy Griffin's schedule was proving capricious) and, oh I don't know, a couple of hundred cups of coffee. The weeks would fly while he was away having a wonderful time learning stuff and meeting people (though I hoped not glamorous women with second-wifehood ambitions).

Bonuses abounded for me, too. Without mentioning the obvious brownie points, the girls and I would have early dinners every night. We'd slurp takeaway noodles in front of *How I Met*

Your Mother (until Lydia excused herself to go upstairs and meditate).

I'd also be able to devote more time to my scheme to enthuse Lydia about the shallow vanities of Generation-Y womanhood. Not that it was having much effect. On the rare occasions Katharine and I managed to coax her along to a rom-com at the movies, she'd sigh her way through it. The "hot" male stars left her cold. She wasn't interested in manicures. If I bought trashy magazines targeted at women in their twenties, they'd quickly appear in the recycle bin.

While Philip was away, I'd sleep without earplugs, stay in my dressing gown all day if I felt like it, and do crosswords in bed without having to explain it was for my brain cells.

Besides, it was Katharine's last year at school. Even though my publishers were keen for me to get started on another book, I'd decided to put everything on hold for a final stint at full-on mothering.

A diligent student, Katharine was determined to excel in the International Baccalaureate. She deserved all the support she could get, especially during the notorious buildup to end-of-year exams. I wanted to be there for her, not just as a full-time servant.

Several times a week, I'd get urgent texts from Katharine asking if I could bring forgotten books or her lunch to school. After school, she'd be welcomed home with hot chocolate and Jonah wrapping himself around her neck and telling her (in cat language) she was doing just fine.

Things started to go wrong early on the morning after Philip's departure when he began his usual thumping at our bedroom door. I climbed out of bed to open it. Fishing rod jingling between his teeth, Jonah leaped joyfully onto the bed—but there was no Philip. Not even a warm pillow symbolizing Philip's temporary absence while he made tea and toast in the kitchen. Staring at the cold, unwrinkled pillow, Jonah was confused. Crestfallen, he dropped the fishing rod onto the covers and stared mournfully toward the window.

"It's okay, boy," I said. "I'll play with you."

Jonah's eyes narrowed in disdain. In fishing rod sport, I was lowest of the low. I didn't swing the stick violently or high enough. My reactions were too slow and I made catches too easy. He sprang off the bed, disappeared out the door, and returned with a length of pink florist's ribbon, which he laid over my hand. So I was in the pink ribbon league, I thought, flicking the ribbon to try and make the game exciting for him. But clearly my lack of technique frustrated him. I just didn't play like a man. He was soon bored, and skulked away moaning. Not since Maria abandoned the Von Trapp children to return to the nunnery had there been such a theatrical demonstration of dejection.

A couple of days later, while wielding an unreasonably hefty pair of weights in the Marquis de Sade room with Peter the personal trainer, a nasty, acidic odor seared the back of my nostrils. Peter said he couldn't smell anything.

After he left I checked the wardrobes and central heating vent in case something had died. The smell, pungent and sharp, seemed to be emanating from somewhere near the windows, but I couldn't see any obvious cause. Maybe Peter was right and it was my imagination. I suspected he was too polite to be reliable.

When he returned on Thursday, the smell was worse. I asked again if he noticed anything. Peter's denial was even more vehement. He swore he couldn't smell A Single Thing . . . so there *had* to be a pong!

After he'd gone, I closed my eyes and searched the room. It's surprising how effective nasal navigation can be once your eyes are shut. The smell was definitely stronger near the window, near the curtain . . . no, in fact *on* the curtain! When I opened my eyes, the top part of the curtain hung in innocently pristine folds. Clambering down on my knees, I lifted the fabric that touched the floor. The pong became so aggressive, I recoiled. Holding the curtain as far away as possible, I inspected a large incriminating yellow stain. It smelled like something the devil might choose as room spray.

Inspecting the shape of the stain, it reminded me of something—the streaks on the laundry room wall! When I'd asked the painters to give the stains a second coat and the marks never went away, I'd assumed they'd forgotten to do the job. They were such amiable blokes I hadn't wanted to nag. It hadn't occurred to me that maybe they *had* blotted out the old stains, and a malevolent force had replaced them with new ones.

The stains weren't modern art, but something I'd thought no civilized cat would stoop to.

The curtains were sent to the cleaners and hung up again. The stains reappeared. The curtains went back to the cleaners and Jonah was officially banned from the workout room, which he found hurtful because he loved rolling around on the mat for tummy rubs and doing yoga stretches in front of Peter twice a week.

Our pet exacted revenge. He targeted the areas that would cause maximum stress—Lydia's bed, Katharine's shelf of beloved books, her violin, and under my desk. And then, horror of horrors—the portable cot!

The girls and I became like cats, crawling the house sniffing corners for evidence. Katharine turned out to have a particularly acute sense of smell. We bought an ultraviolet light, hospital-strength disinfectant, and a bewildering array of biodegradable cleaners.

We also bought special cleaning fluid from the vet's. Its scent was sweet, almost as nauseating as the one it was designed to neutralize. My heart sank when I noticed it was available in jumbo size. I wondered who needed to buy it in such bulk. Did they have a thousand cats? Or was their problem ongoing and . . . unsolvable?

"Spraying," Vivienne announced when I called her about Jonah's new problem.

"Cleo never did it," I said. "Well, only once."

"Yes, but she was female. Spraying is what male cats do. It's why people prefer female cats, and why Jonah was probably the last of his litter to be left in the pet shop."

"The shop assistant said it was conjunctivitis," I reminded her.

"As I said before, it's more than likely someone bought him when he was little, couldn't handle his behavior, and returned him to the shop," Vivienne reminded me. "He's probably inbred as well. Have you heard of puppy farms?"

"You mean when backyard breeders raise dogs in slum conditions and keep the females pregnant all the time?" I asked.

"Yes; the same thing happens with kittens. They're bred indiscriminately, sometimes siblings joined with each other, and sold on to pet shops. That'll be one of the reasons your pet shop didn't sell Jonah with papers."

A sprayer *and* inbred? Vivienne's words were harsh, but I trusted her. She was devoted to cats as a species and understood them at levels I couldn't fathom.

"Will he grow out of it?" I asked.

"Not necessarily," she replied.

My heart sank. I asked why he'd started doing it now.

"I think several things have triggered it," Vivienne replied. "Jonah's world's been turned upside down. From what you've said, he's jealous of the new baby and he's missing Philip. It's quite possible he's feeling overwhelmed by the responsibility of becoming the household's Alpha Male."

Alpha Male? What responsibility does an Alpha Male have these days apart from lying around waiting to be fed?

Vivienne e-mailed a page and a half of advice, with information about the three main causes of inappropriate spraying. They were: (1) medical reasons; (2) litter-tray related; (3) anxiety/stress. While Vivienne was pretty sure Jonah's problem was due to this, she thought it would be worth a vet's check to be sure there was nothing physically wrong with him. The litter tray had to be kept impeccably clean and well away from his food bowls. Whatever the cause, she said, scolding and punishing wasn't going to work.

The vet's window was filled with photos of missing cats. The receptionist said they were usually found run over and killed. For all our doubts and failures, our struggle to keep Jonah indoors was vindicated.

Jonah stood regally on the vet's table, tail aloft and awaiting adulation. King of the World, the vet called him, which he rather liked—until she started prodding and probing. Jonah rolled his lips back and emitted a loud hiss. He then crumpled like a hopeless sissy, moaning and howling so loudly I felt ashamed.

The vet took him "next door" to conduct further tests. She returned with a somewhat deflated version of the cat we knew and loved. Unable to find anything wrong with his insides, she repeated Vivienne's advice and sold us a magic spray bottle. When plugged into an electric socket it emitted calming pheromones that remind cats how safe and happy they felt when they were kittens. Almost all her feline patients had responded to it, she said.

Hopeful that our troubles might be over, I hurried home. After plugging the bottle into an electric socket in a corner where Jonah had performed several misdemeanors I called the girls downstairs to admire the new miracle cure. We watched mortified as he backed up against the electric plug and gave the vet's bottle a thorough showering.

The girls and I did everything Vivienne, the Internet, and the vet suggested—from the orthodox to the wacky. We bought (even) more toys, gave Jonah Rescue Remedy, placed crystals under his cushion, and took him for evening outings on his lead down the street. Nothing worked. We tried a different vet, and then another. The third vet recommended medication. Cat Prozac. No way. I drew the line at putting Jonah on drugs.

It was difficult not to take his behavior personally, especially the day I discovered he'd desecrated Dad's piano. Tears welling, I cleaned what I could and trussed the family heirloom in layers of cling wrap.

I hesitated before inviting anyone over the front doorstep. Yet most of the time Jonah was charming and lovable as ever. Sometimes I felt like one of those wives who endures abuse from her handsome husband, knowing that after he's given her a black eye he's going to dazzle her with charm and chocolates the next day.

Lydia found the phone number of a cat psychic in Queensland. Seeing I was paying for it, I didn't feel too guilty lifting the receiver in my study to listen in. The cat psychic's tone was rustic and cheerful. I imagined her in a condo by the sea tuning into feline frequencies.

"Jonah's talking to me now," she said down the line. *"Oh my heavens!* I've never heard so much complaining! Nothing's good enough for this one. Your cat's too big for his boots. You need to treat him less like a king and more like a cat."

After we'd hung up, the girls and I agreed the psychic was talking sense. At bedtime Jonah was demoted to a leopard-skin cushion in the laundry room. He accepted the indignity of being shut away. In fact, he had an active night life barrelling through his outdoor run to exchange insults with possums.

While keeping Jonah safely removed from our soft furnishings through the hours of darkness limited some of his excesses, part-time exile had no noticeable effect.

"He's doing *what*??!!" growled Philip when he phoned from his Stanford apartment, which, judging by his e-mailed photos, was enviably stainless and smell-free.

"It's nothing," I lied. "We'll have it sorted by the time you get home."

Which was like saying the war would be over by Christmas.

Rejection

Rehoming a cat. Or husband.

The night Philip was due to return from Stanford, Jonah paced the house—impeccable as always at intuiting something special was about to happen. When he wasn't stalking around on his chocolate-colored stilts, he was perching on the living room window ledge scanning the darkened street below. Maybe someday a scientist will find out how animals know when one of their humans is coming home. Is it to do with the power of love, an ability to tune into subtle energies—or a combination of both?

He emitted a series of urgent meows. I joined him at the window and together we watched a set of taxi headlights glow like a cat's eyes and grow larger. Before the taxi had even stopped, Jonah bustled to Shirley's front door and stretched his length up toward the handle.

Lydia bundled him into her arms and opened the door and we all ran down the path to welcome Philip. Jonah was over-whelmed with joy. His purring was thunderous as he buried his face in Philip's hand, reveling in having his ears flattened, his chin stroked, and his nose rubbed all at the same time.

I felt sure everything would be fine now our Alpha Male was home. The star was back in Jonah's sky and he could comfort-ably revert to being secondary male in the household. Nevertheless, to be on the safe side, he slept in the laundry room that night.

We started next morning with the old routine our cat loved so much. Jonah, fishing rod between his teeth, burst through the bedroom door while Philip went out to make tea. He quickly made himself comfortable on Philip's pillow and waited for the games to begin.

But it was Saturday and Philip didn't have to hurry off to work. Besides, he was jet lagged. Philip wasn't interested in being relegated to a chair to have his tea and toast while Jonah had pride of place. He moved Jonah gently aside and climbed back into bed next to me.

Jonah emitted the nasal "hrrrrumphing" noise he made when he was put out, and dropped to the floor.

"Don't worry about him," I said. "He'll soon get used to you being home again."

Fixing Philip with a steely glare, Jonah raised his tail and backed up menacingly against the bedroom curtains. I watched helpless as his tail trembled delicately in the motion I'd come to dread.

"Oh no!" I cried. "Stop him! He's going to . . ."

It was too late. Staring Philip straight in the face, the cat unleashed himself.

Philip's one of the calmest people I know. It's one of the reasons I fell in love with him. He almost never loses his cool.

"*That's it!*" he yelled, leaping out of bed and chasing Jonah out of the room. "*That cat will have to go!*"

Stomping down the hall after them, I saw Jonah's tail flash through the laundry cupboard into the safety of his outdoor run.

"Go!? What do you mean?" I asked, my voice trembling.

Breathing heavily, Philip ran his hand over his scalp. "We can't spend the next ten years like this," he said, turning away from me, his voice etched with ice. "He'll have to find another home."

The air turned suddenly cold, as if a fridge door had been opened.

"But what if we can't find him one?" I asked.

"Then he'll have to go to a farm."

Farm? The word echoed across the years from my childhood. That's what grown-ups said happened to pets who'd disappeared. It took years for me to realize they weren't talking about romping over grassy fields in the company of cows and geese.

"Just look at the damage he's caused," Philip continued. "He's destroyed the new stair carpet; we've had to get the curtains cleaned umpteen times. There's that smell in Lydia's room . . . He's got to go."

An unfamiliar shiver ran through my veins. For the first time in twenty years I felt a chill toward Philip. How could a man who'd opened his heart to my two older children and raised them as his own, who'd been such a great husband and father, be so heartless?

Jonah wasn't perfect, but neither were we. For all his faults and dysfunctional behavior, he belonged with us.

The instant Philip left for work I grabbed the phone and punched in Vivienne's number. We'd tried every form of therapy—conventional and otherwise. Our house was vandalized. My piano was mummified in cling wrap and my marriage was teetering on the edge of an emotional Grand Canyon. As Vivienne answered, I had a sudden flash of inspiration.

"Is there such a thing as nappies for cats?" I asked.

After what I took for amused silence, Vivienne said she didn't think so. She wasn't surprised when I told her about Philip's ultimatum.

"You've tried almost everything," she said. "I know it's hard. Spraying's the number one reason cats are put down."

A boulder settled in my chest as I watched Jonah roll nonchalantly in a patch of sun on the family room rug. He seemed to know his fur blended beautifully with its pattern of soft greens and browns. Stretching his pipe cleaner body in a graceful curve, he blinked at me and yawned. I adored our madly affectionate, funny, crazy cat. We *all* did—well, most of us, anyway. I could never take him to a vet to be "put down."

As well as all her other work, Vivienne was involved in the

rehoming of cats. Her website's heart-tugging photographs of abandoned kittens and strays always worked their magic. She and I discussed the sort of household Jonah might be comfortable in. Certainly not a family of noisy young kids, and he'd drive a little old lady insane. A farm, even if one genuinely existed, would result in physical and emotional collapse.

"Tell you what," said Vivienne with a mischievous giggle. "I could always put a photo of Philip on my website and see if I can find *him* a new home."

When I told the girls about Philip's decree their mouths dropped. Katharine gathered him in her arms and buried her face in his fur.

"He can't go," she said. "We love him."

Oblivious to the drama he was the center of, Jonah purred raucously. I wished I could envelop our daughters and cat in some magical maternal apron and promise everything would be okay. But so much was out of my control.

The girls swore to work even harder monitoring his litter tray, keeping him away from his most frequently visited corners and sniffing out the faintest hints of smells.

After they'd left for classes, I decided to clear my head with a brisk walk. Bare winter trees clawed the sky. Gray rags of clouds hung over the buildings. Almost on automatic pilot, I boarded a tram and rattled across the river to the pet shop.

Letting Jonah into our lives now seemed like a blunder made when I was too weak and vulnerable to have any idea what we were letting ourselves in for. If we'd wanted a cat, we should've researched and stayed well clear of the pet shop. We should have been sensible and gone to a shelter and rescued a mixed-breed moggy that'd have been grateful for a home. We'd been fools to fall for Jonah's good looks and kittenish charms.

Peering through the pet shop window I could see a new batch of kittens was in. They were all identical to how Jonah had been—blue-eyed, sleek, cappuccino circus artists leaping about on elastic legs. Irresistible. One of the kittens danced across the cage while another crouched low and quivered, waiting for the moment to pounce on his sibling. A small group of people gathered to admire the spectacle.

A young couple, bundled up against the cold, stood beside me. They were captivated, just the way we'd been.

"Let's ask if we can take that one home tonight!" said the young woman, her face ablaze with infatuation as she pointed at the kitten who was flying through the air about to land flamboyantly on his friend.

I turned to the couple, so in love they believed the only thing that could enhance their happiness was a kitten.

"Don't do it," I told them. "Get a puppy, or have a baby. Anything's going to be easier than one of those kittens."

They looked astonished. They must've thought I was a fruitcake. Burying my head in my pashmina, I hurried on to the vet's. There was only one jumbo-sized bottle of cat urine neutralizer left on the shelf. We weren't the only ones with a problem.

I knew when I got home Jonah would be at the window. Then he'd be at the door and meowing under my feet. My nose would be on high alert for fresh layers of ammonia in the air. I'd be scouring the house for spots on the window ledge or against the stair railings.

When I opened the gate I saw his silhouette against the lead lights. His noble head, the elegant tapering limbs, the sublimely long tail—how could a beautiful creature inflict such misery? His eyes flashed when he saw me, and his mouth opened in a pink diamond shape as he emitted an accusatory yowl. I couldn't face him. Not just now. After heaving the jumbo bottle of neutralizer up the path and dumping it on the veranda, I strode across the road to the sanctuary of Spoonful.

Household tension was at an all-time high that evening. I was vaguely aware that Lydia was sporting the unflattering beanie (note to self: find appropriate moment to tactfully let her know that a hat with a brim would suit her face shape better).

When Philip arrived home from work, the topic of eviction was carefully avoided. The girls and I presented Jonah's day in the most exemplary light. He hadn't peed anywhere. In fact, we lied, he seemed to be settling down. He'd eaten a housefly and slept for several hours without stalking or yowling at anyone. Glossing over the more disturbing aspects of my conversation with Vivienne, I explained the morning's misdemeanor was just a nervous reaction to the return of Jonah's most favorite person on earth. It wouldn't happen again.

After dinner, the girls and I kept Jonah shut out of the living room while the four of us settled in front of the television in case he reverted to more unacceptable behavior. As we watched the day's news unravel, I tried to ignore Lydia's maroon beanie and the persistent meows on the other side of the door. A pair of paws appeared under the door. The pleading meows gave way to thumps. The girls and I exchanged glances. Philip's face was grim and immobile. Lydia stood up and opened the door. Jonah ran forward. Snared dashingly between his teeth was a purple glove, its fingers waving happily at us. With head and tail lowered he trotted toward Philip and laid the glove respectfully at his feet.

"See?" Lydia said to Philip. "He's saying sorry."

Jonah jumped onto Philip's lap and licked his hand. My husband lowered his gaze. For a moment I thought he was going to shoo Jonah back out the door. Philip hesitated, almost as if this was a first-time encounter, then raised a hand and ran it over the cat's silky spine. Jonah yawned and curled himself on Philip's knee. A flame of affection flickered in Philip's eye. A smile rippled on his lips. Maybe the battle wasn't lost.

Next morning, using my newly developed nasal radar I homed in on Lydia's altar. A dark stain trickled down its side toward the floor.

It couldn't go on.

Cleansed

When drugs aren't all bad.

Vivienne's voice was warm and sympathetic over the phone.

"If he was my cat I'd put him on a medication like Prozac," she said.

"But . . ." I began, hearing Mum's voice booming from her plastic urn: *"Prozac! For a CAT??!!"*

"Look, I'm sorry. I know we've discussed it before and you're against it, but Jonah's problems can't be cured behaviorally. He's got into a pattern you won't be able to break."

I felt a total failure. If pets reflect the personalities of their owners, what kind of lunatics were we?

"It's not your fault," Vivienne continued. "Orientals are nearly always high-maintenance."

I drew a quivery breath. Our bag of options was empty. "Will he have to stay on it for the rest of his life?" I asked.

"Not necessarily. After a few months it might change his brain chemistry and he'll start behaving normally again."

Months?!

When I talked to the vet, she said not to feel guilty about having a chemically altered cat. She had a pair of Orientals at home and she'd had to put them on it every now and then.

Back home, I guiltily placed half a yellow pill in a dish of Jonah's favorite tuna. When I returned several hours later, the tuna had gone. All that remained was half a pill gleaming in the bowl.

I ground the other half of the tablet into a powder and spooned it through his next meal—which he refused to touch. In desperation, I pummeled the medication to a pulp, added it to an eye dropper filled with milk, and tried to squirt it down Jonah's throat. He put his head back and sprayed it all back at me.

Vivienne paid an emergency visit and taught me how to hold Jonah firmly, pry his jaw open, and drop the pill into the back of his throat as quickly and neatly as possible. She made it look easy, but when I tried it next day Jonah wriggled and squirmed like a seal before spitting the pill on the floor. Then he pretended to swallow it, after which he let it drop discreetly onto a cushion. After a gladiatorial battle, I finally won, stroking the pill gently down his gullet the way Vivienne had shown me. As Jonah skulked away, his tail lowered, I felt terrible.

Over the following days, Jonah became a quieter, more amiable cat. The spraying stopped almost immediately. I started trusting him enough to let him back into rooms he'd been banned from during daylight hours (though not enough to unravel the piano's cling wrap protection). He spent most of the day in the living room, dozing in the sun on top of the alpaca rug. While he still ran to greet people at the door and jumped at sudden noises, he was altogether calmer and easier to live with. We were happier. He was more content in himself.

The person I'd expected to voice the most disapproval of the new drug regime was Lydia. I thought she'd urge me to seek some other psychic or maybe an animal shaman. But she'd been working in a psychiatric ward lately. Medication, she said, could change lives.

Hoping we were on the brink of a new, odor-free life I embarked on a full-scale house clean. With her impeccable nose, Katharine helped me discover tiny spots on the skirting boards and stair rails that I'd missed before.

We were ready for a new phase.

Sainthood

If your daughter wants to cling to an altar, don't fight it.

Lydia sailed through end-of-year university exams in October. I assumed she'd keep her caregiving work going through summer before embarking on her final year of psychology in March. It was a great plan. I was perplexed when her response to my cheerleading was lukewarm.

Philip, Katharine, Jonah, and I were watching *Big Bang Theory,* one evening when Lydia hovered at the door to say good night. Television was too crass for her. I respected that. She was going upstairs to commune with higher energies. As she turned to go, I noticed she was still wearing the same maroon beanie—the one I'd knitted with leftover wool ages ago.

"You don't have to wear that hat night and day do you?" I asked.

"Not really," she said, slowly pulling off her beanie. "Though it does get rather cold."

The noise of the television faded to a murmur. The living room walls turned gray. Philip's hand froze on Jonah's back. Our mouths dropped open in unison. My beautiful, feminine daughter was completely bald. Her face seemed unaccountably small without its usual frame of hair.

She'd been looking so pretty lately. We'd been buying good shampoo. I'd lent her my hair dryer and heard its reassuring roar every morning.

"Your hair!" I finally choked.

I wondered if she was making a statement—or if it was something more worrying.

"Cool!" chirped Katharine, the eternal mood smoother. "Did it hurt?"

Lydia shook the pale boiled egg that was her head. The old volcano of anxiety rumbled in my gut.

Whatever the cause or her intentions, I knew overreaction would be futile. Any explosion on my part would push her further in whatever direction it was she was toying with.

"Wow!" said Katharine, patting her sister's scalp. "How did you do it?"

"I borrowed an electric razor."

"Did someone help you?" Kath asked.

"No. Did it myself."

"*Whose* electric razor?" I asked stupidly.

"Just a friend's," Lydia replied blankly, clearly indicating further questioning wasn't welcome. I imagined curtains of her glossy golden hair dropping to the floor of Just A Friend's flat.

"Lots of boys have electric razors, don't they, Lyds?" Katharine cajoled.

"Was it Ned's razor?" I asked, almost hopeful she was seeing him again.

"No, he's getting married."

Just as I began conjuring up the possibility that she'd shaved her head in reaction to his upcoming nuptials, Lydia read my mind. She told me not to worry. She was relieved, in fact happy, that he'd found someone else.

The last time I'd seen the full shape of her head had been when she was a baby after she'd shed the first dark fluff she'd been born with. Her head was pretty then, rounded and curved in gracefully over the back of her neck, ears daintily tucked in at the sides. But even then, I'd waited eagerly for her hair to grow.

Now my daughter's head glistened under the halogen lights. I was reminded of the ancient Egyptian statue of Nefertiti. She looked so . . . vulnerable.

"Are you doing it for a fund-raiser?" I asked, trying to sound casual.

"No. I'm going back to the monastery."

The sentence hit me like a landslide. Lydia and I had grown closer through my illness and building the garden together. Even though I'd been nervous about the intensity of her spiritual aspirations, I understood them on some levels. But this announcement summoned all my old fears of losing her and, worse, Lydia losing herself.

Philip showed no emotion. Jonah blinked up at her from his lap. Katharine became suddenly engrossed in an outdated magazine.

My daughter was bald, devout, and heading to a monastery for the third time. It could only mean one thing.

"You've decided to become a nun?" I asked.

"I'm not sure," she answered. "I just want to see how it feels for a while."

I asked what she meant by "a while." A few weeks? Months? A lifetime?

She said she wasn't sure. Again. How I loathed those words.

"Can't you wait till you've finished your degree?" I asked.

"I can do that any time," she replied offhandedly.

I'd thought her rebellion phase was over. If there was anyone behind this I knew who it had to be. That monk. Why couldn't she be honest with me?

Trying to assemble my emotions, I wondered what she was thinking. Caring for disabled people and vegetarianism were fine and admirable. Shaving her head and becoming a Buddhist nun was a step beyond the realms of normality. Was she aiming to become a Generation-Y saint?

I'd been researching saints. They tend to come from middle-class families. The Buddha himself, Saint Francis of Assisi, and his sidekick St. Clare were raised in comfortable homes. They'd all rejected the abundance their parents had provided.

St. Clare's parents were devastated when she refused to marry. Their anguish is recorded on a fresco in the church dedicated to St. Clare in Assisi. While the facial expressions aren't

particularly informative (apart from one nun glowering at St
Clare's mother), the title says it all—"Clare clinging to the altar
to prevent her family bringing her back home."

It would be the same for us if we tried to drag Lydia away
from her altar of choice.

Gazing at our bald daughter, I tried to dredge positives out of
the anxiety. Number-one consolation was that the Sri Lankan
civil war was over. The likelihood of her being in mortal danger
had reduced. Bizarre as it seemed, at the age of just twenty-five
Lydia was already a seasoned traveler who knew how to avoid
trouble. Going by the phone calls I'd overheard, she had reasonable mastery of Sinhalese. Her Teacher and the nuns would be
meeting her at the airport and taking her straight to the monastery, which she knew well.

And if this strong-minded young woman really wanted to
shut herself away from the world for the rest of her life on some
remote island, I couldn't stop her.

Weariness washed over me. Truth to tell, I'd run out of fight.
There was no point railing against the more outrageous aspects
of our daughter—nor, for that matter, our cat. All I could do
was live my life—and allow them the freedom to do the same.

Besides, Lydia had helped celebrate and soothe me through
all the changes I'd been through recently. It was time I stepped
back and accepted she was a woman in her own right.

"Well . . ." I said, sensing the others were waiting for me to
explode in one of my old-time tirades. "If you want to be a nun,
and it's the right thing for you, I won't say I'm over the moon,
but I'll fully support you."

And, to my surprise, for the first time I actually meant it.

Needled

A cat's scratch can be a badge of honor.

Watching Lydia pack over the following week, I became increasingly curious. Not in the old way, when I'd been threatened by every aspect of Sri Lanka. I longed for a better understanding of the world she wanted to be part of and began to wonder what it would be like to visit the monastery. Physical hardship, possibly even danger, might be involved.

Closer to home, I had more prosaic challenges to contend with. While Lydia prepared for her departure, I was gearing up for the final phase of breast reconstruction: the nipple tattoo.

Philip claimed that, as the fake nipple's chief inspector, he was perfectly happy with it, but it looked albino alongside its partner. Having got this far, I figured the job might as well be finished.

But tattoos involve *needles.* Plus there's no man in a gown to knock you out during the process.

While I was mulling this over, Jonah insisted on a fishing rod session. Watching him spiral through the air, I wished I could be more like a cat. Even a neurotic one like Jonah didn't waste time fretting over needles.

When he finally collapsed on the rug, his glossy sides heaving in the sun, Katharine gathered him up.

"Oh, Jonah!" she said, burying her nose in his fur. "You're such a good de-stresser!"

Maternal alarm bells jangled.

"What's worrying you?" I asked.

"My IB presentation on immigration," she replied, running a finger down Jonah's nose. Our cat adored nose rubs.

Katharine was demonstrating a passion for refugees. On weekends she taught English to children from the Sudan. I'd already noticed an accusatory glint in her eye. Just as Lydia implied we didn't do enough for the disabled, Katharine was disappointed by our lack of commitment to refugees. I'd been made uncomfortably aware that Shirley's proportions were generous enough to accommodate several Sudanese families.

I was concerned about our younger daughter. Her face had grown pale and thin with shadowy semicircles under her eyes. The plaster on her elbow seemed to get bigger every day, covering either a fungal infection or a rash. Either way it was a manifestation of stress. I asked what time she'd finished her homework the night before. She said 11:30, but I knew it would've been much later. She promised to get to bed earlier tonight.

Jonah's paws were dry, she said, unfolding him on top of his scratching post. He flashed me a look of self-pity as I lifted his front paw. The pad was cracked like an old riverbed. While I couldn't improve Katharine's opinion of my commitment to refugees, I could do something about Jonah's paws. He watched intrigued as I lifted his leathery pads one after the other and massaged them with hand cream. Then he promptly licked it off.

When Lydia came downstairs, she offered to drop Katharine at school and take me on to the tattoo parlor. We accepted without hesitation.

The tattoo parlor was a disheveled old worker's cottage with a discreet sign on the fence. Lydia waited for me while I disappeared down a brick path lined with plants.

A blond woman opened the door. With no moles, marks, or wrinkles, her face was technically perfect. It was almost as if someone had penciled her features in on a blank canvas. Devoid of the myriad faults that make a face real, she resembled a daytime soap star.

She asked me to take my top off and lie down on her massage table.

"It doesn't hurt, it just buzzes," she assured me, placing a blue plastic sheet over my exposed breast.

I tried not to look at her tattoo needle. It resembled a dentist's drill in a brown plastic jacket.

"It's just coloring in," she reassured me. "You might feel a tweak if the nerve endings have started joining up. I use anesthetic cream for that."

Anesthetic *cream*? I'd have the sleep of Morpheus any day. To my relief the procedure was painless. It just sent assault waves of vibration through my body as she drilled away. Every few minutes she paused to dab her artwork with little white squares of gauze.

"It shouldn't bleed," she said. "The trick is not to dig the needle in too deep, otherwise you get deep tissue bleeding and the tattoo goes blurry after a few years like my dad's did. But they didn't know that back in the war days."

Too much information. I asked if she had any tats.

"Oh no," she replied. "Except for my face."

"Your face?"

"Yes, eyeliner and eyebrows. I had a natural color done for my lips. Lips can be tricky. If you choose a strong color it goes out of date."

Forty minutes later I stood in front of a mirror to admire her work. The colored-in nipple looked darker than its partner. She said it would fade. I'd have to keep it dry and covered in ointment for four days. I could expect a visit from my old friends swelling and discomfort.

"You'll be able to sunbathe topless soon," she chirped.

While wearing the bikini bottoms Greg had mentioned, no doubt. Were these people *insane*?

I asked what she'd recommend in the way of facial tattoo. She said I had lovely eyes, so she'd do the eyeliner first. Imagining myself the Cleopatra of the old people's home, I squinted in the mirror. The bright red veins in my eyeballs hardly needed highlighting.

A bunch of yellow roses from Philip was waiting beside the front door when Lydia and I got home. Sweetheart. I opened the card and read: "I hope your feeling better." The florist needed a stint at apostrophe school.

To celebrate my coffee-colored nipple, Lydia and I went to a new café down on Chapel Street. With its concrete floor and primitive benches posing as seats, it resembled a nuclear shelter. The clientele was studiously hip. Men wore gray T-shirts. Improbable patches of hair on their chins and cheeks suggested a mange epidemic. Women were bent over laptops or pecking birdlike at their phones. Almost everyone bore that compulsory badge of twenty-first-century youth, at least one tattoo.

A ringlet of steam rose from the machine. Rich, nutty aroma hovered over the tables. The barista shook his dreadlocks and beamed me a telepathic message—"Uncool." Responding in kind, I sent one back—"I could have rinsed your nappies, son."

"Great tats," I said, admiring the impressive coil of red and blue rats twisting up his arm. "That must've hurt."

"Not as much as the one I had here," he said, tapping a spot just above his right breast.

I felt an urge to tell him we were brother and sister in ink.

"Why did you have it done?" I asked instead.

"To prove I could master pain," he replied.

"Oh," I said, staring down into my coffee.

I could've told him pain takes many forms. The most excruciating manifestation isn't from a tattoo needle, or probably even knives and guns. It isn't the wave of panic you experience when a doctor uses the c-word, or the jab of surgical wounds. Real anguish happens when things go wrong for your kids.

But he'd written me off as old and boring. He was looking through me to his next customer.

Back home, watching the usual run of funeral insurance advertisements on afternoon television, I caught a snippet of an American sitcom—one of those modern ones where it's hip to be gay.

Lydia brought in a mug of tea and glanced at the screen.

"You want rebellion!???" roared the television teenager whose parents were furious about his new pornographic tattoo. "I'll show ya rebellion. I'll run away and be a monk in Thailand!"

As canned laughter filled the room, Lydia and I exchanged glances—and a hint of a smile.

Blessed

I'm not religious but . . .

Suitcases were Jonah's enemies. To him they were as bad as the big black cats down the street. A suitcase or a backpack meant someone was leaving.

B.P. (Before Prozac) the sight of them had sent him into a frenzy. With tail boofed, he'd sprint up and down the hallway, his meows changing key into pitiful "Ne-ooooos!"

Anyone who tried to catch him to calm him down would be left in the dust as he shot upstairs and down again. Up down, up down. Don't go, don't go . . .

If a bag was left open and partially packed, he'd leap into it, dig in, and refuse to budge. Zipped-up luggage ready to go beside the front door was even more vulnerable. Jonah would seize the first opportunity to back up against it, ensuring the owner would take more of our cat away with them than they'd intended.

Managing Jonah's suitcase phobia had been a challenge. I didn't want to do anything to tip him back into his bad old ways.

We stored all forms of luggage out of sight these days, in the attic or bulging on top of each other in one of the cupboards of my study. Whenever one of us needed to pack to go away, another family member would divert Jonah's attention with ribbon, fishing rod, or flattery. The traveler would then stealthily remove the suitcase from its hiding place, slide into their bedroom with it, and shut the door.

We tried to hide it from him, but Jonah always knew, even A.P. (After Prozac). So it was as Lydia prepared to leave for Sri Lanka again. Shut behind her bedroom door, she folded her modest garments along with gifts for the monks and nuns. We'd had a brief scuffle over a blanket of ugly gray and crimson squares I'd knitted. Originally, it had been made to order for the homeless through Katharine's school. Then it turned out the homeless didn't want it, so I'd started taking it to yoga. I was briefly affronted when Lydia asked if she could take it to Sri Lanka—until I decided it was a compliment. She wanted to take something of me with her.

Desperate to be let in to Lydia's room, Jonah went on fast-forward, a Pink Panther on speed. Hurtling around the upstairs family space, he leaped from one window ledge to another, across the sofa backs, then down on the floor. He threw himself at her door and stretched a paw up to pat the handle.

When Lydia emerged, a vision in white crowned with a maroon beanie, Jonah lunged at her and begged to be picked up.

"It's all right, boy," she laughed, holding him like a restless baby. "I won't be far away. I'll beam you golden light every day."

Jonah stopped writhing and blinked up at her. Lydia and Jonah seemed to float away on a shared wavelength for a moment or two. Maybe they would be able to communicate in some other dimension while she was absent. Who knows what filtered through her brain during all those hours of meditation? Maybe the same trippy stuff wafted through Jonah's mind when he dozed on the alpaca rug.

Whenever I'd tried to discuss her religious views with Lydia she still closed me down. The most I could get out of her was that the purpose of Buddhism was to achieve enlightenment.

If I asked if that's what she was aiming for—to become enlightened—she'd clam up. That was when I'd fight an urge to take her by the shoulders, shake her, and tell her to stop dreaming. But I'd read enough quasi-spiritual books to know the answer to that one. She'd say it was *I* who was half awake and locked in the dream.

After Lydia kissed Jonah good-bye, I helped her hoist her backpack on her shoulders. The rosemary hedge brushed our clothes with its oily perfume as we headed down the path. Watching her beanie glide gracefully ahead of me, I wanted to explain I had an inkling of understanding of why she was doing this, even though I wasn't religious.

She heaved her backpack into the car's trunk.

The car coughed to life. Leonard Cohen bellowed "Hallelujah!" at full volume over the speaker system. I hushed his mouth.

If she'd wanted to hear, I'd have said: I'm not religious but . . .

I always light a candle in old churches in memory of friends who are suffering or loved ones who've moved on.

Lydia studied her hands. She was already in another world. It's always easier being the leaver than the leav-ee.

The motorway unraveled under our wheels. She wasn't going to change her mind. Not now.

I'm not religious but . . .

Certain places on Earth have incredible atmosphere. In the tomb of St. Francis in Assisi I wept tears from a cave somewhere deep inside me. Maybe some locations are portals. Or imbued with goodness because of the person they're associated with. Perhaps the bricks and stones become consecrated simply because they remind human beings of the potential for goodness within themselves.

We entered the concrete esophagus of the airport parking lot. Finding a place to park was surprisingly easy. But it always is with Lydia on board.

I stood back while Lydia checked herself in at the counter. Passport, customs form. She was an old hand.

I'm not religious but . . .

Even though Sam was killed in 1983, I never lost him. The older I get the more I understand people are never lost. They're always with us.

Likewise, if you go ahead and became a Buddhist nun in Sri Lanka, I won't be losing you. Not really.

We stood at the shiny good-bye doors. She kissed my cheek.

"Why don't you come and stay at the monastery?" she asked.

Go to a Third World joint run by a monk who'd caused me so many sleepless nights? And let's not forget the primitive toilet arrangements, leeches, and the rat.

The psychologist had told me to put my health first. I had no intention of disobeying orders.

Surely Lydia knew I only went to places that had fluffy towels. She had to be joking.

"You know I'm not religious but . . ." I said, kissing her back. "I'll think about it."

Serendipity

If you want to know what to do, ask a cat.

The first I ever heard of Sri Lanka was at primary school. The teacher unraveled the wrinkled map that hung over the blackboard and pointed to an island shaped like a teardrop off the coast of India. It was colored reassuringly pink like most of the world (the important parts, anyhow). Like our own country, it belonged to that eternal force, the British Empire.

"Ceylon's famous for tea and these," said the teacher, holding up her engagement ring for us all to see. The sparkly blue stone in it was a sapphire, she said.

It wasn't fair. Ceylon had precious gems. As for tea, there was enough British blood left in our veins to know we'd practically die without it. I was jealous of Ceylon. In New Zealand all we were famous for was mutton and cheese.

Before it was known as Ceylon, the island had the even more romantic name of Serendipity. Straight out of a fairy tale, the word Serendipity has Arabic roots. Oddly enough, Serendipity has been voted one of the ten most difficult words to translate from English. Serendipity happens when a person discovers something they weren't expecting to find. A happy accident.

Sri Lanka was the opposite of serendipity as far as I was concerned. Since Lydia's fascination with the place, not to mention tsunamis, war and poverty, I'd thought of the teardrop island as a Land of Tears.

A text bleeped to life on my phone. It was Lydia saying it was raining in Sri Lanka. I sent one back saying the roses were out in our Gratitude Garden.

My days had become full keeping Katharine afloat for her last few weeks of school. The poor kid had pushed herself so hard she'd developed chronic tonsillitis at the beginning of the final term. I'd never seen anyone so sick from a sore throat.

Every time she started to get better, she was struck down by a bout worse than the one before. One doctor said it was the most severe case she'd seen in thirty years. Antibiotics stopped working after a while and Katharine started getting infections on top of the infections she already had. After twelve blood tests and five different GPs, she finally went to a specialist. He put her on steroids to get her through the exams on the understanding she'd have a tonsillectomy the day after school was out.

It had been heartbreaking watching our sunniest child languish in a mist of illness and misery for three months. At the beginning of the year she'd hoped to achieve marks high enough to get into medicine. With so much time away from school sick, she'd tearfully let that dream go. Besides, she'd seen so many doctors lately she wasn't sure she liked them as a breed. Their thinking was too narrow and scientific, she said. They didn't see the whole person.

Every time I dropped her off at school for another exam, I half expected a phone call saying she'd collapsed. Yet with unbelievable tenacity she managed to slog through.

Jonah excelled himself during her illness, switching to super-hero mode and watching over her constantly. He stood sentinel beside her on her desk while she studied, classical music pouring from her stereo. Devoted to the depths of his fur follicles, our cat pretended he really didn't mind Bach's cello suites so much after all.

When Katharine staggered home from exams and collapsed on her bed, not knowing if she'd flunked or passed, Jonah leaped onto her duvet, nestled into her neck and sang to her in a honeyed purr.

My wrists were sore from squeezing oranges. The blades of

the smoothie-maker went blunt. Every packet of Panadol in the bathroom cabinet was empty.

Time after time, I delivered Katharine lectures on how unimportant exam marks were, saying they were just one square in the knitted blanket of life. If she didn't do as well as she'd hoped, she could take off to cooking school in Paris or do an art history course in Florence and become a connoisseur of finer things. Smiling weakly, she asked if I'd include performing in musical theater in that list.

Of course . . . anything, darling girl . . . just please get well.

When the exams were finally over, she was in no state to celebrate with her friends.

"I just want to be separated from my tonsils," she croaked.

Which she duly was—and sitting up in a hospital bed on a post-operative high.

"It was nothing, Mum. I feel great!" she said.

The first night she was home, Philip and I were woken by the sound of Jonah galloping up and down the hall, yowling loudly. We opened the door. His eyes, a pair of black orbs in the shadows, glowed up at us. He led us upstairs, springing up them two at a time. Katharine was in bed, crying with pain. The hospital drugs had worn off. She was in agony.

"Thanks, boy," I said, stroking Jonah's silky back.

Our feline sat neatly on Katharine's pillow while Philip phoned the hospital and arranged to collect stronger medicine. Devil cat no more, Jonah was Katharine's guardian angel.

A couple of hours later, after Philip had returned with the hospital painkillers, we opened Katharine's bedroom door a crack. Through a beam of light from the bathroom we could see her comfortably asleep with Jonah curled up beside her.

Jonah raised his head as if to say, "It's okay. I've got everything under control. You two can go back to bed now."

"Still want to send him to a farm?" I asked Philip as we stumbled downstairs, drunk with tiredness.

Philip shook his head and put his arm around me. There was no need to answer. Jonah was our daughter's greatest round-the-clock comforter. For all the ups and downs we'd been through, from carpet destruction to cat Prozac, from grandchild envy to incontinence, he was part of our family.

Next morning, another text message came through from Lydia saying it was still raining in Sri Lanka. For all I knew, she might've taken her vows and become a full-fledged nun by now. That was exactly the sort of sanity-challenging information she'd choose to withhold from me in favor of weather reports. I replied quoting a cover story from *Newsweek* saying meditation helps the brain grow. No answer. Perhaps she was meditating.

As Katharine grew stronger, the calendar flicked over into January, and her astonishing exam results came through. Her marks were so high she could go straight into medicine if she wanted. I was relieved when she opted for a science degree instead. A few years of broader studies would give her time to kick back and consider her options.

Meanwhile, Sri Lanka had crept like a cat into my mind. The teardrop island kept turning up everywhere—in my dreams; on the news. (Terrible flooding this time, displacing a million people. Lydia's weather reports hadn't been exaggerated.) When Philip and I went out for a night at the opera, it was to *The Pearl Fishers*, a doomed romance set in, of all places, Sri Lanka. I opened a biography of Virginia Woolf's husband, Leonard, to learn that before their marriage he was a British official in Sri Lanka, overseeing public executions and indulging in local women.

If Lydia *had* become a nun, I mused, there wasn't much I could do about it except offer my support. If, on the other hand, she was still thinking about it, well, that was up to her. The least I could do was visit the monastery and take an interest.

Though I had previously had no real desire to go to the teardrop island, it mattered a great deal to Lydia. And if it was important to her . . .

★   ★   ★

As I lay on the bed with Jonah one afternoon, he rolled playfully on his back in a shaft of sunlight. I grasped his front paws gently between my thumb and fingers and stared down into his serious blue eyes.

"What do you think I should do?" I asked, lowering my forehead to touch his.

Gazing up at me without a blink, he beamed a single word: *Go.*

"But what about my health?" I asked, rubbing his nose.

My energy levels were still pathetic. On outings, the family sprinted ahead while I trailed in their wake, pretending to admire the scenery. I was slower. My lungs seemed to have shrunk. I still huffed and puffed.

Viruses invited themselves into my system more often and took longer to go away. I no longer sailed around mindlessly inside my body. I'd started experiencing numbness down both arms, which an MRI revealed was due to compression in my upper spine, but (the doctor added cheerfully) no tumor.

The enormous smile scar across my abdomen wasn't without issues, either. If I sat up suddenly, or twisted in an unusual way, I'd seize up with paralyzing pain. I Googled the symptoms to find others who'd had the same surgery got it, too. "Charlie horse cramps" they were called. It was indeed like being kicked in the stomach. According to the Googlers, the cramps got worse with time.

Countless what-ifs whirled around my mind. My creaking, panting, cramping, infection-prone body was hardly up to Sri Lanka. What if I couldn't make it up the monastery steps? Or if I caught a horrible bug and died in the jungle?

One morning while I was chomping through my muesli, Jonah winked at me and sent some more words: *Does a brush with death mean you're going to stop living?*

He's right, I thought. I could stay home drinking green tea, avoiding stress, and being obsessed with the fact I wasn't going to live forever, or I could follow my daughter's example and live.

Seizing the phone, I punched in the nonsensical sequence of

numbers needed to reach the monastery. The line crackled, then buzzed, and for once the call went through. A melodic female voice answered. Probably a nun. Tropical birds whooped and chortled in the background as she went off to find Lydia.

"Is it still raining?" I asked our daughter. "Has the monastery been swept away by the floods?"

Lydia assured me she was fine. Even though it was raining a lot where she was, the actual flooding was farther south. She always made it seem the trouble was somewhere else.

"I'm thinking of coming over in February," I said.

"To stay at the monastery?" Lydia asked, sounding pleased and nervous at the same time.

Drawing a breath, I pictured the 200 steps. *And* the hole in the ground that would most probably be my toilet. *Plus* the nonexistent towels, fluffy or otherwise. (Guests were instructed to bring their own linen.) Then there was the information Katharine, in an uncharacteristic fit of kid-sister brattiness, had recently confided—Lydia had discovered a leech "on her vagina." (I'd managed to raise two daughters who didn't know the difference between a vagina and a vulva.)

"Yes."

Three nights at the monastery would be enough, I told her. After that I'd move to a four-star hotel, where she'd be welcome to join me. To my surprise, she was enthusiastic about staying in a luxury hotel.

One of the things I dreaded most about going to Sri Lanka was having the inoculations (my pathetic needle phobia again). I even toyed with the idea of not having any. Then Heather next door told me about a friend of hers who'd just returned from Sri Lanka with typhoid *and* malaria. Frankly, the prospect of falling ill in Sri Lanka didn't worry me as much as being a nuisance.

Steeling myself I went to the doctor's. She seemed perplexed when I told her where I was going.

Her list of recommended vaccinations was sobering. Adult

diphtheria and tetanus, hepatitis A, hepatitis B, polio, rabies, typhoid, swine flu, varicella (for those who haven't previously had chicken pox) and possibly malaria tablets. "Typhoid," "cholera," "malaria"—romantic sounding names engraved on headstones throughout the Empire.

Seeing my expression, the doctor said I could *maybe* get away without some of them. Fixing her gaze tactfully on her prescription pad, she asked if the trip might involve an exchange of bodily fluids. I was flattered, but in a monastery? At my age? I was more likely to have a heart attack on the 200 steps.

She talked me into several jabs and a fizzy drink for cholera. Disease prevention dealt with, I asked Lydia what gifts to bring. The nuns' feet were dry and cracked, she said. They'd appreciate soap and coconut body butter. Sweets, pens, and mini flashlights (with batteries) for the boy monks. She asked if I'd bring her singlet top and sarong for the hotel pool. Remembering how she covered her arms when she came home from the monastery, I took this as a hopeful sign.

As for her Teacher/guru, he could do with a new pair of maroon sheepskin slippers, size 9, she said, then sent a photo of the slippers she had in mind. I couldn't find maroon scuffs anywhere, so Katharine and I went to a shop that made them to order. When I explained the circumstances, the shoemaker nodded wisely.

"I've met monks," he said. "I went to a lot of monasteries in Asia until I realized they were just like the Greek Orthodox churches I grew up with. Bowing, lighting candles, and praying. It's all the same."

He went out the back to find a sample of maroon leather. The color was perfect. He recommended lining the slippers with the darkest fleece because "they go barefoot most of the time." Monks have harsh lives, he said, and it's tougher for them when they get older. He'd once made sheepskin boots for an elderly Tibetan monk whose feet got terribly cold.

"Asian monks are trained to be very tough mentally," he added. "I had one in Thailand who used to hit me. He'd yell at me to get down on the floor. You can't argue with them. They see the world from their perspective and that's how it is. They're not open to looking at it any other way."

I told him what size we needed and paid the deposit.

"Lots of people leave Buddhism because they realize they're just sitting there observing life, not living it," he added. "Don't worry about your daughter."

Easy for him to say.

"The slippers will be ready tomorrow. Would you like to meet *my* monk?" the man asked, guiding us to the front of his shop and parting a row of moccasins on the second shelf.

Curled asleep in the shadows was a large tabby cat.

"She's seventeen years old and she knows everything. She tells me when to calm down and she knows when I'm sick. She talks to me all the time. When she's hungry she winks at me."

We admired the sleeping cat together for a while.

"I don't need those monks when I can have this cat," he said.

I wondered if someday Lydia might feel the same about Jonah. It didn't seem likely.

Following advice from a well-traveled friend I visited the drugstore for orange pills to block me up in case I got diarrhea and yellow ones for the opposite effect, if necessary.

Next stop was an outdoor shop redolent with canvas and insect repellent. Philip adored those places but I'd spent my life avoiding them.

A Man vs. Wild type greeted me. "You're going *where*?" he asked.

He asked me to repeat the name of my destination, and was perplexed when told why I was going there.

He'd camped in Namibia, and we exchanged information about mosquitoes. Nasty buggers, he said, then talked me into buying a full-sized mosquito net soaked in repellent as well as a smaller net to go over my hat. Man vs. Wild had been grateful for his silk sleeping-bag liner (also impregnated with insecticide) in Namibia, so I bought one of those, too. And while I was at it, some debugging powder to soak my clothes in. It was a major pesticide binge for someone who'd spent their adult years shopping organic.

Lydia had told me that a halogen lamp to strap around my head was essential for power cuts (and more important, to fend off the rat and to get to the loo during the night). I added a camping pillow (presumably no sheets meant no pillows), a fancy-looking tick remover, and brightly colored mosquito-repelling wristbands.

"Enjoy," said Man vs. Wild, loading my stuff into bags.

He can't have meant it.

Jonah was intrigued when I got home and spread my wares out on the table. He dabbed his nose in the packages, savoring the unfamiliar perfumes.

Katharine, on the other hand, was appalled.

"*Please* tell me you're *not* going to wear a hat with a mosquito net!" she groaned.

"It'll be in Sri Lanka. You won't have to see."

"But Mum, it's sooooo uncool!"

Following Man vs. Wild's instructions, I took the mosquito net into the back garden and draped it over garden loungers to air for twenty-four hours.

Jonah's calming medicine wasn't working so well as my departure approached. With his usual impeccable instincts about people's comings and goings, he was getting clingy. Katharine took him outside for a walk on his lead in the back garden. Glancing up from the kitchen counter, I saw the mosquito net floating sideways like a ghost on a mission. Jonah had caught it between his teeth and was dragging it away.

On the night of 9 February, before I was due to fly out, Jonah deluged the curtains in the Marquis de Sade room. My nearly packed suitcase was mercifully spared.

With his jaw set, Philip unhooked the curtains to soak them in a bucket in the laundry room. It was no time for ultimatums.

I reminded Philip it was Jonah's first crime since Christmas.

That night I ran through my checklist—gifts, sheets, towels,

pillow, clothes (mostly white to conform to monastery requirements), long white socks and Marcel Marceau gloves (to repel
insects), mosquito nets, torch, toilet paper, antiseptic wipes,
plus enough pills and potions to fill a drugstore.

Then I remembered the monastery's food quota of two vegetarian curries a day! No way would I survive on that. I'd be
gnawing the woodwork by 8 p.m. Lucky the supermarket was
still open. Two packets of nut bars and I was ready.

Next morning, I put on my compression socks and the
moonstone earrings that'd been a birthday gift from Lydia. As
Philip wheeled my suitcase to the car, Katharine stood on the
veranda holding Jonah, lifting one of his front paws to wave
good-bye.

"He's not purring," she said.

Island of Tears

Daughter am I in my mother's house,
But mistress in my own. —*Rudyard Kipling*

As the plane shuddered off the tarmac, I experienced an exhilarating combination of fear and liberation. Whatever lay ahead, whether it was witnessing Lydia's taking of robes or an inconvenient death from some romantic-sounding disease, there was no turning back.

I slid my shoes off and dozed, picked at a meal, watched a movie, and checked the flight monitor. We were *still* over Australia! The country below resembled a rock pool—brown with flecks of blue and green. It was surprisingly beautiful.

The size of my shoes alongside those belonging to the tidy Malaysian man sitting next to me was embarrassing. To him, I must've seemed a mountainous, unruly woman. Yet he was friendly and accommodating.

Toward the end of the flight my newfound Malaysian friend passed me his business card, possibly to thank me for not rolling over and crushing him in my sleep. Together we stepped out of the plane into the spa-pool heat of Kuala Lumpur, where I had a twenty-four-hour stopover. Colored lights festooned the skyscrapers for Chinese New Year. People kept asking in concerned tones if I was alone. In restaurants waiters hurried to find newspapers and magazines to ease the nonexistent discomfort of being a solitary woman.

One thing I'd deliberately forgotten to pack was Lydia's old singlet top. In a glamorous department store I found one with a

Calvin Klein logo twinkling in fake diamonds in the lower left-hand corner. A risky choice. I hoped there was enough of the old Lydia left to appreciate the glitz.

In the same shopping center I visited the loos. A sign said QUEUE HERE. The five cubicles were silently occupied. When I finally gained access I found out why. The toilet was a glistening white throne with foot holes either side of the bowl. There was no seat. It seemed to require removal of all the clothing on my lower body. Prickly with defeat, I bolted for the hotel. If I couldn't handle a pristine loo in Malaysia, how on earth was I going to manage the plumbing of a Sri Lankan monastery?

"Is the music the right temperature for you?" asked the pretty masseuse at the hotel when I lay down for a much-needed rub.

A few minutes later I was wishing I'd avoided the "Traditional" massage, thinking the only reason some massages are called "Traditional" is that they're too violent to become mainstream. My masseuse tugged my toes till they clicked out of their sockets. In one split second of agony my shoe size went up another notch.

The stop-over had been recommended to help ease jet lag, but staggering on to the midnight flight to Colombo I was still disoriented. In line behind young men wearing beach hats and the inevitable tattoos, I noticed their legs were hairy but their beards were barely perceptible. They smelled of bubble gum and brandished plastic bags of duty-free vodka. The world was their kindergarten. As they exchanged indecipherable banter, I thought the cabin announcement mentioned Colombia. Such was my dazed state that I momentarily imagined I'd made a mistake and was heading for the cocaine capital of South America to star in *Banged Up Abroad*.

I fell asleep watching the racehorse movie *Secretariat* and woke to the sound of the plane's engines changing. The street-lights of Colombo were strung like pearls along the coast below. The country that had entranced my daughter and been witness to so much pain over the years was surprisingly peaceful.

The captain apologized for the bumpy landing. He said it was due to flood damage on the runway. I'd been too busy examining the other planes at the airport to notice. They were decorated like birds in an ancient painting. An illuminated Buddha statue glowed through the velvet darkness. We seemed to have landed in an exotic fable.

Adjusting my watch to three in the morning, I waited for the cabin crew to open the doors. With the monastery four hours' drive away along difficult roads, Lydia and I had agreed I'd wait in an airport hotel until she reached Colombo around lunch-time. Someone from the hotel was supposed to collect me from the Arrivals area. I hoped he'd be out there already holding a sign with my name on it.

Stepping into the terminal, I steeled myself for the throngs of hustlers I'd encountered in places like Bali and Mumbai, but the atmosphere was surprisingly calm. I made my way past quiet, watchful faces—family groups, women wearing jewel-colored saris—and another Buddha statue. A group of men held up a forest of placards emblazoned with names. My heart sank. Mine wasn't among them.

A grandfatherly chap with distinguished white whiskers came to my rescue and guided me to a car outside. The night was hot, but not unbearably soggy. Preparing to experience the perfumes of Sri Lanka, I opened my lungs. All I got was a waft of jet fuel.

The floods hadn't been too bad around Colombo, the old man said, but in the east and north of the country it had been like another tsunami.

"You've had terrible floods in Queensland, too, have you not?" he asked gently.

I was momentarily speechless. Certainly, the Queensland floods had been devastating, but nothing on the scale Sri Lanka had been suffering. It was incredibly gracious of him to express concern for people in a more fortunate country than his own.

"Yes, but we didn't have a million people lose their homes the way you have," I replied.

I was surprised the old gentleman was so well informed about our part of the world. Australia's media had all but ignored the Sri Lankan emergency.

He hailed a car and a young driver sprang out to take my luggage.

"The main road has been closed for renovations," the older man explained. "You will be taking the back roads. It'll take about ten minutes to get to the hotel. Don't be alarmed."

Inside my head I store a list of famous potential last words: "Red light? What red light?" "It's not loaded." "These snakes aren't poisonous." Climbing into the unmarked car I added a new one to the list: "Don't be alarmed."

In the darkness it was impossible to have any idea where we were going. We swung past a military checkpoint, another Buddha statue (Sri Lankans put the Italians to shame in the religious shrine department) and a wide stretch of road that appeared to be barricaded off. Presumably that was the main road the old man had mentioned.

We veered into a narrow street lined with advertisements for cough lozenges. Dogs and people on bikes were just visible in the shadows. I wondered what they were doing up at this hour.

The car turned sharply and plunged into a narrow, winding road with no streetlights. We approached a bridge—not much wider than a footpath and half broken. The driver slowed down, as if he was evaluating the risk—then suddenly put his foot down and charged forward. Once we'd rattled across the bridge, the driver glanced over his shoulder and smiled victoriously. Craning my neck, I peered down at a silver ribbon of water shimmering far below. We appeared to have cleared a ravine.

In pitch darkness at 3:30 in the morning in the back streets of Colombo with a complete stranger driving an unmarked car, my thoughts turned to abduction. If I was being kidnapped, and my life was about to come to an end, I decided there wasn't much to complain about. I'd had a good life—rich and wonderful in many ways. There'd been time to love, give birth to four fantastic children, and experience joy, sorrow—and cats—in all their complexities.

On the other hand, my body organs would be unsaleable and there wasn't a thing worth stealing on me, apart from several tons of mosquito repellent. I was probably safe.

A splash of lights ahead glowed yellow and welcoming. We were back in civilization. Minutes later, we pulled up outside the hotel gates. In case I was about to mistake it for nirvana, a guard ran a metal detector under and over the car. After he'd waved us through, we hiccoughed over speed bumps and pulled up outside the hotel foyer.

Two gentlemen greeted me warmly. Omar Sharif's twin brother fetched my bags, while his colleague informed me I'd been upgraded to a suite. He escorted me to a series of rooms, each the size of a small tennis court. The bed would've accommodated Hugh Hefner and at least six Playboy Bunnies. The curtains, opera-house sumptuous, spilled theatrically over the floor. The Raj lives on.

After a few hours of fitful sleep, I trekked the distance between my bed and the windows to drag the curtains open. The Indian Ocean fixed me with a silvery gaze, shimmering with heat. I'd always imagined such a legendary sea would be blue. Palm trees glistened along a flat, seemingly endless shoreline. In the distance, a tiny fishing boat nudged across the water. Below my window, two men in white uniforms cleaned a garishly turquoise swimming pool. The hotel and the land beyond its imposing walls were two different countries.

A text buzzed in from Lydia. They weren't far away.

Hoping to make a good impression, I dressed in my whitest clothes and waited anxiously in the hotel foyer. While a procession of taxis and limousines glided past the front doors, I prepared myself mentally for the reunion with Lydia.

I hoped she wouldn't be too thin—though I knew better than to say anything. And if she turned up wearing nun's robes, I was *not* going to overreact. This was her world, or one she'd chosen to be part of. Mother's authority, whatever that was at this stage in our lives, had to be put on hold. I was a mere visitor.

A ripple of excitement ran through the foyer as a battered van pulled up outside the hotel's doors. Dented and dusty, the vehicle was hardly up to hotel standards so when security guards rushed forward I thought they would move it along as fast as possible.

To my surprise, instead of reaching for their guns, the guards started beaming like babies, clasping their hands in prayer and bending down deeply before the van.

A doorman reached for the passenger door handle as if it was part of a royal carriage. I glimpsed a flash of maroon behind the van's dusty windows. Then, elegantly and with perfect timing, out stepped Lydia's Teacher, grinning like a rock star.

The concierge left his post and dropped to his knees in front of the monk, pressing the hem of the maroon robe to his lips. I'd heard the expression "kiss the hem of his garment" but never seen it in action before.

The monk accepted the adulation with radiant dignity. Magnificent in his robes, he *belonged* in this setting. In Australia, he was held in awe by a few but mostly ignored or regarded as an oddity; a representative of an alternative religion. Here in Sri Lanka, the monk was part of a belief system that was the life-blood of much of the population. It was suddenly easier to understand why, when he'd been staying at our place, he'd expected the sort of deference that I hadn't been able to provide. Bestowing benevolence on all who bowed before him in the hotel lobby, he was treated as a demigod.

For all the mixed feelings I'd had in the past, I was pleased to see him—and honored he'd made the arduous journey down from the monastery to meet me. As a non-Buddhist and an old friend, I lowered my head respectfully, and hoped it was enough.

Close on the Teacher's heels followed the two nuns, who graciously accepted the (slightly shallower) bows they were offered. At last, a familiar figure unfolded herself from the van's backseat and ran toward me. Smiling broadly, Lydia enveloped me in her arms and kissed my cheeks. I couldn't remember receiving such a warm embrace from her since she was in primary school. All the resentments and brinkmanship of recent years seemed to dissolve. Something in her feelings toward me had shifted.

Hugging her, I noticed she was still dressed in white—a student, not a nun. And to my astonishment, she'd actually let her hair grow! Still, it was too early to make assumptions. Perhaps she was saving her initiation for my visit.

"If there is a pearl in all the world, Lydia is our jewel," said her Teacher, beaming at me. I wasn't sure whether to interpret the remark as flattery. Either way, there was ownership in it.

The van and its passengers needed rest and refreshment before embarking on the long journey back to the monastery. Fortunately, they'd arrived just before noon so Lydia's Teacher and the nuns were still able to eat. Hotel staff respectfully arranged tables so the monk and his driver could sit together at one table while Lydia and the nuns sat with me at another. When Lydia chatted to the waiter in Sinhalese his eyes bulged with surprise, and his smile became incandescent.

"Don't be too impressed," she said as he walked away toward the kitchen. "It's just country dialect."

"You mean hillbilly talk—like 'them thar grits'?" I asked.

Lydia led me to the buffet where she pointed out some local delicacies, which she assured me were delicious. It was too early in the trip to take gastronomic risks and become a health care liability, so I quietly avoided them in favor of pasta. Over lunch I asked Lydia if any other Westerners were staying at the monastery. She said no, it would just be us.

Soon after, with much bowing and hem-kissing from hotel staff, the monk and his entourage climbed back into the van. He slid into the front seat next to the driver, with the nuns sitting down behind him. Lydia and I took the backseat. No seat belts. We'd have to rely on the Buddha perched on top of the rearview mirror, along with the protection beads and (Christian?) cross dangling below it. Sweating already, I glanced hopefully at the air-conditioning unit sighing luke-warm air above our heads. Whatever lay ahead was going to be an exercise in trust.

The engine coughed to life with an explosive backfire. There was enough rural blood left in my veins to diagnose the scraping noise as clutch trouble. Staff waved a royal farewell as we roared and spluttered out the hotel gates. We rumbled over potholes past stands selling coconuts, bananas, brightly colored blow-up toys, and (I was getting used to them now) the omnipresent Buddha statues.

I asked Lydia about the rows of brand-new airplane seats that lined the roadsides. She said they were everywhere. Apparently, there was a tax exemption for vans imported with no windows or seats. Enterprising locals had got around the loophole by importing these vans like ours, drilling out holes for windows and putting in the seats. She pointed out the impromptu finishing in our vehicle.

Some villagers bowed when they saw the saintly beings in our van. Others kept going about their business—shopping, gossiping, or carrying loads on their heads. We passed a handsome young man with no legs in a wheelchair, soldiers with machine guns slung like afterthoughts over their shoulders, boys playing cricket, girls with bright umbrellas strolling beside a railway line, a white heron in a river. A man with a box on his head smiled through our window and offered us evening shoes studded with jewels.

Sri Lankan roads aren't for the fainthearted. They're mostly two lanes with an invisible third lane down the middle, which is disputed territory. Traffic from either direction claims the middle of the road with as much speed and aggression as his vehicle and the condition of the road allows. Drivers charge forward blasting their horns, daring anyone to challenge them. Even a bull elephant on the back of a truck doesn't get right of way. It's a combination of bluff and split-second negotiation—and a miracle head-on collisions don't happen every two minutes.

In the back of the van without a seat belt, I was probably in more physical danger than I'd ever been. There was no point worrying. A monk and two nuns on board put the odds in our favor.

Halfway up a hill, we lurched to a halt outside a bank so I could withdraw money for the van hire. When the driver tried to start the vehicle up again it refused to budge. Helpful bank guards gave us a push start up the hill—heavy work, and beyond the call of duty. The engine heaved reluctantly to life. Triumphant and sweating, the guards waved us off.

Villages gave way to rice paddies, pineapple fields, and stands of banana trees. Landscape unfurled in shades of green ranging from gloomy to fluorescent. As the road became steep, winding its way toward Kandy, the senior nun pulled her hood up over her head and slept like a caterpillar. The other nun's smooth head gleamed in the steam-bath atmosphere of the van. The air-conditioning had died. Opening the windows would've been futile. Inside and out were equally hot and dusty.

We passed trees with leaves the size of dinner plates, a truck graveyard, and a roadside box with the Buddha radiating a pulsating neon light aura. Despite the intensity of the heat, I was taken by the colorful spontaneity of the place. Roadside advertising posters were refreshingly free of the semi-pornographic images we've become inured to in the West. Women were portrayed as wholesome and modestly dressed. Anorexic models didn't have a chance.

The clutch jerked violently as the road became even steeper and more perilous. Toiling up a hill through a village selling nothing but pottery, I was reminded of the first time I visited Ubud in Bali twenty-five years earlier. People always say Bali was better twenty-five years ago. If they want to find out what it was like before tourism took over, they should visit Sri Lanka.

"Sri Lankans don't think of themselves as poor," said Lydia. "They just think Westerners are ridiculously rich. When you look at any distribution-of-wealth chart, that's a fact."

My spiritual daughter has a way of presenting things with

surgical clarity sometimes. She was right. Compared to Sri Lankans we're awash with wealth, yet we mentally impoverish ourselves focusing on what we don't have.

The people of this flood-ridden, war-torn, tsunami-drenched island seemed to have a humanity the West had somehow lost in its consumerist thrall. I found myself wanting to share Sri Lanka with the world and protect it at the same time. If tourists swarmed there, the country would gain monetarily but potentially lose a lot.

The monk instructed our driver to pull over at a sweet shop for tea. After the internal massage my organs were getting from the road, it was a relief to stop and get my legs moving. Curious faces watched the monk, nuns, Lydia, and I make our way to the sweet store.

My eyes took a while to adjust to the store's darkened interior. The decor was stark, but the ambience was friendly. I felt immediately at home. It was a Sri Lankan version of Spoonful. We chose homemade sweets from a counter near the door and sat down on a bench. Overstaffed by Western standards, the service was impeccable. There was one person to bring our sweets, another to pour the tea, and at least three assistants to watch.

A photo of a stern, handsome man with a handlebar moustache glowered down from behind the counter. An older, even more distinguished version of him stood at the door. I tried a smile. His eyes flashed handsomely back.

We gorged ourselves on strong tea and delicious sweets. Mouth-wateringly nutty, the sesame sweets deserved to be world famous. Jaggery sweets made from unrefined whole cane sugar came a close second. As for the coconut ice, I was an expert connoisseur because Dad used to make it when we were kids. The sweet shop's version, layered in lurid pink and white sprinkled with fruit, was the best I'd ever tasted.

Back in the van, our driver made a brave assault on the last few hills to Kandy. Though he was willing, the clutch was not. It screeched, clunked, and finally expired on a steep bend. Hot and tired, despite all the sugar we'd consumed, we piled onto the side of the road while the van driver and curious onlookers stared into the bowels of the engine.

An amiable café owner invited us to sit at tables with red and white checked cloths. We ordered cans of Coke and waited. The monk produced his cell phone and called a mechanic. Flies circled above our heads and mosquitoes buzzed around our ankles. I reached in my handbag for the high-grade insect killer only to find its pump was missing. I'd brought it all the way from Australia and it didn't work!

Under normal circumstances I'd have freaked out, wondering: How long would it take to get a mechanic? Would he know how to fix the van? Would we still be in this café in three days' time? Was I going to get one of those mosquito diseases and die? But it was pointless worrying or looking at my watch. I had no control and therefore no responsibility. The sensation was surprisingly liberating. I hadn't felt this free and on the edge of things since I'd traveled alone in Samoa in my twenties.

As Lydia and I sipped our Cokes and chatted, she was warmer and more open than she'd been for years. She wanted to hear about everyone at home—how Annie's crawling was coming along, and if Jonah's "little problem" was still driving us nuts. Heartened, I realized that if she was going to become a nun and live in this country she'd still want to stay connected to us.

More time passed as we sat in the café on the road to Kandy. Hours and minutes, lateness or earliness, became irrelevant. If we were still stranded there at nightfall, the owner might be kind enough to let us sleep on the floor. And that would be okay.

The mechanic miraculously showed up and managed to fix the clutch with minimum fuss. In the meantime, the monk had been busy on his phone. He'd just found out he had important business in Kandy. A car collected him and he disappeared in a plume of dust, leaving the nuns and us to complete the final leg to the monastery with our apologetic driver. I'd hoped the monk might spare some time so we could have a serious discussion about Lydia's future. Maybe tomorrow.

Sri Lanka is remote by many people's standards. A lot of those living in Colombo regard Kandy as out of the way. I was soon to learn that most people in Kandy would have difficulty locating the simple forest monastery that was our destination.

Once we'd passed the turnoff to Kandy, the road became even narrower and bumpier, winding around the edge of a river canyon.

"Just pretend you're on a four-wheel-drive tourist excursion for this part," said Lydia as we veered off the main street up a perpendicular track. I gripped the side of the van as it carved through dense jungle. We were rocking so violently, I wondered if my abdominal scar might spasm. But anxiety would be counterproductive. People in this country had far greater concerns.

The driver beeped his horn for a woman with a child on her hip, a man in a sarong, and another carrying a sack of flour on his head. Their smiles lit the dark green gloom. We passed a sign for "Computer Repairing" which seemed incongruous in the depths of the jungle. After we'd negotiated a hairpin bend and lurched over a particularly large hump, the senior nun turned to me, her eyes ablaze.

"Look, Sister Helen!" she cried. "There's our mountain!"

If we'd been in a movie, heavenly voices would've surged over the background music just then. The heroine (Doris Day? Julie Andrews? No, Meryl Streep!), her eyes sparkling with tears, would have raised her face to the clouds.

Monastic

Old people bring many blessings.

Laden with tropical growth, Boulder Mountain rose sharply above us. Its slope appeared to be held together by enormous stones, many of them larger than elephants. While a few creepers had the audacity to scramble over them, most of the rocks were bare and lined with age. Immovable sculptures of the forest, the boulders were both beautiful and forbidding in the heavy shadows of evening.

Other monks had tried to make a home here in the past, the nun explained, but they'd been frightened away by evil spirits. The current monk, Lydia's Teacher, was made of sterner stuff. Meditating in the cave near the summit for several years, he claimed the place.

Though the mountain air was cooler than it'd been at sea level, it was still and lifeless. I longed for a breeze, especially knowing 200 steps were hiding in the forest. My suitcase was ludicrously large. I wished I'd settled for a backpack.

As we slid out of the van, the driver gallantly hoisted my suitcase on his shoulder and disappeared up some mossy steps. We followed him, climbing and climbing. Jungle plants wrapped themselves so voraciously around the path that there was no view of the valley below. All I could see was the next set of steps ahead. Soon my eyes were stinging and my chest pumping. Stopping to catch my breath, I waved the others to go on ahead. To my relief, they vanished into the folds of the jungle. Only Lydia remained, waiting patiently behind me. I apologized for holding her up. She said not to worry, she felt like a breather herself.

When my lungs returned to normal, Lydia shadowed my footsteps with no sign of annoyance or frustration. Dad, who'd been an enthusiastic mountain climber, had a saying: "Always let the slowest go first." With gratitude, I realized it's exactly what Lydia was doing. I made an effort not to count the steps, concentrating instead on scaling one set at a time without worrying how many more might be lurking on the slope above us. It was a good exercise in living in the present—perfect for the ascent to a Buddhist monastery, really.

Shadows grew longer as we reached the plain two-story building that was the nuns' quarters. I slipped my shoes off at the door and stumbled into a harshly lit room.

"Sit," said the senior nun in a tone that wasn't to be argued with.

Dusty and sweaty, I lowered myself onto a plastic chair covered with gold fabric. Not a word was said, but I later found out that seat was reserved for monks only.

A ginger kitten trotted toward me and rubbed against my ankle. As it gazed up at me through amber eyes, I thought of Jonah and wondered how he'd enjoy monastic life. Jonah's personality was so pervasive I saw him everywhere these days, even in the eyes of racehorses and wild animals. His beauty and intensity seemed to be part of every animal.

"What a lovely kitten!" I said.

"It's not a kitten, it's a cat," Lydia explained quietly. "The nuns found her mewing in the forest eight years ago. She's had several litters, but none survived. She's vegetarian."

A vegetarian cat? I didn't like to say anything. Maybe she was a high-minded feline. Or she was just conforming to monastery rules.

"What's her name?"

"Puss. Just Puss."

The van driver said good-bye and bowed deeply to both nuns. To my great embarrassment, he then turned and bowed just as deeply to me. Heat prickled up my neck. I must've been blushing.

"It's what we do for the oldest person present," the senior nun explained.

Looking at her, it was impossible to tell how old she was—thirty or forty? She had one of those unlined ecclesiastical faces. I later discovered she was just two years younger than me—we were closer in the walking-frame stakes than I'd thought.

Bow to people—just because they're *old*? It was a complete reversal of cultural priorities.

"Old people bring many blessings," she explained with a radiant smile.

My first day in Sri Lanka had been filled with so many unfamiliar experiences I was beginning to feel like Alice in Wonderland. Strangest of all, coming from a culture that worships youth and detests gray hair, was to be actually *revered* for having a few wrinkles. Not that I liked to think of myself as ancient, just mature with a chance of wisdom.

Once the driver had handed over my suitcase, apologized again for the van breaking down, and left, Lydia escorted me up some outdoor steps to our rooms. Too weary to take much in, I registered apricot walls, a bare lightbulb, a table with a white plastic chair, and a bed with a blue mosquito net hovering over it.

The air was thick and warm. Lydia opened the windows, saying she hadn't had any trouble from mosquitoes in her room next door. Just as she was about to explain where to find the bathroom, we were plunged into darkness. The senior nun glided into the room with a lit candle creating a halo around her.

"It's just an electricity cut, Sister Helen," she said, placing the candle on the table and floating out the door again. The candle promptly went out and fell on the floor.

"Did you bring a headlamp?" Lydia asked.

There was a dull thud. Lydia assured me it was just her tripping over the candle.

Once our halogen lights were strapped around our heads we

lit up like glowworms. I followed Lydia's silhouette outside onto the balcony, then around a corner over a potentially treacherous hump to what she tactfully described as a "French-style" toilet—a tiled floor with a hole in the ground—plus a bucket and scrubbing brush; flushing mechanisms nonexistent. Compared to this, the lavatory in Kuala Lumpur had been the pinnacle of hygiene technology. What a prissy, screwed-up fool I'd been twenty-four hours ago!

I decided the hole in the ground was manageable providing it wasn't a breeding ground for scorpions. Actually, even if it was I wasn't about to go and pee in the jungle among snakes and whatever else was lurking out there. For the next few days it was going to be my hole in the ground—and Lydia's and whoever else had claim to it. I was simply going to have to learn to use a bucket and scrubbing brush.

Back downstairs I showered under a dribble of tepid water with a large cockroach for a friend. As the grime of the day trickled away, I decided it was one of the best showers of my life.

It was intriguing to see how simply Lydia had lived for weeks, sometimes months, at a time. My bedroom was identical to hers, the bed just a mattress on plywood about the right length for a ten-year-old boy. Once smoothed down with sheets from home and the travel pillow it looked incredibly inviting. After a day playing human tumbleweed inside the van, I was grateful for its stillness.

Lydia brought mugs of tea, so hot and strong they almost passed as soup. With trepidation, I produced a small parcel from my suitcase and handed it to her.

"Wow!" she said, holding up the singlet top so the diamonds twinkled in the shadows. "Calvin Klein! How exciting!"

Her delight at the crass glitziness of the garment was wonderful.

After a while, Lydia kissed me good night and said to knock on her door if I needed her. Alone in my room with my headlamp, I smiled at the electronic bleeping coming from her room. In these strange surroundings it was reassuring she had the same old quirks—like forgetting to turn her alarm clock off, and tripping over things.

Outside, the night had turned black as onyx. I'd naively assumed darkness in the jungle would mean silence, but a hypnotic chorus of male chanting echoed across the valley. The sound resonated through me, carrying me back through generations to anonymous forebears who lived before the Industrial Revolution, the Age of Enlightenment, and the Renaissance.

After the chanting ended, other more insistent noises took over. Lowering myself onto the bed, I heard crickets (several types), birds, frogs, dogs, and an unidentified range of creatures that trilled, squawked, honked, clicked, whistled, quacked, and chirped. Competing loudly against each other, they took me back still further to a time when the prospect of evil spirits was feasible.

After a while, unnerved by the spooky symphony, I sprang off the bed and reached for my iPhone. A clearly pixelated image of Jonah draped like a beret over Philip's head flashed to life once I pressed a button. I was relieved it still worked. For a moment I'd imagined I'd slipped into another century.

By the light of my headlamp, I dug my earplugs out of my toilet bag, thanking whoever was CEO of the heavens right now that I'd remembered to bring the orange plugs of sanity. Next, I counted out my nut bars. Two for each night. I hoped they'd get me through. If not, I'd just have to regard the monastery as a fat farm.

Sifting through my carefully thought out luggage, I felt ridiculous. Almost everything I'd brought for "protection" was proving useless. I draped the pesticide-soaked net over the window in case Lydia was being optimistic about mosquitoes. As for the silk liner, mozzie bands, Marcel Marceau gloves, knee-length white socks, and hat net—I needn't have bothered. The blocking and unblocking pills languished inside their packets. I was almost hoping I'd meet a tick, so the tick remover hadn't been a waste of cabin space.

Still, I thought, easing cautiously back on the bed in case it was more fragile than it looked, the trip wasn't over. There was plenty of time for things to go wrong. Even through the earplugs, I could hear the screeching jungle—but was too tired to care.

I'd hardly fallen asleep when I was woken by the sound of a woodpecker drilling a tree. After a while, I realized it wasn't a woodpecker at all, but a drumroll—the monks' morning wake-up call. Soon after, their eerie chanting began. Using harmonies even Schoenberg couldn't have dreamed up, their mahogany voices drifted across the jungle canopy. The sound was from another world—music a shoal of fish might make if they could sing.

Pink light filtered through the curtains. Over more than three decades, motherhood had taken me to all sorts of places—from pinnacles of joy in maternity wards to utter desolation at a graveside. Through all those years I'd never imagined it would bring me to a remote monastery in Sri Lanka.

I was relieved that the monks hadn't issued an invitation to attend the predawn chanting. Maybe it was a male-only thing. Monastery life didn't seem to encourage mingling of the sexes. The monks were housed across the hill well away from the nuns' accommodation.

Getting back to sleep was impossible. I lumbered out of bed and wondered what Trinny and Susannah would recommend under these circumstances. White trousers and a mostly white long-sleeved top seemed logical—and of course I was happy to take on the role of student, whatever that might mean. Pale clothes deflected heat and kept insects at bay. Pulling on the knee-length white socks, I toyed with the idea of the Marcel Marceau gloves—and put them back in my suitcase.

Lydia escorted me downstairs to the dining room, which was a simple space with two small tables covered in plastic tablecloths, a sink, and a microwave. A wall of windows overlooked a mass of plant life glistening happily in the sun. I recognized a banana tree and some coconut palms, but they were squashed together, bigger and greener than anything I was used to, as if they were on growth hormones. Most of the trees and plants were unfamiliar. Not for the first time, I felt overwhelmed by ignorance.

The table was laid out with flat bread, dhal, delicately flavored rice balls, and bananas. There was also a tub of garishly labeled margarine and a jar of Vegemite. Apart from these two imports, almost all the ingredients were fresh from the monastery surrounds. The breakfast was wholesome and filling. When I commented it felt health-enhancing Lydia explained it was based on Ayurvedic principles of food being medicine.

Approaching the day ahead with an open mind, I wondered if Lydia's Teacher might hold some classes I could sit in on. It turned out he'd had to stay in Kandy on business overnight and sent his apologies. Lydia offered to show me around, and suggested we could maybe go into town with the nuns later on. Oh, she added, and a fortune-teller was coming up from the village mid morning.

After we'd washed our dishes and put them away, Lydia showed me the meditation hall farther up the hill. She'd spent many hours alone there, sometimes more than twelve hours a day, doing sitting and walking meditation. The room, largely unadorned, was steamy and still.

Trying to understand what she'd been doing there, I asked her to give me a short, guided meditation. Perched on a blue cushion on the floor, I closed my eyes and listened to her voice. Sounding strong and authoritative, she urged me to concentrate on my breathing; I tried but a river of sweat trickled down my back and I started to feel dizzy.

Like an uncooperative schoolchild, I interrupted to ask if she'd mind if I stretched out on the floor. She nodded graciously. Even horizontal I was still uncomfortable. My right leg twitched and my throat was dry. Maybe it was jet lag, but I was relieved when the session finished.

Lydia showed me her Teacher's house, a pleasant cottage with a view over the valley. We then wandered past the monks' quarters, where maroon garments were draped over a clothesline. Nine monks currently lived there, she said. Most of them were teenage boys ranging in age from twelve to nineteen. We strolled past the classroom—an open-sided hall with benches and a whiteboard—where she taught the young monks English and neuroscience. *Neuroscience?*

Some monks were more interested in neuroscience than others, she confessed, but the links to meditation and its effects on the brain were particularly relevant. Apparently, happiness can be measured by heightened activity in the orbital frontal cortex. Scientists had discovered that the man with the happiest brain in the world happened to be a Buddhist monk.

Before there was time to ask more, we needed to hurry back to the dining room to meet the fortune-teller. Neuroscience to fortune-telling seemed an easy leap in this unworldly place.

I'd expected a village fortune-teller to have white hair and no teeth. But she was a good-looking woman in her thirties with prominent hooded eyes and long dark hair tumbling over her shoulders. She looked like the sort of woman I might've made friends with at a playgroup not so long ago. Unfortunately, she spoke no English.

The senior nun, who'd had her fortune told with surprising accuracy on a previous occasion, agreed to translate while Lydia took notes. The psychic didn't ask to look at my palm. She gazed disinterestedly out the window instead.

"You make a lot of money, but you waste it," she said.

I couldn't argue with her there.

"Your family lives near you. Brothers, sisters—some over the back fence, some next door."

Well, even the best fortune-tellers miss the mark sometimes.

"In your house there is the ghost of an old man," she continued. "He is followed up and down the stairs by a cat. Do you have a cat?"

I nodded.

"The cat and the old man's ghost—I think it is your father. They are good friends."

Lydia and I exchanged glances. Perhaps Jonah had been trying to tell us something when he'd sprayed Dad's old piano. Dad had always liked cats.

"You've had a very hard time with your health lately," the

fortune-teller went on. "But things are okay now. You'll get another health problem when you're sixty but don't worry. It won't be serious. You'll live till . . ."

She took the pencil from Lydia's hand and wrote "82" on the paper.

I was happy with that.

"You had a terrible time when everything was very bad," she added, her eyes suddenly veiled with a memory of pain. "You wanted to end your life, but you became strong instead. You lost all fear and started a new life."

It's only natural to want to catch a fortune-teller out. I asked how old I was when I had this experience. Without hesitating she replied "28"—exactly the age I was when poor Sam was killed. She was right. There was no doubt I'd felt suicidal.

I asked her about my work.

"I see two books," she said. "They will spread sunshine over the world."

I was hoping the woman would go on to tell Lydia's fortune, but she seemed to have run out of energy. She said Lydia would have three children and needed to be careful driving her car.

The fortune-teller then asked if Lydia and I might be interested in buying gems to clear impurities from our blood. Her partner, who happened to be waiting outside, sold such gems and would make them up into pendants for us at an excellent price, much cheaper than we'd pay in our own country. While I was happy to do anything to support the local economy, Lydia put her hand on my arm. Despite her spiritual tendencies, she'd always been astute with finances. Thanking the psychic, and paying her several times the going rate, she said we'd think about cleansing gems.

After the fortune-teller and her partner had left, Lydia and I savored a lunchtime banquet of potato curry, green vegetables, salad, lentils flavored with turmeric, and soybeans. Thanks to the Sri Lankan sweet tooth, dessert was equally sumptuous— dry noodles decorated with yogurt and honey, then drizzled with jaggery syrup. In case that wasn't enough, papaya and bananas had been added to the table. The monastery cook was a food poet, a culinary Cézanne. And to think I'd considered starvation a possibility!

The Sri Lankan tuk-tuk is basically a lethal weapon on wheels. As a motorbike with a small cabin attached behind the driver's seat, it offers several forms of torture. If you don't choke to death on the exhaust fumes, it can shatter your bones as it bounces along goat tracks disguised as roads. It has potential to topple over and hurl you into a river, or simply smash head-on into a truck full of livestock. Alternatively, you can try fitting three people into the cabin and risk having the life crushed out of you.

"Are the three of us going to fit in that thing?" I asked, peering at a passenger seat wide enough to accommodate three budgerigars.

The senior nun and Lydia assured me we would.

"Just hold on tight," said Lydia as the driver plummeted down the hill into the jungle. If the van had been adventurous, the tuk-tuk was plain suicidal. We crashed over potholes, through lakes of mud, then spun around corners, narrowly avoiding toppling over precipices. When we finally staggered out onto the village street, it felt as though my heart had rearranged itself to somewhere in my abdomen and that my bowels had been transplanted to my chest.

As we started walking, two girls wearing headscarves stared at us as though aliens had landed. A group of women in saris nodded and smiled curiously. It felt strange to be pale skinned in a village of Sri Lankans. Almost everyone I encountered was friendly and polite. I quietly hoped Sri Lankans felt equally welcome when they visited our part of the world.

The senior nun led us into a supermarket to buy jelly for her ailing mother. Apparently, two weeks before, the eighty-three-year-old had felt dizzy. Sitting on her bed, she'd fallen sideways onto the covers and had been lying there ever since. Jelly was all she could eat.

Searching the shelves, I was surprised to see a range of

skin-whitening creams, potions, and even pills. Once again, priorities were the opposite to those back home, where young women dedicated much of their lives to making their skin darker, if not orange.

When Lydia found the jelly section, the senior nun asked her to check the best-before dates. Satisfied the product was in good condition, the nun made her purchase and led us out of the supermarket to a T-shirt shop.

Contrary to my assumptions about nuns, this one proved a wily shopper with a keen eye. She had no doubt the purple top with paisley glitter would be perfect to take home for Katharine—and her taste was spot-on. The shopkeepers were surprised when Lydia joked and laughed with them in fluent Sinhalese. I took a step backwards and pretended I knew exactly what they were talking about.

On the way back up the hill, the tuk-tuk lurched to a halt outside a modest house half hidden in the trees. A group of people stood outside smiling and waving. Lydia explained they were members of the nun's family.

"Would you like to meet my mother?" asked the senior nun. "She is very weak."

Moving through the front door, I recognized a house close to mourning. Women sat talking quietly together. Men stood around hoping to appear useful. Children played upstairs. No matter what culture they're from, the warmth and tenderness of people at such a time is profound. To be in a household in the presence of death is to see the human heart at its most somber and loving.

Family members welcomed us warmly and the nun beckoned us to a room toward the back of the house. The space was small and darkened. Even though the window was open it felt hot and airless.

Lying on the bed was an elderly woman so wasted she was barely a shell. Bending tenderly over her mother, the nun adjusted a cotton blanket to cover her sticks of legs. A primitive drip was attached to her mother's thin, leathery arm. Her lips were drawn back from her toothless mouth as though in a state of permanent thirst.

Yet her eyes blazed as if she was living with greater intensity now than she had all her life. Her smile was so luminous it filled the room with light. With a withered hand, she reached for Lydia's sleeve and spoke to her in Sinhalese.

"She says she's very pleased to meet you," said Lydia. "And she wishes you a long life."

I took the old woman's hand and stroked her corrugated skin, which was surprisingly soft and warm. To receive a blessing for long life from someone so close to the spirit world was a great privilege.

The closeness I felt to her reminded me of the circle of women who'd helped me through cancer and of the immense capacity we have to give strength and light to one another. I hoped someday I'd be able to pass the blessing the nun's mother had given me on to other women, young and old—to wish each one of them a long life brimming with love.

After we thanked the nun's family and started walking away from the house, I was unable to speak. I'd dreaded coming to this country yet, in the short time I'd been here, Sri Lanka had showered me with unexpected riches. The fluffy-towel-addicted, fear-obsessed person I thought I'd become had given way to the life-loving adventurer I used to be.

To be embraced so warmly by the nun and her family had been a gift beyond price. Receiving a blessing from her dying mother made the circle of women seem more powerful than ever. No matter how old we are or what country we're from, women have great strength and compassion to offer each other.

Not only that, I'd found a place where old people weren't despised but regarded as a source of blessings.

Most important of all, I'd grown closer to the daughter I'd thought I'd lost.

No wonder the island had been called Serendipity, land of happy accidents.

Disciple

Secret nuns' business.

As the tuk-tuk gasped and sputtered to a halt below the monastery, dark sponges formed in the sky. Chanting floated across the valley—male voices, slightly more melodic than the ones that had woken me before dawn.

Lydia explained they were Muslims in the mosque on the nearby hill. I lowered my head and smiled. People in this country lived and breathed religion. If in doubt, chant.

Raindrops tapped on the steps and pattered on the trees. As the drops grew larger, they drumrolled on leaves the size of pancakes. We hurried up the steps as the clouds squeezed together and unleashed torrents, the sound of which drowned the distant chanting, and every other human and animal voice.

The senior nun smiled warmly as we removed our shoes and scurried into her quarters. I found a non-monk-designated chair and sat to catch my breath.

Suddenly, the junior nun's eyes widened. She drew a breath and pointed to a spot on the floor near the door. A glistening scorpion the size of a large crab marched across the tiles, his tail raised in an aggressive curve.

"Don't move!" the nun whispered, reaching for a broom. "The rain brings them inside."

Scorpion stings kill thousands of people a year. It's said that for every person killed by a poisonous snake, ten die from scorpion stings. James Bond was scared of scorpions. This particular Buddhist nun was not.

With her broom poised over her shoulder, she crouched low and stalked the well-armed arachnid. Her concentration and muscle tension reminded me of Jonah on a hunt. At first I assumed she was aiming for the kill, but I gradually realized the situation was more complex. Killing a creature, even a scorpion, was against her belief system. Somehow this fearless woman would have to keep all of us from danger by removing the scorpion without taking its life.

Keeping her distance as much as possible, she nudged the creature with the broom. It stopped and raised a warning claw at her. The nun then sprang into action. With one hand on the broom, she swept the scorpion vigorously forward, using her other hand to lean forward, open the door, and sweep the creature safely outside.

As the younger nun slammed the door shut, the senior nun, Lydia, and I clapped and cheered. It had been a remarkable performance of courage and coordination.

Beaming modestly, the nun bowed and put the broom away.

We laughed and drank sweet tea to celebrate. The junior nun asked if Sister Lydia and Sister Helen would like to do some chanting. When in Rome . . .

While the junior nun prepared the chanting room, I asked her superior how she'd found her vocation.

"I was good at school," she said. "My father didn't want me to take robes. He wanted me to get a job. But I wanted to find peace and happiness inside my head and help others."

She was in no way dissatisfied with her choice. Much of her life was spent visiting hospitals and being an important member of her community, doing what she could for women in particular. There were just two years between us, but our lives couldn't have been more different.

"Lydia my daughter!" she said, touching her heart with her hand, her smiling face pure with love.

Lydia smiled back at her. Not so long ago I'd have felt a stab of jealousy if another woman claimed my daughter as her own. Not any more. The whole point of parenthood is that in the end you *have* to let them go. If any of our kids found love outside our immediate family, no matter what form it took, I would rejoice for them.

I still hadn't found the right moment to ask about Lydia's long-term plan. If becoming a nun here was on her agenda, I realized she would be loved and well cared for.

The holy women escorted us to an alcove off the main room. A statue of Buddha smiled benignly from a nest of flowers and candles. Lydia handed me what appeared to be a prayer book written in curly script that could've been squeezed out of an icing bag.

I'd never been much good at sitting through church, and I wasn't too comfortable cross-legged on floors anymore, but I wanted to be part of the chanting session. A kitchen worker appeared and sat on the floor alongside us.

As the nun sat facing the altar reciting hypnotic phrases, I started nodding off. Lydia nudged me in the side and pointed at English phonetic pronunciations in the prayer book. I tried to keep up with her, but the words made no sense. It took me back to childhood Sundays in St. Mary's church when Mum would point out hymnbook words that were equally indecipherable.

Religion was scary back then. The vicar had created some kind of kinky universe inside his head. What was he doing talking about Death's Dark Vale when we had a perfectly nice park with a duck pond? According to him the entire town was overrun with sinners. I wished we could move somewhere without so many evildoers. Afterwards, when he waited at the church door to say farewell to his congregation, I'd do anything to avoid his soft paw enveloping my hand.

The chanting nun extended a white cotton thread to the kitchen worker, who passed the end of the thread to Lydia, who handed it on to me. Holding the one long cord zigzagging across the room like a spiderweb, we continued chanting. When it was felt enough chanting had been done, the thread was gently recoiled and returned to the nun.

Yet again, I was taken back to childhood where mysterious rituals occurred during my short, unsuccessful stint at Brownies. Smart in our brown uniforms and polished badges, we had to line up and take turns jumping over a toadstool. I obliged of course, but had no idea what it meant. Chanting with the cotton thread left me equally mystified. It meant Special Blessings, according to Lydia.

The nun then chanted and tied a bracelet of plaited cotton around my wrist for Very Special Blessings and Protection. Bowing and thanking all concerned, I headed back to my room.

Instead of showering "Western style" under the tepid dribble with the cockroach downstairs, I decided to go local. Pouring a bucket of cold water over myself inside the "French-style" bathroom was much simpler and more refreshing.

I hadn't realized how busy monastery life was for Lydia. Apart from the hours she spent meditating and teaching the young monks, she guided her Teacher through the intricacies of the Internet. She also wrote e-mails and helped fill out forms for anyone eager to communicate with the English-speaking world.

When the van driver for the monastery had to make travel arrangements to import a van from Malaysia, Lydia helped him out. She was assisting the nuns with an application to attend a conference in Thailand for women in Buddhism. These and other undertakings involved much discussion and negotiation interspersed with occasional emotional outbursts. She handled them all with good humor.

When I talked to Lydia about the demands on her, she said some of her earlier stints at the monastery had been physically demanding. Carrying bricks up the slope for a new building, renovating an old cottage, and sweeping had been a hard slog that was part of her service.

I would have happily stayed on at the monastery; well, at least another couple of nights. It had been so important to see why it occupied such a special place in Lydia's life and a delight to share the nuns' world. I loved the way their solemn expressions could melt in girlish giggles. The discipline of their lives was interwoven with lightheartedness. Their commitment to religion and their Teacher was enriched by their love of family and the village around them. Though familiar with suffering, they savored the joyful aspects of being alive.

Fond as she was of the monastery, Lydia surprised me by confessing she was looking forward to a few nights in the hotel on the outskirts of Kandy. I figured the drive to get there would take about an hour. But Lydia's Teacher, who had finally disentangled himself from his other commitments, was determined to show us the tea plantations.

"You mean they're on the way to the hotel?" I asked.

"Not exactly," he replied in a voice both melodic and authoritative.

Once our bags were packed, I finally had a chance to meet some of the monks—smooth-skinned youths, each with a single bare shoulder showing. One had a crutch from a hernia operation. While he claimed not to be in pain, he was pale and could barely shuffle up the steps.

I wondered how their mothers felt. Were they relieved their sons were being fed and educated—or did they simply yearn for their boys?

The young monks listened attentively while Lydia gave them a neuroscience lesson using PowerPoint on her laptop. As she explained how brain cells cannot be replaced after being damaged, but sometimes reroute themselves, it was hard to judge her audience's response. While some boys were more engaged than others, they were all immensely polite and showed no obvious signs of boredom.

Farewells and gifts were exchanged and photos taken. I returned to my room to collect my suitcase but it had disappeared—miraculously transported down the slope into the trunk of a waiting car.

As we followed Lydia's Teacher down the slope, he warned us the steps were slippery after last night's rain. Though the lure of a flushing toilet and jet-stream shower was strong, I was sad to be going. My stay at the monastery had been short, but I was leaving it a more openhearted, less fearful woman than the one who had arrived.

Settling into the backseat of the car, I told the monk we'd be more than happy to go straight to the hotel.

"But you really must see the tea plantations," he insisted. "It'll only take an hour or two and it's very beautiful. Also, it's nice and cool up there in the high country."

Considering how close to the heavens the monastery was already, it was hard to imagine there was much more of an "up there" above us.

The monk made it clear there was no room for argument. Maybe he wanted to use the time to discuss serious matters concerning his "disciple" Lydia.

The Question

Hungry ghosts and radiant happiness.

As we snaked through towns with the windows down, I started to feel nauseated by the combination of heat and petrol fumes. The monk was uncomfortable, too. He leaned out the window and spat theatrically onto the road. The driver assured us we'd be in cooler, more pleasant country soon.

Outside a shack on the side of the road, a boy sifted through his mother's waist-long hair. This touching scene reminded me of the ongoing battle we'd had with nits during primary school years.

The car rattled up into hills steep and green enough to have been digitally enhanced. Rounding a bend, we encountered a heavily armed soldier with a whistle pressed to his lips. He raised his arm and gestured for us to stop. My heart thumped, as I thought about how at least nineteen journalists had been killed in Sri Lanka since 1992. I didn't consider myself a journalist anymore, just a housewife with an accidental bestseller, but the idea of encountering Sri Lankan military was unnerving. The instant the soldier saw our monk, however, his smile became so broad the whistle dropped from his mouth and he waved us on.

"Look, Miss Lydia!" said the driver, pulling to the side of the road. "A waterfall!"

We paused alongside a group of brightly dressed locals to admire the torrent charging over huge rocks. As I leaned out of the window to take a photo, an ancient arm thrust itself into the car, the fingers curved up in the unmistakable shape of want. The arm belonged to a gray-haired woman, her eyes milky with age. Another beggar hovered ghostlike outside Lydia's window.

The driver urged us not to give them anything, but it was my first encounter with begging in Sri Lanka. If I'd stayed home in Melbourne, I'd have met more beggars on Chapel Street by now. I rustled through my wallet for an appropriate note to offer, but the hand pointed to another note, the equivalent of $10—a fortune by local standards. I gave it to her.

The driver grumbled as we roared away. Those people they do nothing, he complained. They expect others to do everything for them. But the monk reminded him beggars provide an opportunity for dharma.

Tea plantations rolled like plush green carpets over the hills. No wonder the British had loved it up here—a cool retreat away from the confusing bustle of the lowlands, with an endless supply of tea. Dotted among the rows of tea bushes were women workers wearing saris with large white sacks draped over their backs. Their bodies seemed permanently bent from picking tea, all for $2 a day.

It was getting near the magic hour of noon, before which the monk needed to eat. The driver pulled off the road and puttered up a driveway toward a graceful white building adorned with art deco swirls. Straight out of colonial times, it oozed refinement.

Stopping outside the gleaming entrance, our driver hooted the horn and waited. A smartly dressed waiter hurried out to the car with a menu for the monk to inspect. A cluster of staff gathered anxiously around our vehicle to await his verdict.

Although he thought there was a better restaurant farther up the hill with a more open feel, the monk decided this one would do. Visibly relieved, the staff ushered us into their establishment.

A gracious building with a foyer bedecked with columns and armchairs, the place was straight out of another century. I admired the high pressed-metal ceilings as we scaled wide stairs to an empty dining room overlooking the hills. Lydia and I were escorted to a table near the window. The monk and the driver were shown to another table several yards way. I was getting used to this arrangement. In fact, I'd decided that separate-gender dining had the potential to enliven some social occasions back home. The blokes could drone on about sport while women exchanged free-range gossip.

Lydia and I ordered soda water and waited our turn to choose from the buffet. I was beginning to realize local food was far more delicious and safer to eat than Sri Lankan interpretations of Italian cuisine. The delicate flavors, as well as the variety of textures and colors of Sri Lankan cooking, had me hooked.

As we sat at our table admiring old photographs from Empire days, the driver approached us. He seemed almost distraught.

"I'm sorry to say this, but your Teacher is not well," he said.

We glanced across at the monk gazing thoughtfully out the window. He didn't appear in extreme pain.

"He must go to hospital immediately," the driver continued. "It may be something to do with his blood pressure. He has been too busy lately."

We offered to help, but the monk and driver assured us there was nothing we could do. The monk stood up and said there was probably nothing to worry about. He seemed okay, but I knew that people can feel much worse than they look. The monk swept out of the restaurant with the driver in his wake.

Lydia and I exchanged glances across the table. Being abandoned in the Sri Lankan highlands hadn't been on my itinerary. The old control-freak me would've had a meltdown under these circumstances. Phone calls would've been made. Taxis called. But if being in this country had taught me anything, it was to chill out and let things evolve. It was a perfectly pleasant restaurant.

"How long do you think we'll be here?" Lydia asked, smiling.

"If he gets admitted to the hospital it could be a while," I replied. "They might forget about us altogether."

The lightness of not knowing what was going to happen was surprisingly liberating. We finished lunch and ordered a large pot of tea. A visit to the bathroom (Wow! Flushing toilets!) was followed by another pot of tea.

An hour or two later, we talked about finding our own way to the hotel, figuring it was probably only about four hours' drive away and that getting there wouldn't be impossible. Just as we were about to leave, there was a flourish of maroon at the entrance to the dining room and Lydia's Teacher sailed toward us, benevolent and trouble free as ever.

"There is absolutely nothing wrong with me," he confided.

The driver reinforced the hospital doctor's diagnosis. After careful examination the conclusion was that the monk was in perfectly good health.

"We will now go straight to the tea plantation," the monk added.

"You can't possibly take us," I said, thinking wistfully of sinking into a hotel swimming pool. "You need rest."

But the monk would have none of it. We climbed back into the car to wind on up and over more hills to Mackwoods Tea Plantation, which had "Over 165 Years of Excellence."

At the tea plantation parking lot we had our first glimpse of tourists. Staring out of their white flabby bodies through designer sunglasses, they resembled creatures from another planet. Disgorging from buses and rental cars in khaki shorts, stout walking shoes, and sun hats, they huddled in fearful groups. In almost any other circumstances I'd have been just like them.

Traveling in some kind of cultural submarine, they snatched bite-sized glimpses of the sights around them before turning their attention back to each other, reassuring themselves theirs was the Real World.

They worked themselves into a frenzy inside a shop selling alluringly packaged tea, as if there might soon be a world shortage. In the canteen they drained pots of tea and chocolate cake down their white saggy gullets. Hungry, always hungry for food and shopping.

In the Buddhist Wheel of Life, Hungry Ghosts are tormented by cravings that can never be fulfilled. Not fully alive, they're incapable of appreciating the present moment and are therefore in a constant state of rage and desire. Whoever painted Hungry Ghosts with thin necks and bulging bellies must have been thinking of tourists.

Outside the canteen we saw a rarity in Sri Lanka—an overweight child. Pasty faced with eyes like raisins, the young boy waddled about in a brand-name T-shirt and a cap that was too small for him. Weighed down by the consumerist society he came from, he was a pitiful sight.

While tourists took photos of themselves buying tea, drinking tea, and standing outside the tea factory, Lydia's Teacher started feeling much better. He was keen for us to embark on a guided tour of the factory, which exuded a sweet, trippy aroma.

A charming young woman explained the tea manufacturing process, which was surprisingly unencumbered by modern technology. It took less than twenty-four hours from leaf to packet. After admiring conveyor belts of green leaves destined to end up brewed in pots all over the world, we headed back to the parking lot.

While the others visited the bathrooms, the driver took me aside and fixed me with an earnest look. He would, he said, give me a house with furniture and *every*thing, if I could find a nice man to marry his daughter. I'd want for nothing if I could find her a man with a good heart.

Struggling to respond, I thought of all the women I knew, ages ranging from sixteen to seventy-five, who lamented the difficulty of finding a decent bloke, and assured him it was a universal problem.

With the tea tour completed, we assured the monk and driver we'd be more than happy to be taken to the hotel now.

"But you must see Little Britain!" the monk urged.

For a fleeting moment I thought he was referring to the television comedy.

"Nuwara Eliya was built in the nineteenth century and it's

just like an English town with redbrick buildings and hotels on a lake," he continued. "It's very beautiful. And we must go to the botanical gardens."

The car twisted and surged until we reached Little Britain. To complete the Englishness of it all, shafts of rain fell into the lake. We stopped at a handsome old hotel where Queen Victoria still reigned. A pianola in the lobby played Christmas carols even though it was February. Out in the garden, white-haired couples from Surrey swayed to Engelbert Humperdinck under a magnolia tree while women in saris and men in white jackets kept them topped up with tea.

The scene was unexpectedly touching. All participants, both foreign and local, were taking part in a game of Let's Pretend the Empire Never Died. The British tourists were ecstatic to relive the glory of their ancestors. And locals, dressed in ethnic clothing, were content to nurture the foreigners' fantasies with tea from a silver urn . . . for a price. As the skies opened they scurried for the shelter of the magnolia.

A man on the roadside assured us the botanic gardens were a thirty-minute drive out of town. Concerned it might be past dark by the time we got to our accommodation, I suggested perhaps we didn't need to see the gardens. But the monk insisted they were unmissable.

On the way we encountered devastating flood damage. An entire hillside had collapsed into a valley. Bulldozers and diggers clawed the earth trying to reclaim a track that could eventually become a road again. For once the magic of traveling with a monk didn't work. A man in a hard hat held up a stop sign and made us wait . . . and wait. About forty minutes later we were finally waved through and it was nearly 4 p.m. by the time we reached the garden gates, ten minutes away from closing time. The entrance fee would be US$10 per person plus an extra fee for the car. Daylight robbery by local standards. In no mood to argue if it meant we could head for Kandy straight after, I opened my wallet.

We glided past a white concrete pillar engraved with 1861,

passing wrought-iron gates and heading up the driveway. The gardens were lovely, but not much different in layout to any of that era. The monk and driver agreed it wasn't the best time of year for flowers.

After a quick circuit of the gardens we were finally allowed to start the five-hour journey to the hotel. Lydia seized the opportunity to ask her Teacher to bestow a Buddhist name on her.

I squirmed uncomfortably while he hummed and hawed, running through several options aloud. Lydia had been named after Dad's mother, an equally determined woman by all accounts. A lot of thought had gone into calling her that. A name is a brand, a theme song. Hers was a good one with a worthy heritage. The ancient land of Lydia (in the region of modern Turkey) was the first country to produce coins. In the Bible there's a Lydia who sells purple cloth.

If our daughter was going to reject everything else she'd grown up with, it was logical she'd discard her name. But surely if she was going to do something that serious, and take on a new one, it would happen in a temple, not in the backseat of a Japanese car? The monk eventually decided on the title Nanda, meaning Radiant Happiness. Maybe that's who she was going to be from now on: Sister Radiant Happiness.

To my embarrassment, Lydia asked him for a Buddhist name for me. Then again, if he was comfortable bestowing a Buddhist name on someone who didn't belong to the religion, maybe it wasn't such a big deal. After more deliberating, he settled on Ramani, meaning One Whose Blessings Come from Nature. I was secretly pleased with it. Maybe the monk understood me better than I'd imagined.

As darkness enveloped the car, the driver's eyelids became heavy in the rearview mirror. He'd had a demanding day, what with kamikaze traffic on farcical roads and the mercy dash to the hospital.

To keep him awake, Radiant Happiness and Blessing From Nature encouraged him to talk about his passion—cars. According to him, a Toyota was the best brand in Sri Lanka. He asked what sort of vehicle we had back home. He shook his head at the thought of a Subaru. Spare parts were too expensive. He'd once driven a Ferrari, but his dream car would be a Lamborghini.

"By the way," he asked. "Do you know the way to this hotel?"

Thank Buddha for Google Earth. The instructions were clear, but as the driver said, we seemed to be on the safari route. As we reached the outskirts of Kandy the map told us to scale a cliff face. I'd heard the road to the hotel had been closed during the floods. Maybe this was an alternative approach. Jolting through the obsidian night, I was starting to tire of unpredictable adventures.

Eyes glowed along the roadside. When the driver asked them for directions they shook their heads or vanished into the jungle. A bus hurtled down the hill, nearly tossing us into the chasm. While both drivers stopped to regain their composure, the bus driver told us we were on the right road, and to keep going up.

Near the summit, a well-lit sign for the hotel shone reassuringly. A figure slid out from the shadows and approached our car; the driver wound down his window. The man tried to give him a piece of paper, but the driver put his foot down and charged up the rest of the hill.

"These people are dangerous," he said. "He wants us to find someone in the hotel who probably doesn't exist. He's selling drugs. He'll have us all killed. They'll call the police and we'll end up in the same cell. Two Sri Lankans and two foreigners."

As we finally lurched into the hotel grounds, I was relieved beyond words. I prepared to bid farewell to the monk and his driver, but they said they had time for refreshments before leaving.

Inside, I reveled in the Muzak, the unnatural glow of the swimming pool, and the staff uniforms with their pseudo references to Sri Lankan traditional dress.

As we sat down at a table, in my dazed state I noticed how versatile monastic robes are. They can look just at home in the lobby of a flash hotel as in the depths of a forest monastery.

After we'd had some tea, the monk cleared his throat. I was too tired and disoriented to imagine he might be about to say something important.

"Lydia," he said, radiating his charismatic smile. "If you want to come to the monastery and be ordained as a nun you can stay and be the meditation teacher."

Suddenly alert, I leaned forward and waited for Lydia's response. This was the moment I'd traveled half the world for. If she was going to say yes, it would be okay. I might even get a shack in Kandy and spend several months a year in this crazy, beautiful place. But still . . .

Lydia stirred her lime and soda with her straw.

The monk, the driver, and I waited for her to say something.

But, apart from the clink of champagne glasses at the next table and Elton John over the loudspeakers—there was silence.

Reverence

An enemy is sometimes a friend in disguise.

The young man who cleaned our hotel room fell violently in love with Lydia. When she first spoke to him in Sinhalese, his eyebrows rose and parted like a drawbridge. His amazement melted into delight, solidifying into passion when he discovered she'd spent months living devoutly in a monastery.

When Lydia's new admirer wasn't lingering in the corridor outside our room, he was inventing an endless list of excuses for tapping on the door. The tea bags had forgotten to replenish themselves. Our pillows weren't straight. The curtains needed closing.

Though he was very good-looking and charming, he was approximately six inches shorter than Lydia. However, the difference in their heights did nothing to dampen his ardor. Like her, he said, he was Buddhist and, he added earnestly, hoped to visit Australia someday.

Elvis was in nappies the last time I'd witnessed such a severe affliction of lovesickness. I warned Lydia the signs were blazingly obvious, but she shrugged me off. Since her religious phase had begun, she'd lost any ability to read mating signals. Any men who looked at her with interest were simply ignored. Unlike her sister, she was immune to bulging biceps and aftershave. While she could speak four languages, she'd become flirt illiterate.

Sinhalese is notoriously complicated. About the only word I could recognize was "oh" for "yes." Lydia and the young man chatted animatedly saying "oh" and nodding a lot. Feeling like a spare incense stick in an ashram, I asked what they were talk-ing about.

"It's Poya day," Lydia said, as if I should have known. "Full moon is a special day on the Buddhist calendar. It's the best time to visit the Tooth Temple."

The young man smiled in a besotted fashion at Lydia and promised that while we were away at the Tooth Temple he would do "something special" with our room. He then excused himself and wheeled his trolley of forgetful tea bags down the corridor.

"What does he mean *something special*?" I asked Lydia. "Is he kinky?"

"Don't worry about it," she sighed, inspecting my red linen shirt. "Just change your clothes. We'll need to wear white."

Thinking the religious part of my adventure was over, I'd scrunched all the white clothes in the bottom of my suitcase. Oh well. The crinkled look was so far out it was probably in.

Yet another demented tuk-tuk driver took us on a thrill ride over potholes the size of craters down the rutted precipice into town. He stopped outside different shops every now and then, explaining that this was the place he and his family bought all their gemstones/antiques/designer-label clothes and if we'd like to go inside and look around he would happily wait for us. Lydia explained this was common practice with tuk-tuk drivers. They'd revisit the store later to collect a percentage of anything we'd spent.

She waved him on good-naturedly, keen to get to the Tooth Temple before the day's heat set in and the crowds became overwhelming. I hadn't appreciated the importance of the Temple of the Sacred Tooth Relic in Kandy. Housing a tooth (or more accurately, the remains of one) that once belonged to Buddha himself, the temple is one of the most religiously signif-icant places in all of Sri Lanka.

The incisor was wrenched from Buddha's funeral pyre in 543 BC and smuggled to the island in the hair of a princess in the fourth century AD. Whoever holds the tooth relic is said to have the right to rule the country. Because of its importance, the Tooth Temple has been bombed several times, most recently in 1998 when eleven people were killed in a suicide truck explosion. The buildings have been restored every time, so they give no hint of a troubled past.

Every Sri Lankan Buddhist aims to make a pilgrimage to the Tooth Temple at least once in their lifetime. Though Lydia had been many times before, she had never been on Poya day.

Rising above limpid Kandy Lake, the Temple buildings and royal palace complex were every bit as imposing as I'd expected. Thousands of people, almost all dressed in white, thronged toward the entrance.

I've always been claustrophobic, which is one of the reasons I stay away from rock concerts and soccer games. When I saw the Tooth Temple crowd, I toyed with the idea of sitting under a tree with a cool drink while Lydia went inside and merged with the multitude. But I'd stared down other phobias during this trip. I could surely conquer one more.

We hired a guide, took off our shoes at the door, and shuffled up a broad marble staircase. Crammed against so many others in stifling heat, I felt the beginnings of a panic attack. I concentrated on staying calm—it was essential to maintain dignity; for my daughter's sake, if nothing else.

"Keep moving with the people," our guide instructed repeatedly, his tone reassuringly matter-of-fact.

My shirt turned clammy and clung to my back. A rivulet of sweat trickled down my cheek as Lydia bought three white lotus blossoms for offerings to the Buddha. She handed one to me, and one to our guide. Clutching the flower, he stared at the floor, embarrassed. A security guard laughed and teased him.

I dropped my flower and stooped to pick it up.

"No! You mustn't do that!" snapped the guard. "The offerings must be clean and pure, not off the ground."

At the top of the stairs we were shepherded into an open space interspersed with columns. Brightly colored banners hung from a ceiling made of gold lotus flowers. Musicians wearing white caps and sarongs, the latter tied with red sashes, stepped into a shaft of light. Drums set up a mesmerizing

rhythm. Wind instruments wheedled out a haunting melody—
music to trance by.

Climbing more stairs, I kept concentrating on staying calm
while moving forward. By the time we reached the casket room
I was too busy focusing on breathing to take much notice of our
surroundings. Lydia placed her flower on the tooth casket and
we shuffled downstairs before stepping outside into searing
white daylight. I've rarely felt more relieved.

Outside we encountered an imposing bull elephant the size of a
large garden shed. I assumed the creature was a fine example of
a taxidermist's art. When his trunk swayed to life and drifted
toward me, I almost bolted up a tree. The elephant's eyes twinkled mischievously. A man held out a stem of bananas, and the
creature unfurled his trunk, wrinkled and worn like an old
vacuum cleaner hose, and deftly retrieved them. We watched
amazed as the elephant devoured the whole lot in one mouth-
ful—bananas, skins, and branch.

The guide escorted us through a courtyard filled with
hundreds of women in white sitting under trees while a recorded
male voice droned teachings over loudspeakers. Some women
were alone and giving the appearance of listening, but most
were in groups talking softly to each other.

"Why are they here?" I whispered.

"Because women know more about suffering than anybody,"
our guide explained. "They give their lives to their family and
then they come here to catch up on time they missed out on."

A pair of grandmothers nodded and smiled over a shared
amusement. A group of middle-aged women sat in companion-
able silence. Their life stories were written on their faces. No one
had discovered pain-free childbirth. They'd all worried themselves
sick over their children—husbands and parents, too. They were all
givers, taking time out together for a little peace and kindness.

The courtyard had such a gentle ambience I wished I could sit
in the shade and linger with them. Even though our lives were
different on superficial levels, we were sisters under the skin.

Some of the older women stayed all night long, the guide continued, talking and drinking tea. Younger ones left early, around 5 p.m.—meaning they'd still spent most of the day there.

It was a living, breathing circle of women. In the way I'd found loving support from my yoga group, Mary and my women friends, these Sri Lankan women had formalized the union. I wished there was a place like it in Melbourne where women could go—and just be.

After another white-knuckle tuk-tuk ride up the hill, we returned hot and dusty to our hotel room.

"Oh my goodness!" said Lydia, opening the door to behold the sight before her.

Our beds were covered in red flowers painstakingly arranged in geometric patterns contrasting against triangular crimson leaves. Three red flowers had been placed in a row on each of our pillows. Lydia's pajamas had been lovingly folded into a rectangle beside her pillow.

Her admirer had certainly done something special.

We changed into our swimwear and walked through the warm evening air toward the pool, passing a sign advertising the hotel fortune-teller. Sri Lankans translate English into a more refined language. Tables have signs saying PROMISED rather than RESERVED. Activity organizers are called "animators."

A German woman called her toddler away from the water's edge. A French couple sipped cocktails at a table. The luxury of this place was surreal compared to the monastery.

Sun drifted down toward hills across the other side of the valley. Clouds rose like temples lined with gold. Slipping noiselessly into the pool, Lydia and I were anointed in its turquoise cool.

Climbing out of the water refreshed, I shook my hair and sat on a lounger to admire the spectacle across the valley. There was no point getting my camera. No photo could live up to the reality. If any great artist—from one of the ancient Greeks to van Gogh—had seen this sunset, he would've put down his brushes and walked away.

Monks' voices wafted from a nearby monastery, chanting in velvet unison. Giant rays of gold radiated from the sun and stretched across the sky.

Lydia stepped out of the pool, slipped into her Calvin Klein singlet top, and walked toward me.

"I can't remember when I last watched a sunset," I said. "I mean *really* watched one."

"I suppose you could regard it as a form of meditation," she said, toweling her hair. "The beauty of every second melting into the next."

I stood up and walked with her to the edge of the terrace to get a better view. As the sun sank into the clouds, majestic bands of color flattened out to form red and gold brush strokes across the sky.

"It is a magic country," I said, gazing across the hills silhouetted in the distance.

She nodded in silent agreement.

"You'll have to find another island to run away to now I've found you here," I said, only half joking.

Lydia smiled.

"If I was your age, I'd have done the same," I added. "Especially if I could speak the language . . . except maybe not the nun thing."

The scene was perfect now. I wanted everything to stop and stay frozen in this moment. This golden sky in the warm blanket of a tropic night with my beautiful, grown-up daughter in the land she'd chosen to be part of.

There'd been other times when I'd wanted to capture time—a summer when I was insanely in love; an autumn morning near a duck pond where baby Lydia toddled toward me, her arms open for me to catch her soft weight in mine.

But clinging to moments, or for that matter daughters, is futile. The trick is to appreciate their beauty, do your best by them, and let them go as graciously as possible.

Life is always in movement. One beautiful moment can evolve into another, more precious form. Every second, even when colored with sadness, has potential to be richer than the last.

The mastery is in awareness and trust; in having enough wisdom to step back to allow space for the new to unfold. To avoid becoming a Hungry Ghost mourning the past and always craving for the future.

The red and gold brushstrokes slowly darkened to crimson. The monks' voices enveloped us in their liquid harmonies.

"I love it here," Lydia said, as we watched the hills turn a misty lilac. "But I've done enough."

Her words left me momentarily speechless.

"When I first started meditating, I thought if I tried hard for long enough something incredible would happen," she continued, her voice fractured with emotion. "You know, scientists have done tests and they've found physical changes in the brain when people approach higher levels of awareness. I thought I'd be able to achieve that. Maybe even find . . ."

The rest of her sentence hung in the air between us. *Please don't say it's hard to explain.*

"Enlightenment?" I asked quietly.

The Frenchman lit a cigarette and the German woman gathered her toddler in a towel.

A tear formed a crystalline river down Lydia's cheek. Her pain was deep.

"I just thought if I sat there long enough . . ." she said, then started weeping.

I put my arm around her.

All the time I'd perceived her as being rebellious, Lydia had been focusing on the unattainable goal of perfection. It was the same determination she'd used to achieve high distinctions at university. Once she set her mind on something, her willpower was relentless.

I wondered what had instilled this drive and if it was to do with being born into a household grieving for an older brother she'd never met. While she was in no way a replacement for Sam, it's true she would never have been born if he hadn't been run over that day. Perhaps the darling girl really had burdened herself with the task of healing hearts.

Although I'd always made a point of not portraying Sam as a saint, maybe he'd seemed that way to her. Perhaps on a subconscious level she'd grown up measuring herself against an older brother who was untainted because he was dead.

"I've wasted the last five years of my life," she sobbed quietly. "I could've been going to parties and having fun with my friends instead of striving so hard, meditating hour after hour."

Rocking her gently in my arms, I pieced the past few days together. The fact that she'd let her hair grow, and the silence after her Teacher had publicly invited her to become a nun, now made sense. Far from being manipulated into committing herself to an ancient religion, Lydia was still in charge of her life.

"I need to come home," she said.

Now I'd finally understood her love for the monastery and Sri Lanka, she was coming home?

"Really?" I asked. "No maroon robes?"

God, what was I doing? Trying to talk her into being a nun?!

"This place will always be part of me, but . . ."

Her voice trailed off. I resisted the urge to try and finish her sentence.

"But what?"

"I don't feel right here anymore. I'm sure I'll come back someday, but not for a while. I want to do a master's in psychology. I've been in touch with Melbourne University and they've got a place for me. I want to combine what I've learned here with Western knowledge somehow . . ."

She buried her head in my neck and asked if she could fly back with me in a few days' time and live at home for a while.

My time with Lydia in Sri Lanka had taught me so much. All the energy I'd put into worrying about primitive toilets, vegetarian curries, and mosquitoes had been wasted. The terrifying island of tears had turned out to be an oasis of delightful contradictions. Not only that, it'd taken me back to the adventurous woman I'd once been.

Most important, this beautiful island had helped me to understand Lydia. The tensions between us had been more about our similarities than our differences.

The sky became a crimson blanket, then purple.

"I feel terrible about coming here when you were sick," she said, her cheeks glistening in the fading light. "I didn't know what I was doing."

"But you came home when I really needed you," I said, rocking her gently. "You looked after me beautifully, thanks to your dad paying the fare."

She straightened her back and wiped her eyes.

"But it was my Teacher who paid for the fare," she said.

"*Your Teacher?!*" I gasped. "I thought he was the one trying to keep you here!"

She shook her head.

"He never did that. He refused to teach me anything that time. In fact he hardly spoke to me. He made it clear he thought I should be with you. Buddhism regards family as very important."

The island of Serendipity had saved its biggest surprise till last. The charismatic monk I'd suspected of trying to ensnare my daughter and steal her away from us had been far more generous and understanding of family ties than I'd given him credit for.

I'd been a fool for misjudging the man so badly. He'd had our family's interests at heart all along. No wonder Steve hadn't replied when I'd sent him the thank-you note.

Through all the turmoil, one thing had been consistent— my daughter's determination to make a meaningful impact on the world.

The profound darkness of the tropics enveloped us. The monks' voices faded away. Night birds and insects started up their own musical homage to the glory of being alive.

Completion

Happiness is the weight of a cat on your lap,
and a contented daughter.

As the car pulled up outside Shirley, a double rainbow arced in the sky above. The colors were so vivid and clearly defined in the lower arc I could pick them out individually. I'd never seen such a brilliant rainbow.

High above it, a hazy second rainbow formed a protective curve. A mothering arc, watching over her daughter, content to bask in her offspring's beauty.

A familiar silhouette sat in the living room window. The moment Jonah saw us he stood up on his toes, arched his back, and flicked his tail. Bending intensely, he peered down at the car. As he pressed his face against the glass we could see the blue flash of his eyes.

"Someone's pleased to see you," I said to Lydia.

As she ran up the path, Jonah jumped down from the window ledge and hurtled off to wait on the other side of the front door. We could hear him meowing. Lydia turned the key, and Jonah pushed the door open to spring into her arms.

"Oh, I missed you, boy!" she said, sinking her face in his fur.

Jonah's purr was so deep and resonant it reminded me of something I'd heard just a few nights earlier—the monks chanting at sunset. I thought of the slipper maker and the cat that was his monk. Jonah would be more than willing to take on the role of Lydia's guru.

★ ★ ★

Adjusting back to "normal" life was more difficult for Lydia than I'd realized. In her search for spiritual perfection, so many things had been sidelined. The first thing she did was update her Facebook page. Her old profile, featuring photos of her in monasteries or managing fund-raising events, made her tearful. "I hardly look like a real person!" she wept.

She shut herself in the bathroom and emerged twenty minutes later wearing full makeup.

"Please take my photo," she said, thrusting a camera in my hand.

I was engrossed in my study writing a new book but there was urgency in her voice. We went into the back garden where she smiled self-consciously under the tree. Unlike most of her generation who practiced flashy smiles taking self-portraits on their phones, Lydia had forgotten how to perform for a camera. She took the camera from me and deleted most of the photos. If I told her what I really thought, that she glowed with rare beauty, she'd have recoiled uncomfortably. Her Teacher's words echoed inside my head—"If there is a pearl in all the world, Lydia is our jewel."

Getting back into the social scene was painful to begin with. Some of her friends only seemed to laugh, talk, and drink. She found it hard to fit in. A couple of times she came home tearful, again regretting how she'd spent the past five years. I tried to assure her that while the benefits of her experiences mightn't seem obvious to her yet, they'd added great richness to who she was and would stay with her forever.

Walking along Chapel Street with her one Saturday night, she glided along the pavement, oblivious to admiring glances from men. When I nudged her and asked if she'd noticed that cute guy trying to make eye contact, she seemed almost startled.

Katharine, Philip, and I were delighted when she came along to operas, musicals, and the occasional trashy film with us. During her devout phase she'd rejected entertainment as a "diversion."

It was wonderful to see her wearing clothes that weren't

from a charity shop. To my surprise, she developed an addiction to a boutique specializing in conservative outfits with cashmere and leather accessories. Jonah was particularly pleased about that. He scurried into her bedroom whenever he could to steal her scarves.

"I'm ashamed to confess it," she said one day. "But I have a weakness for animal-skin prints."

I bought her a fake leopard-skin handbag. Jonah naturally assumed it was his and started carrying it around the house.

Lydia took her cooking skills to new levels. Not only could she re-create Mum's ginger crunch to perfection, Julia Child and Nigella Lawson became household friends.

Jonah galloped eagerly into the kitchen whenever he heard her rattling in the pot cupboard. It meant no end of games—jumping up on the counter and being shooed off again. Lydia solved the situation peaceably, placing his tallest scratching pole in the middle of the kitchen so he could supervise. This involved much "talking," answering every question with a meow or a cluck—or, if he disapproved for some reason, one of his snitching sounds.

"I'm just his under-chef," she chuckled.

Pausing at the bottom of the stairs, I almost missed the smell of incense. She wasn't meditating much anymore. I suggested maybe she shouldn't give it up altogether.

Since Katharine had moved out to residential college at university, the house was quiet with just the three of us—four, counting Jonah. After a few months, Lydia was ready to move into a flat with people her own age. She and three friends found a modern apartment above an art gallery in Carlton. Sunny and spacious, it was ideal. Now she'd decided to do a PhD as well as a master's in psychology, she planned to stay there a few years.

She left home on one of those brilliant sunny days we sometimes get in winter. Her bed was fine to go once Philip had sawn out the piece of wood that had been saturated with Jonah's misdoings.

The apple tree waved its bare branches in farewell as a pair of movers trudged down the path with her desk, chair, and boxes of clothes. After they'd driven away, she called me upstairs. Her room was empty except for a cluttered bookshelf. I ran my hand over the apricot walls. They still had an other-worldly quality.

"We've had quite an adventure," I said, picking up a plump meditation cushion. "Aren't you taking this?"

"You can keep it if you like," she said.

"Meditation," I said, turning the cushion in my hands. "It does sometimes help me tune out after I've been writing."

"You're not thinking of becoming a nun, are you?" Lydia chuckled.

I shook my head and laughed. She put her hands on my shoulders and drew me close.

"Thanks for everything, Mum."

My ears went hot. I couldn't believe what I'd just heard.

My stroppy, strong-willed daughter who'd only ever called me Helen had finally called me Mum.

Tail's End

Set them free . . . within reason.

That afternoon, I clicked Jonah into his harness and carried him into the back garden.

As I stretched on a lounger and closed my eyes, the cat jumped onto the sunbed next to mine. Purring and rolling ecstatically in the golden warmth, he invited me to rub his tummy. Like all good concubines, I obliged.

Half a tablet of cat Prozac had become part of his daily routine. He was still demented, charming, and bossy but the medication had made a big difference to his "little problem." He only sprayed these days if one of the black cats from down the road glowered through a window at him, or he caught someone packing a suitcase. Dad's piano was still a source of unwholesome interest, so, to the curiosity of visitors, it remained in its protective covering.

"You're a good boy, aren't you?" I said, as he lay on his side and slid his eyes shut.

Our feline seemed so calm and happy I decided to risk giving him what he'd always craved. He hardly seemed to notice when I undid the harness. We lay side by side, savoring the sunshine and each other's company. He was free now, and he'd chosen to stay with me. Flattered, I closed my eyes and drifted into a haze.

Except I couldn't relax entirely. Every few seconds I checked Jonah was still lying next to me. He appeared comatose. Once, when I opened one eye I caught him examining me with a piercing gaze, as though ascertaining whether I was asleep.

Pretending to doze, I watched the crafty creature check me out again. Satisfied I was unconscious, he sprang off his lounger, gave himself a congratulatory shake, and trotted stealthily away. My heart sank as his tail disappeared around the side of the house.

Sighing at the thought of another neighborhood gadabout, I rolled off the lounger and plodded after him. That cat couldn't be trusted.

As I rounded the corner, he was pattering past the trash bins. Too far away for me to catch, even if I broke into a sprint.

"Jonah!" I whined. "Come back."

The cat stopped in his tracks, turned his handsome face to me and blinked.

"It would be nice if you stayed home," I said.

The feline hesitated. I waited for him to bolt. But, to my astonishment, he lay down on the path, rolled on his back and put his feet in the air as if to say, "You might as well come and get me."

Bundling him into my arms, I kissed his furry forehead. In return he honored me with a good-natured purr. He'd enjoyed the joke.

Cats and daughters. Let them roam a little.

But keep an eye on them.

Acknowledgments

Becoming an international author has brought some amazing people into my life. Michaela Hamilton and her team at Citadel have done a tremendous job introducing my books to American readers. I had no idea our family stories would be embraced so warmly in the United States. Michaela's a cat person from way back, and I'll always be grateful for her dynamism and enthusiasm.

Heartfelt thanks to the wonderful U.S. readers who sent e-mails. I've loved reading your stories and tried to respond to them all. Thank you for recommending my books to your friends. It's the kindest thing you can do for an author.

I've often wondered why authors thank their agents. Since the divine Elizabeth Sheinkman of William Morris took me on I've understood why. Along with her assistant, Jo Rodgers, Elizabeth is an author's dream—cheerleader and visionary rolled into one.

Gratitude to Louise Thurtell of Allen and Unwin in Sydney. And to the many international publishers who translated *Cats and Daughters* and *Cleo* into their own languages.

To the medics who guided me through breast cancer, thank you is not enough. Scribbling a book or two is nothing compared to the work you do saving lives.

People sometimes ask how the members of my family feel being the subject of my books. They're incredibly tolerant and bighearted. Philip, Katharine, Rob, Chantelle, and babies Annie and Stella—you are the jewels of my life.

Deepest thanks of all to Lydia for so generously agreeing to be central to this story. No doubt you'd tell it differently from your perspective. Perhaps someday you will. In the meantime, I hope you appreciate this book for what it is . . . a kind of love story.

And Jonah, if you're reading this, that goes for you, too.

www.helenbrown.com